Cropping Pattern and Socio-economic Development of Tribal Areas in Himachal Pradesh

Cropping Pattern and Socio-economic Development of Tribal Areas in Himachal Pradesh

Dr. Heera Bhagti

KUNAL BOOKS
New Delhi-110002 (India)

KUNAL BOOKS
4648/21, 1st Floor, Ansari Road,
Daryaganj, New Delhi - 110002.
Phones: 011-23275069, 9811043697
E-mail: *kunalbooks@gmail.com*
Website: *www.kunalbooks.com*

Cropping Pattern and Socio-economic Development of Tribal Areas in Himachal Pradesh

First Published 2021
ISBN: 978-93-89224-77-1

Published in India by Prem Singh Bisht of Kunal Books and printed at **Trident Enterprises**, Noida, (U.P.).

Dedicated

to

Lord Shiva

Foreword

The book titled 'CROPPING PATTERN AND SOCIO-ECONOMIC DEVELOPMENT OF TRIBAL AREAS IN HIMACHAL PRADESH', is one of the arduous and academic excellence attempt of Dr. Heera Bhagti to depict and generalize socio-economic development of the tribal areas in relation to cropping pattern which is the major occupation of the tribal regions and has a special usage due to the features of excellent land fertility of these areas. Dr. Heera being a researcher and an enriched academician, has contributed this academic venture to ameliorate and obliterate accomplishment of economic prosperity and with this intention, has recommended measures which is obviously a sincere and noble attempt on her part. The concerned organizations and government bodies should sincerely go through the measures recommended in the book and should come forward to the common cause and development. I am sure and wish that the book will be preferred as one of the key academic documents for the readers and researchers. I wish and expect that in future she will continue working on such academic and research ventures as a good academician and will enrich readers.

Dr. Devinder Sharma

Professor, Department of Commerce,

Himachal Pradesh University, Shimla

Preface

India is endowed with the most diverse topographical features, such as high mountains, extensive plateaus and wide plains traversed by mighty rivers. Majority of Indian population resides in villages and agriculture is the primary occupation of rural India. Hence a wide range of crops are grown in the Country. As the study relates to the tribal areas of Himachal Pradesh, it becomes important to have an understanding about the demography of tribes in the Country, in general and Himachal, in particular. What makes this study analytical and interesting is the fact that tribal pockets are scattered around different topographical set-ups. Moreover, this variation is both inter-regional and intra-regional in nature. There are a number of tribes in India, spread all over the country right from the foot hill of Himalayas to the land tip of Lakshadweep and from the plains of Gujarat to the hills in the North- East.

The tribal people constitute 8.61 percent of total population of India according to 2011 census. The word tribe denotes a group of persons having a common character, occupation, culture, tradition and interest. These tribes are also known as the 'adivasis' and 'vanvasis', who are dependent on hunting, agriculture and fishing. Some of the major tribal groups in India are Gonds, Santhas, Khasis, Angamis, Bhils, Bhutias and great Andamanese. The tribal groups of Himachal Pradesh include Kinnauras, Lahaulas, Gaddis, Jads, Pangwals and Swangwals. These tribal people have their own culture, tradition, language and lifestyle. Amongst all tribes, the tribes of Himachal Pradesh are mostly engaged in agricultural activities.

The present empirical study is a modest attempt to analyse the Cropping Pattern of Tribal Areas of Kinnaur and Lahaul- Spiti districts of Himachal Pradesh with respect to their socio-economic development. Kinnaur is one of the border district of the State, having certain peculiarities of language, history, culture and climatic conditions. Similarly, Lahaul - Spiti, is in the eastern corner, having congenial climatic conditions for agriculture. The main occupations of Kinnauras are agriculture and horticulture whereas, Lahaulas are mainly engaged in agricultural activities.

The main crops produced in Himachal Pradesh include; wheat, maize, rice, barley, seed-potato, ginger, vegetables, vegetable seeds, mushroom, hops, olives, fig and off season vegetables that includes; ginger, potato, soyabean, oilseeds, and pulses etc. The Climate of Kinnaur is cold and dry and is ideally suitable for the production of temperate and dry fruits. Apples, apricot, almond, walnut etc. are found almost all over the district. People of Lahaul -Spiti cultivate buck wheat, cauliflower, cabbage and cash crops like kuth, potato, hops, peas, mustard, raddish, trench bean, tomatoes, soyabeen etc. Barley is the staple food of the people of this region.

The present book has been divided into five chapters. The first chapter provides an outline of the cropping pattern in the tribal areas of Himachal Pradesh with an understanding of the diversity of tribal groups residing in these areas.

The second chapter includes the review of existing literature, finding the research gap and research methodology used for the undertaken study.

The third chapter deals with the outturn of cash crops in Kinnaur and Lahaul - Spiti districts of Himachal Pradesh during the study period. This chapter gives a reflection on the total cropped area, total irrigated area under different crops and crop intensity and outturn of different crops in the study area as well as Himachal Pradesh.

The fourth chapter empirically analyses the cropping pattern and socio-economic development of the areas under study. An attempt has been made to empirically examine different factors affecting cropping pattern along with the status of employment in context to the cropping pattern which affects the socio-economic development of the tribals. The dependence of tribal population on cropping pattern and the socio economic life of the tribal areas is also studied in this chapter. The last chapter gives the conclusion of the whole study, along with findings of the study and certain suggestions regarding the improvement in cropping pattern to increase the productivity to uplift the social-economic life of the tribal people.

Dr. Heera Bhagti

Acknowledgements

It gives me immense pleasure to convey the intensity of my feeling of high gratitude to all the people who have directly or indirectly contributed to the successful completion of this book. This intensive research project would have remained incomplete if the sentiments of those who contributed directly or indirectly are not acknowledged. First and foremost, I bow my head in reverence to "Bhole Shankar" who blessed me with this opportunity of higher education and gave me the courage and confidence to follow the right path.

It is indeed my great privilege to express deep sense of gratitude to my distinguished and esteemed research supervisor Dr. Devinder Sharma, Professor, Department of Commerce, Himachal Pradesh University, Shimla -05, for his unvarying supervision and guidance in nurturing this study from conception to completion. His wide range of knowledge, critical understanding and research expertise has been of invaluable help in my research work. In this regard, from start to finish, I have received great inspiration, steady encouragement and affectionate guidance from my respected supervisor.

It gives me immense pleasure to place on record my deep sense of gratitude to Prof. O.P. Verma, Prof. S.S. Narta, Prof. Kulwant Singh Pathania, Prof. Kulbhushan Chandel, Prof. Vijay Kumar and Dr. Raj Kumar Singh, distinguished teachers of Department of Commerce, Himachal Pradesh University, Shimla -05, whose ever willing cooperation and inspiration helped me to complete this work in right perspective.

I want to express my deep gratitude towards all those respondents who have been a source of information and without their kind cooperation; it would not have been possible to carry out my research work.

I am also indebted to the librarian and staff members of various libraries, particularly, Himachal Pradesh University library; Indian Instituted of Advanced Study library, Shimla; Dr. Y.S. Parmar University of Horticulture library, Nauni Solan; State library Shimla; Jawaharlal Nehru University library, Delhi; and various departments such as Tribal Development Department, Himachal Pradesh Government, Shimla; Directorate of Land Records Kasumpati, Shimla; Directorate of Horticulture, Navbhahar, Shimla; Directorate of Census Operations, Himachal Pradesh, Shimla; for providing me every help to consult all relevant study material.

I am highly indebted to my father Shri Dharam Pur Bhandari and my loving mother late Smt. Karan Butit Bhandari, my elder brothers and sisters: Shri Bana Singh Bhandari, Mr. Anil Bhandari, Smt. Sewti Kusha, Mrs. Rupa Dhanshyan, Mrs. Sarita Jha and my sisters in law Smt. Yankhub Bhandari and Mrs. Chitralekha Bhandari, who supported in pursuing my higher education by providing me moral and financial help and also gave me liberty to do anything.

I express my sincere thanks to Dr. Keshav Sharma, Dr. Bharti Sharma, Research Fellow Mr. Anupam Sharma, Dr. Munish Ribalta and Mrs. Suman Ribalta for their resourcefulness and help extended by them in completion of my book.

I am also deeply indebted to all the authors whose books and research papers I have read consulted and cited in the book. I am obliged to all those who helped me in all possible ways in bringing my research work to a fruitful conclusion.

Dated:

Place: **Dr. Heera Bhagti**

List of Table

List of Figure

List of Maps

Contents

1

Outline of Cropping Pattern in Tribal Areas of Himachal Pradesh

India is characterized by great diversity in terms of provincial attributes, agro-ecological characteristics, and social and economic identities of those involved in agriculture. It has been admitted that the agricultural extension system has generally not succeeded in reducing the gap between crops yields that could have been obtained through improved practices. The government of India has launched the National Food Security Mission and the Rashtriya Krishi Vikas Yojna to rejuvenate agriculture and improve farm income. Out of India's more than one billion people, 69 percent[1] population lives in rural areas where the main occupation is agriculture, which plays a significant role in the process of socio-economic development.

In the pre-independence agrarian system at the time of the arrival of the British, Indian economy was, self-reliant, possessing a fine balance between agriculture and industry. Large portions of population, (about three-fourth) depended on agriculture which was a subsistence occupation. Agricultural activities were mainly devoted to food-crops like paddy, wheat and millets. Most of the food produced in the villages was consumed by the village population itself and the raw material produced by the peasants fed the needs of handicrafts. Apart from agriculturists, there were other classes of people like weavers, carpenters, potters, oilmen, washer man, cobblers and barbers. People engaged in these hereditary occupations, were paid out of the crops at the time of harvest for the services rendered by them either in terms of cash or in kind. There were three distinct classes in the villages. These were; agriculturists, village artisans & menials, and Village officials. The villages were isolated and self -

contained units, appropriately called by economic historians as small republics.

1.1 Consequences of British Rule

The British rule in India can be divided in to two periods: (a) The period of East India Company from 1757 to 1858, and (b) from 1858 to 1947. The British interests in India were governed by their requirements due to industrial revolution. These requirements were two fold: (a) to secure raw materials from India for factories in Britain and (b) to ensure permanent market in India for the British manufactures.

The British pursued a trade policy which encouraged exports of raw material and imports of manufactured goods. The farmers were forced, through Zamidars and British agents to switch-over from food-crops (wheat, paddy, millets) to cash-crops (cotton, jute, tobacco, indigo) and sell the latter to be exported to Britain. The process of commercialization of agriculture was intensified by the development of railways. These all initiatives were although favouring British yet encouraged cash-crops in India.

1.2 Independent India and the Land Reforms

The most important natural resource of India is land which is the base for agricultural production. It is the prime resource of the vast majority of the poor deriving livelihood from agriculture. Since independence, land reforms have been recognised as a crucial element of the poverty removal strategy and for modernisation of agriculture. The two types of legislations brought forth by the national government where; one, against the feudal hangovers in order to encourage the capitalist form of agriculture, and second, to put limits on the maximum amount of land owned so that, in the name of social justice, 'teeming millions' could be contained within the rural areas.[2] The objective of land reforms was to revamp the institutional framework by redistributing land in favour of the poor, providing security of tenure, regulating rents on land, and consolidating small and fragmented holdings.

The Land Reforms constituted the following:[3]

- Abolition of intermediaries.
- Tenancy reforms including security of tenure, regulation of rent, and conferment of ownership rights on tenants.

- Ceiling on land holdings and distribution of surplus land among landless workers and marginal farmers.
- Consolidation of holdings.
- Protection of 'tribals' rights in land.
- Modernization of land administration.

After independence, Land Reform Programme was started with great elaboration to bring social justice to the rural masses. Legislations were enacted in different States for the abolition of Zamindari System by fixing ceiling on land holdings, regulation of rents, and security of tenure.

1.3 Cropping Pattern in Indian Agriculture

Cropping pattern refers to the distribution of cultivated land among different crops. It also reveals the nature of agricultural operations, including the importance of food-crops vis-à-vis cash-crops. Cropping pattern is influenced by a host of factors which can be classified in to two categories.

(a) Physical factors (b) Economic factors

(a) Physical Factors: include soil conditions, extent of rainfall and type of climate.

(b) Economic Factors: include relative prices of agricultural commodities, size of the farms, availability of inputs, demand conditions, system of land holdings and government policy regarding exports, imports, taxes and subsidies. The crops are categorized in terms of physical and economic factors as under:

(i) Kharif Crops: under which crops are planted at the Southwest monsoon in June–July and harvested in September–October.

(ii) Rabi Crops: under which crops are planted usually between October and December and harvested between March and May.

The important cash-crops in the Country are; oilseeds, sugarcane, ginger, pepper, rice, wheat, apple etc[4]. These cash-crops have a great importance in national income. Some of the major commercial crops, which are grown in the states known for higher crop- production and have a great contribution in the national trade, are as under:

1. **Food Grains:** These include rice, wheat, coarse, cereals (like maize, gram, bajra, jowar), and pulses. These crops constitute the backbone of India's food economy. In India, nearly 75 percent of the cultivated area is occupied by food-crops including rice, wheat, millets, and pulses[5]. Paddy is the most important food-crop in India followed by wheat. There has been no significant change in the cropping pattern during the post independence period. The present cropping pattern is unbalanced as it is heavily tilted in favor of paddy and wheat while area under oilseeds and pulses is less than required.
2. **Oilseeds:** There are ten major oilseeds produced in India, namely groundnut, castor seed, sesame, soya bean, sunflower, rapeseed, mustard, linseed and safflower. Of these, groundnut, rapeseed, mustard and soya bean occupy commanding position in terms of total production.
3. **Fiber Crops:** cotton and jute are the chief crops under this category.
4. **Plantation Crops:** These include sugarcane, tea, coffee, tobacco, rubber, cocoa, cardamom, cashew and coconut. Some of these crops constitute important items of cashew in the world. Coconut is tree crop grown extensively in coastal areas providing livelihood to about 10 million people in cultivation, processing and related activities[6].
5. **Horticultural Crops:** India, with its wide variability of climate and soil, produces a large range of horticultural crops such as fruits, vegetables, potato, tropical tuber crops, ornamental crops, medicinal and aromatic plants, and spices like black pepper, cardamom, ginger, garlic, turmeric, and chilies. The variety of fruits grown includes mango, banana, citrus, pineapple, papaya, guava, sapota, jackfruit, litchi, grapes and nuts.

But the cropping pattern varies from region to region. It is influenced by factors like topography, climate, mode of production, cultural ethos etc. As the present study is focusing on the cropping patterns, it is essential here to define, what exactly the term 'cropping pattern' means. Cropping pattern is the proportion of area under various crops. The cropping patterns of a region are closely influenced by the geo-climatic, socio-economic, historical and political factors (Hussain, M. 1996)[7] influencing patterns of crop based land use of a region and are manifestation of combined influence of physical and human environment. Differences in attitude towards the rural land in the level of prosperity and technology have produced changes in emphasis. Their effects on both landscape and land use studies are likely to be far reaching (Coppock, 1968)[8]. It is pertinent to mention that weather plays a decisive role in determining the existing cropping pattern. It is also depending on terrain, topography, slope, soils and availability of water for irrigation use of pesticides, fertilizers and mechanization. In simple words, cropping pattern means the production of various crops at a point of time. It is dynamic concept because no cropping pattern can be said to be ideal for all times to a particular region. It changes in accordance to space and time with a view to meet requirements and is governed largely by the physical as well as cultural and technological factors. The change in cropping pattern in a particular span of time clearly indicates the changes that have taken place in the agricultural development. These changes are brought about by socio-economic influence.

1.4 Crop Diversification in the Indian Perspective

With the advent of modern agricultural technology, especially during the period of the Green Revolution in the late sixties and early seventies, there is a continuous surge for diversified agriculture in terms of crops, primarily on economic considerations. According to R.B.I. "A contributing factor responsible for below potential performance of agriculture, is the failure to sufficiently diversify the cropping pattern." The minimum support price policy has distorted the relative prices between rice and wheat, on the one hand, and other food and non food crops, on the other, giving rise to a deformed cropping pattern. It has contributed to a steep rise in the ratio of procurement to production over the years. The higher increase in Maximum Retail Prices (MRPs) of rice and wheat relative to prices of other agricultural commodities has contributed to an incentive structure that favours production of rice and wheat at the cost of other crops.

However, changes take place in the cropping pattern due to the factors categorised as:

a) Resource related factors covering irrigation, rainfall and soil fertility.

b) Technology related factors covering not only seed, fertilizer, and water technologies but also those related to marketing, storage and processing.

c) Household related factors covering food and fodder, self-sufficiency requirement as well as investment capacity.

d) Price related factors covering output and input prices as well as trade policies and other economic policies that affect these prices either directly or indirectly.

e) Institutional and infrastructure related factors covering farm size and tenancy arrangements, research, extension and marketing systems and government regulatory policies.

These factors are not resistant but inter-related. The adoption of crop technologies is influenced not only by resource related but also by institutional and infrastructure related factors. Similarly, government policies - both supportive and regulatory in nature - affect both the input and output prices. Likewise, special government programmes also affect area allocation and crop composition. More importantly, both the economic liberalization policies as well as the globalization process are also exerting strong pressures on the area allocation decision of farmers, essentially through their impact on the relative prices of inputs and outputs. Although the factors that influence the area allocation decision of farmers are all important, they differ in terms of the relative importance both across farm groups and resource regions. While factors such as food and fodder self-sufficiency, farm size, and investment constraints are important in influencing the area allocation pattern among smaller farms, larger farmers with an ability to circumvent resources constraints usually go more by economic considerations based on relative crop prices than by other non-economic considerations. Similarly, economic factors play a relatively stronger role in influencing the crop pattern in areas with a better irrigation and infrastructure potential. In such areas, commercialization and market networks co-evolve to make the farmers more dynamic and highly responsive to economic impulses.

What is most notable is the change in the relative importance of these factors over time. From a immense generalized perspective, Indian agriculture is increasingly getting influenced more and more by economic factors. This needs not be surprising because irrigation expansion, infrastructure development, penetration of rural markets, development and spread of short duration and drought resistant crop technologies have all contributed to minimizing the role of non-economic factors in crop choice of even small farmers. Further, the reform initiatives undertaken in the context of the ongoing agricultural liberalization and globalization policies are also going to further strengthen the role of price related economic incentives in determining crop composition both at the micro and macro levels.

1.5 Consequences of Crop Pattern Changes

Turning now to the socio-economic and environmental consequences of crop pattern changes, the Green Revolution technologies have among other things, an increasing tendency towards crop specialization and commercialization of agriculture. While these developments have positive effects on land/labour productivity and net farm income. They have also endangered a number of undesirable side effects like reduced farm employment and crop imbalances. Although the expansion of commercialized agriculture has fomented new sets of rural non-farm activities and strengthened the rural-urban growth linkages, it has also weakened the traditional inter- sectoral linkages between the crop and livestock sectors.

Besides, crop pattern changes also lead to serious environmental consequences that take such forms as groundwater depletion, soil fertility loss and water logging and salinity - all of which can reduce the productive capacity and growth potential of agriculture over the long-term. A classical example is the rice-wheat system in North western India replacing traditional crops like pulses, oilseeds and cotton.

1.6 Cropping Pattern and Topographical Conditions of India

India is endowed with almost all the important topographical features, high mountains, extensive plateaus and wide plains traversed by mighty rivers. Hence a wide range of crops are grown in the Country. The topographical factor draws multi-level effects over a community. A particular topography effects climate of that region, which further impacts the level as well as pattern of production (agricultural or horticultural). In this way, topography remains a determining factor in causing the variations in terms of socio-economic conditions of a community too. As the study relates to tribal areas, it becomes important to have an understanding about the demography of tribes in the Country, in general and Himachal in particularly. What makes this study analytical and so interesting is the fact that tribal pockets are scattered around different topographical set-ups.

Moreover, this variation is both inter- regional and intra-regional in nature.

1.7 Indian Tribes

India is the home to large number of indigenous people who are still untouched by the lifestyle of the modern world. As per Census 2011, India has the total tribal population of 1, 04,281,034 which is 8.61 percent of the total population[9]. These tribal people also known as the 'adivasis', who are still dependent on haunting, agriculture and fishing. Some of the major tribal groups in India are Gonds, Santhas, Khasis, Angamis, Bhils, Bhutias and great Andamanese. All these tribal people have their own culture, tradition, language and lifestyle.[10] There are a number of tribes in India, spread over the country from the foot hill of the Himalayas to the lands tip of Lakshadweep and from the plains of Gujarat to the hills in the North-East.

Article 366 (25) of the Constitution of India[11] refers to Scheduled Tribes as those communities, who are scheduled in accordance with Article 342 of the Constitution[12]. This Article says that only those communities, who have been declared as such by the President through an initial public notification or through a subsequent amending Act of Parliament, will be considered to be Scheduled Tribes. Article 342[13] provides for specification of tribes or tribal communities or parts of or groups within tribes or tribal communities which are deemed to be for the purposes of the Constitution as the Scheduled Tribes in relation to that State or Union Territory. In pursuance of these provisions, the list of Scheduled Tribes are notified for each State or Union Territory and are valid only within the jurisdiction of that State or Union Territory and not outside.

1.7.1 Distribution of Tribes

Tribes or tribal communities are deemed to be for the purposes of the Constitution as the Scheduled Tribes in relation to a State or Union Territory. In pursuance of these provisions, the list of Scheduled Tribes are notified for each State or Union Territory and are valid only within the jurisdiction of that State or Union Territory and not outside.

The Scheduled Tribes are notified in 30 States/UTs and the number of individual ethnic groups, etc. notified as Scheduled Tribes is 705[14]. The tribal population of the Country, as per 2011 Census, is 10.43

crore, constituting 8.6 percent of the total population out of whom 89.97 percent live in rural areas and 10.03percent in urban areas. The decadal population growth of the tribal from Census 2001 to 2011 has been 23.66 percent against the 17.69 percent of the entire population[15]. A smaller portion of their population has now settled in permanent villages as well as in towns and cities. On the whole, as per rough estimates, the prominent tribal areas constitute about 15 percent of the total geographical area of the Country.

1.7.2 State-wise Tribal Populations in India

The State-wise population of tribes according to the Census of 2001 and 2011, depicted in the table 1.1, indicates that the population of tribes has grown-up more than the population growth of India from 2001 to 2011. The growth in total population of tribes in India has been recorded 23.76 per cent as against of the total population growth of 17.68 per cent in the Country. In the Union Territories, the population of these communities has not grown much as compared to the states except Lakshadweep where the growth in tribal population has been recorded 7.91 percent against 4.91percent growth in their total population in 2011.

Table-1.1 : States and Union Territory-wise Population of Tribes in India

State /U.T.	Population of Tribes (000s)			Growth	Population (000s)			Growth
	2001	2011	%		2001	2011	%	
Andhra Pradesh	5024 (6.0)	5918 (6.0)	**7.02**	17.79	76210 (7.4)	84280 (7)	**100**	10.58
Arunachal Pradesh	705 (0.8)	951 (0.9)	**68.76**	34.89	1098 (0.1)	1383 (0.1)	**100**	25.95
Assam	3309 (3.9)	3884 (3.7)	**12.44**	17.37	26655 (2.6)	31205 (2.6)	**100**	17.06
Bihar	758 (0.9)	1336 (1.3)	**1.28**	76.25	82998 (8.0)	104099 (8.6)	**100**	25.42
Chhatisgarh	6617 (7.8)	7822 (7.5)	**30.62**	18.21	20834 (2.0)	25545 (2.11)	**100**	22.61
Goa	- (-)	149 (0.1)	**10.21**	-	1348 (0.1)	1458 (0.1)	**100**	8.16
Gujarat	7481 (8.9)	8917 (8.5)	**14.75**	19.19	50671 (4.9)	60439 (4.9)	**100**	19.28
Haryana	- (-)	**0**	**-**	-	21145 (2.1)	25351 (2.1)	**100**	19.89

Contd. ...

Himachal Pradesh	245 (0.3)	392 (0.4)	**5.71**	60	6078 (0.6)	6864 (0.6)	**100**	12.93
Jammu & Kashmir	1106 (1.3)	1493 (1.4)	**11.90**	34.99	10144 (1.0)	12541 (1.0)	**100**	23.62
Jharkhand	7087 (8.4)	8645 (8.3)	**26.20**	21.98	26946 (2.6)	32988 (2.7)	**100**	22.42
Karnataka	3464 (4.1)	4248 (4.1)	**6.95**	22.63	52850 (5.1)	61095 (5)	**100**	15.60
Kerala	364 (0.4)	485 (0.5)	**1.45**	33.24	31841 (3.1)	33406 (2.8)	**100**	4.91
Madhya Pradesh	12233 (14.5)	15316 (14.7)	**21.09**	25.20	60348 (5.9)	72626 (6)	**100**	20.34
Maharashtra	8517 (10.1)	10510 (10.1)	**9.35**	23.40	96879 (9.4)	112374 (9.3)	**100**	15.99
Manipur	741 (0.9)	903 (0.9)	**35.14**	21.86	2167 (0.2)	2570 (0.2)	**100**	18.59
Meghalaya	1993 (2.4)	2556 (2.5)	**86.18**	28.25	2319 (0.2)	2966 (0.2)	**100**	27.9
Mizoram	839 (1.0)	1036 (1.0)	**94.43**	23.48	889 (0.1)	1097 (0.1)	**100**	23.39
Nagaland	1774 (2.1)	1711 (1.6)	**86.50**	-3.55	1990 (0.2)	1978 (0.16)	**100**	-0.60
Orissa	8145 (9.7)	9590 (9.2)	**22.84**	17.74	36805 (3.6)	41974 (3.5)	**100**	14.04
Punjab	- (-)	0	**-**	-	24359 (2.4)	27743 (2.3)	**100**	13.89
Rajasthan	7098 (8.4)	9238 (8.8)	**13.47**	30.14	56507 (5.5)	68548 (5.7)	**100**	21.30
Sikkim	111 (0.1)	206 (0.2)	**33.77**	85.58	541 (0.1)	610 (0.05)	**100**	12.75
Tamilnadu	651 (0.8)	794 (0.1)	**1.10**	21.97	62406 (6.1)	72147 (5.9)	**100**	15.60
Tripura	993 (1.2)	1167 (1.1)	**31.77**	17.52	3199 (0.3)	3673 (0.3)	**100**	14.81
Uttar Pradesh	108 (0.1)	1134 (1.2)	**0.56**	950	166198 (16.2)	199812 (16.5)	**100**	20.22
Uttarakhand	256 (0.3)	292 (0.3)	**2.89**	14.06	8489 (0.8)	10086 (0.8)	**100**	18.81
West Bengal	4407 (5.2)	5297 (5.1)	**5.80**	20.19	80176 (7.8)	91276 (7.5)	**100**	13.84
Andaman & Nikobar	29 (0.03)	29 (0.03)	**7.63**	-	356 (0.03)	380 (0.03)	**100**	6.74
Chandigarh	- (-)	**0**	**-**	-	901 (0.1)	1055 (0.08)	**100**	17.09

Contd. ...

Daman & Diu	14 (0.02)	15 (0.01)	**6.17**	7.14	158 (0.01)	243 (0.02)	**100**	53.79
Dadra & Nagar Haveli	137 (0.2)	178 (0.2)	**51.74**	29.92	220 (0.02)	344 (0.03)	**100**	56.36
Delhi	- (-)	0	**-**	-	13850 (1.3)	16788 (1.4)	**100**	21.21
Lakshadweep	57 (0.1)	61 (0.1)	**95.31**	7.01	61 (0.01)	64 (0.005)	**100**	4.91
Puduchery	- (-)	**0**	**-**	-	974 (0.1)	1248 (0.1)	**100**	28.13
Total	84263 (100)	104281	**8.61**	23.76	1,02,8610 (100)	1,21,0569	**100**	17.68

Source: *Census of India 2011, pp. 15-19 and Socio Economic Indicators of Various States, 2002, pp. 1-6, Department of Economics and Statistics, Kasumpti, Shimla-09, Himachal Pradesh.*

Utter Pradesh, Bihar and Tamil Nadu have recorded the least tribal population (i.e. 0.56, 1.28% and 1.10%) in 2011 as against their total population. In Goa 0.1percent tribal population recorded in 2011 whereas, there was no tribal person in the State as per Census 2001. On the other hand, the total population of all the states and the union territories of India have recorded a positive growth from 2001 to 2011 except in Nagaland where there was a negative growth in the total population in 2011 from 2001 (-0.60 % in total population and -3.55% in tribal population). This indicates that the total population of India has grown up from 2001 to 2011 in all the states and union territories with the exception of a very meagre decline in total population in Nagaland whereas, the growth in the population of tribes in the States and the union territories has recorded a wide fluctuation resulting to more growth in the population of tribes as compared to the growth in total population.

India being diversified in terms of geography, languages, castes, economic structure, religion and culture, the major classifications of tribes in the Country is as follows:[16]

1.7.3 Tribes as per Linguistic Classification

On the basis of linguistic classification, people of India can be classified into the four speech families' viz. the Indo- European (Aryan), the Dravidian, the Austric (Kolar Munda) and the Tibeto-Chinese (Sino-Tibetan) tribes. Regarding linguistic classification, Majumdar opines that so far as the tribal people are concerned, the

Aryans speech comes into the picture only as a consequence of cultural contact since almost all of the tribal people have pre- Aryan or non-Aryan racial affinities and origins. The tribal people of India may be classified chiefly into three speech families.

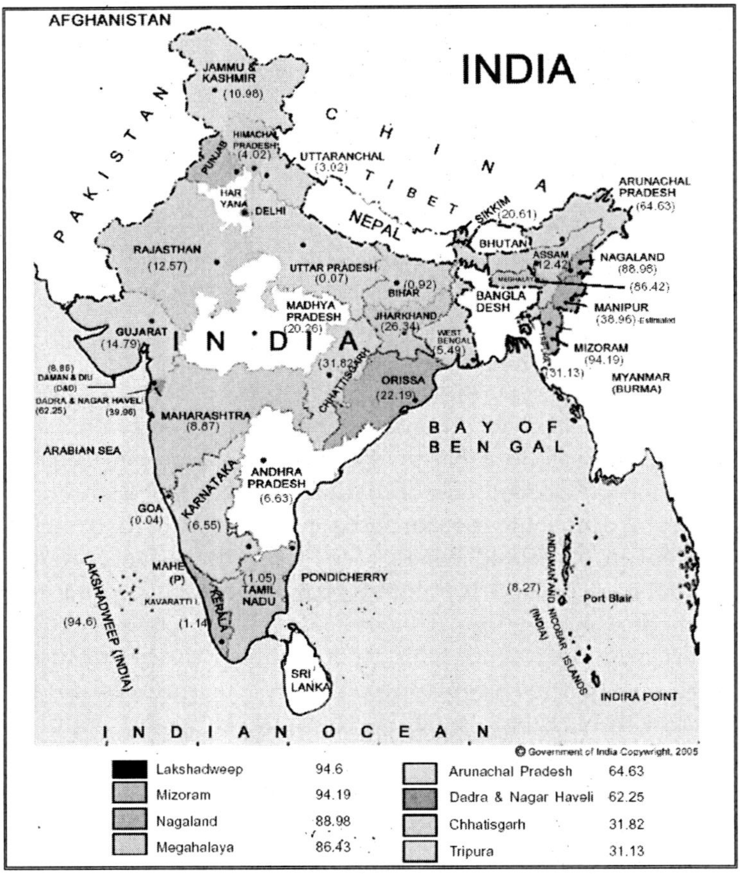

Map 1.1 : Tribal Population in India

The tribal people speaking Dravidian family language inhibit the middle and southern India. The most developed languages of Dravidian family are Tamil, Telugu, Kannada and Malayalam. The speeches of Toda, Paliya, Chenchu, Irula and Kadar are also included in the Dravidian family.

The Austric family of speeches is also known as mund speech family. Speeches of the family are spoken mainly by the tribes of

Chhota Nagpur area but these are also in vogue to a lesser extent, in some parts of Madhya Pradesh, Orissa, West Bengal, Madras and Terai region of Himalayas stretching from Bihar to Shimla hills. The Santhali speech of Bengal, Bihar and Orissa, Mundari, Ho- Kharia, Bhumij and some other speeches of Bihar are also included in this family.

Tibeto-Chinese speeches are spoken most by the tribes of mangol racial stock. The family is divided into two branches viz. Tibeto-Burman and Siamese- Chinese. The tribes of Assam, Meghalaya and some other parts of the north- east India speak are of this family.

1.7.4 Racial Classification of Tribes

On the basis of racial classification, tribes can be classified in to six main races with nine sub-types. These are:

1) The Negrito
2) The Proto-australoid
3) The Mangoloid
    a) Palaco- mangoloid;
    b) Long headed and
    c) Broad headed
4) The Mediterranean
    a) Palaco-Mediterranean
    b) Mediterranean
    c) Oriental type
5) The Western Brachycephals, and
    a) Alpinoid
    b) Dinaric
    c) Armenoid
6) The Nordic

The tribes of the hills of Cochin and Travancere such as Kadar, Irula, Paliyan. Angami naga of Assam and tribes of Rajmahal hills of Eastern Bihar are included in Nagrito racial type which exhibits short stature, black skin colour, black wooly hair, thin lips and broad nose.

The Proto-australoid racial type exhibits short to medium stature, long and high head, small face and small flattened nose. Most of the middle or Central Indian tribes come within this race. Some south Indian tribes like Cheachu, Bhill etc. also exhibit the racial characteristics of this type. As far as Mangoloid racial stock is concerned, most of the tribes of north-east India are included in this racial type. The Naga, Chakma, Lepcha etc. are some of the important tribes of this racial group.

1.7.5 Economic Classification of Tribes

In terms of the economic classification, the tribes in India can be classified as:

- Tribes hunting in forests
- Tribes engaged in hilly cultivation (Shifting or slash and burn cultivation)
- Tribes engaged in cultivation on leveled (plain) land
- Simple artisan tribes
- Pastrol tribes
- Tribes living as folk artists
- Agricultural and non- agricultural labour oriented tribes.
- Tribes engaged in service and trade.

The tribes, who are dependent upon hunting in forests, get their livelihood through collection of edible roots and fruits, hunting and fishing. This class of tribes is found mostly in Southern India. The Chenchu and Chandi of Andhra Pradesh, Kadar, Milapatram and Kurumaba from Kerala and Paliyan of Tamilnadu and Onge, Tarwa, Senteneless and Nicobarese of Andeman and Nicobar Islands are some of the important tribes of this category. The Raji of Uttar Pradesh, Hill Garo of Meghalaya, Bihar, Karw and Hill Kharia of Chhota Nagpur and Juan of Orissa are also some of the notable tribes of this category.

A vast chunk of Indian tribes is engaged in shifting cultivation on hilly or mountainous tracks of north- eastern and central India. This mode of cultivation is different from the conventional settled cultivation. Almost all the tribes of Assam, Meghalaya, Arunachal Pradesh, Mizoram, Manipur and Tripura produce their crops through this mode of cultivation. Some tribes of Orissa and Gonel and Baiga of Madhya Pradesh are also engaged in this mode of cultivation.

Some of the Indian tribes have their livelihood through cottage industries. They are engaged in basket and mat making, weaving, working as blacksmith and supplement the needs of their neighbor tribal and non- tribal societies. The Goffer of Kashmir and Kinnaura of Himachal Pradesh are proficient in such occupations. The Kolam of Maharashtra is the traditional mat weavers and the Irula of Tamilnadu make bamboo baskets. Totally pastoral tribes are very few. Yet Toda of Nilgiri Hills, Gaddi and Backrawal of Himachal Pradesh, Nageshia of Madhya Pradesh, Maldhan of Gujarat and some tribes of northern and southern India are notable examples who are pastoral. Some of these tribes trade milk and bear the cattle like sheep and goat for selling them in the market.

Another class of tribes earns their livelihood by performing dances like acrobatic, snake charming etc. and can be termed as folk artists. The Nut and Spera of Uttar Pradesh, Mundupptu of Orissa, Kota of Tamilnadu and Gonels of Madhya Pradesh are examples of this category.

1.7.6 Cultural Classification of Tribes

According to the cultural classification, the tribes can be mainly grouped into three classes. These are:

- Those who are culturally most distant from the rural and urban groups and are more or less, out of contact from others.
- Those who are under the influence of the culture of the rural and urban groups and have developed discomforts and problems consequently.
- Those who are although in contact with the rural and urban groups but could not adjust with their culture or are isolated.

The Indian Conference of Social Work appointed Tribal Welfare Committee which has suggested the following classification of tribes:[17]

- Tribal Communities,
- Semi- Tribal Communities,
- Accumulated Tribal Communities, and
- Totally assimilated tribes.

1.7.7 Classification of Tribes Based on Religious Beliefs

The religion has variably influenced the tribal communities and they still maintain their native religious purity. The tribes can be classified on religious basis as follows:

- Hindus;
- Christians;
- Buddhists;
- Muslims;
- Jain; and
- Other religions.

In fact, the impact of local and regional Deities plays a key role in the behaviour and practices of the tribes. They have full faith on their Deity and for the purpose of maintaining the purity in terms of the society to be blessed by the Deity; the tribes prefer to be in isolation and to live a life as per their socio- cultural ethos. However, there is a difference in the life styles and socio- cultural value systems in all the tribes.[18]

1.7.8 Region-wise Indian Tribes

Taking in to consideration Indian tribes are categorized in terms of regional classification also. The geographical, ecological, social, economic, administrative, ethnic and racial factors, vidyarthi and Rai (1976) proposed a fourfold geographical region along with one distinct sub region of the islands. These are:[19]

- **Himalayan Region:** it is divided in three sub-regions
  1) **North Eastern Himalayan Region:** It includes Assam, Meghalaya and mountainous region of West Bengal, i.e. Darjeeling, Arunachal Pradesh, Nagaland, Manipur, Mizoram and Tripura.
  2) **Central Himalayan Region:** The Tarai areas of Uttar Pradesh and Bihar fall in this region.
  3) **North Western Himalayan Region:** Himachal Pradesh and Jammu & Kashmir constitute this region.
- **Middle India Region**: It comprises Bihar, West Bengal, Orissa, and Madhya Pradesh.
- **Western India Region:** It includes Rajasthan Gujarat, Maharashtra, Goa, and Dadra and Nagar Haveli.
- **South India Region:** It comprises Andhra Pradesh, Tamil Nadu, Karnataka, and Kerala with a meagre tribal population.

➢ **The Island Region:** The islands of Andaman and Nicobar in the Bay of Bengal and Lakshadweep in the Arabian Sea constitute a distinct sub region.

With reference to the above classification, the present area of study falls in the north western Himalayan region. It is known for its unique topography in the Country so is the socio-economic patterns of life and the cropping pattern in particular. In this context, a brief description about the tribal distribution across the state of Himachal Pradesh is explained below:

1.8 Himachal Pradesh: A Brief Profile

Himachal Pradesh is one the hilly states of India which came into existence as a centrally administered territory on 15th April, 1948 with the merger of 30 former small princely hill states. And presently Himachal Pradesh comprises of 12 districts having an area of 55,673 Sq. Kms with the decennial population growth of 12.81 percent during 2001-2011 having sex ratio of 974 females per 1,000 males. The density of population is 123 persons per sq. km. and literacy rate is 83.78 per cent (2011).[20]

Table-1.2 : Himachal Pradesh at a Glance

Sr. No.	Particulars	Information
1.	Area	55,673 Sq. Kms
2.	Districts	12
2.	Population	68,56509
3.	Males	34,81,873
4.	Females	33,82,729
5	Schedule Tribe Population	3,92,000
6	Literacy rate	82.80%
7.	Per Capita Income (at current price 2015-16)	1,30,067
8.	Land area covered i) Agriculture ii) Horticulture	 9,54,651 Hct. 2,20,706 Hct.
9.	Average rain	1,225.4mm

Source: Statistical Outline of Himachal Pradesh – 2015-16, Economic and Statistics Department, Himachal Pradesh, Shimla-9.

1.8.1 Economy of the State

Before the formation of State, no attention was paid to the economic development and social welfare of the people of the region. The princes were indifferent and the people were helpless. These princes had inadequate financial resources and they were more struck to their inherited occupations. Even the British cared merely for the cantonment towns and for those places which they chose for their pleasure due to which, the rural and tribal regions were left to be covered in the process of development. Since the State is mainly rural and tribal hilly region, people of this region could not get the advantages of the development initiatives. Further, per capita land was scarce due to hilly terrain and the best of it was with the rulers or their relatives. The common peasants tilled less terraced fields, carved out of stony hill sides to make out a precarious living. However, the people of Kinnaur had some trade contacts with Tibet. Even the Punjab hill areas of Kangra, Kullu, Lahaul & Spiti and Shimla were also under the direct administration of the British Government still they lagged much behind the other progressive regions of Punjab and did not witness any substantial economic development up till the integration of this region in Himachal Pradesh on November 1, 1966. It was only after the formation of the State that the people and the Government of this hilly region started making strenuous efforts to improve their own economic conditions. The feature of the State is that rivers flow through the hilly terrains and there is adequate potential of hydro power. The places are worth for tourists' attraction as the customs and traditions, fairs and festivals, temple and monuments, fauna and flora attract thousands of tourists. Himachal Pradesh has emerged as leader in hill area development, horticulture revolution, education, services, investment in industry, power and tourism. However, majority of the population is rural and agriculture and horticulture are still the major occupations and as such, the rural life is still maintaining the traditional value system despite of the fact that the cropping pattern has however changed with the socio-economic influences. The cropping pattern of the state is explained as below:

a) **Agriculture in Himachal Pradesh:** In Himachal Pradesh, agriculture plays a substantial role in the State's economy as it is the chief occupation of people. About 10 percent of the total Gross State Domestic Product comes from agriculture and its allied sectors.[21] The main crops produced in Himachal Pradesh include; wheat, maize, rice, barley, seed-potato, ginger, vegetables, vegetable seeds, mushroom, chicory seeds, hops, olives, fig and off season vegetables that includes; ginger, potato, soyabean, oilseeds, and pulses etc. Agriculture provides employment to around 62 percent of the working population in the State and the agriculture sector including allied activities generates revenue of nearly [22].5 percent of the Gross State Domestic Product.22 The farmers have focus upon generating the cash crops for more revenue earning as it suits the agro-climatic conditions in Himachal Pradesh.[23]

b) **Horticulture:** The State has taken a leap forward to produce different varieties of fruits from tropical to temperate regions which have made it the fruit bowl of the Country. The area under fruits, which was 792 hectares in 1950-51 with total production of 1,200 tonnes, increased to 2, 24,352 hectares during 2014-15 and the total fruit production was 7.52 lakh tonnes.[24] The State is growing the fruits like apple, pear, peach plum, almond, walnut, citrus, mango, raisin grapes etc. Apple is the major fruit accounting for more than 49 percent of total area under fruits and about 85 percent of total fruit production. Commercially apple is the main fresh fruits grown in 1, 09,553 hectares against 400 hectares in 1950-51 followed by 3,025 hectares in 1960-61.[25]

1.9 Tribes in Himachal Pradesh

The tribal communities of India represent colourful traditions and custom and a distinct way of life. The tribes of this State, who are the natives of the borders of other countries, are in the Districts of Kinnaur and Lahaul-Spiti and some parts of Chamba and Kangra Districts. In Chamba district, the tribes are in Pangi and Bharmaur areas. Some of the tribes of Himachal Pradesh are as discussed below:

1.9.1 Gaddis

The Gaddis live in Bharmaur tehsil in Chamba district of Himachal Pradesh and along certain foot hills of the Dhauladhar in Kangra district. They frequently describe their own area as garden, the land of Gaddis or the Shiva- Bhumi. Though the majority of them are in Bharmour in Chamba district because of the migratory life, Gaddis are in Chamba, Kangra and Kinnaur.

1.9.2 Gujjars

The Gujjars are the important pastoral tribes of Himachal Pradesh. According to Crooke, the term Gujjars is from the Sanskrit word which is originally the name of Gujarat. Another interpretation of the term is 'Go- chars' i.e. Cowherds in Gujarat and Kathiawar. In Himachal Pradesh, they are descendents of Prophet Ishaque. Most of them have come from Jammu as it is referred that about 300 years ago, the marriage of the ruler of Sirmaur was settled with the daughter of a Raja of Jammu. The bride insisted that she would go to Sirmaur only when her Gujjars would also accompany her. The ruler of Sirmaur agreed and the Gujjars entered in Himachal Pradesh.

1.9.3 Lahaulis

The inhabitants of Lahaul belonged to a mix race of Mundari aborigins and Tibetans. The earliest history of Lahaulis is Brahmans found in Pathan valley and most probably, are the emigrants from Chamba.

1.9.4 Spitians

The inhabitants of the Spiti are Bhots, with strong infusion of Tartar blood and it is referred that not many years ago, a colony of 200 persons emigrated from the territory of Great Tibet. Usually, there is no caste system in Spiti. But, there is difference in communities as they do not get married with other communities.

1.9.5 Pangwals

The Pangwals are the residents of Pangi tehsil in Chamba district. They are predominantly Hindus and they do not normally migrate from their villages even for grazing sheep. They live in high valleys between the altitudes of 2400 to 3600 metres.

1.9.6 Bodh

The term Bodh has been derived from Tibetan origin. In ancient times, Tibet was known as 'Bhota Desh' and the Tibetans were called Bhots. These tribes were mostly found in Lahaul- Spiti and in the Pattan Valley region. The Bodhs or Bhots are Buddhists whose ancestors came from Tibet in the 7th and 8th century.

1.9.7 The Swangla Tribe

The swangla tribes are confined to the Pattan valley of Lahaul.

These are the people who are living in the Chandra and Bhaga valleys called the Swangla Mon or Muntsi. These people are considered highest in social position and it is believed that in the old times, these tribes belonged to the Brahmin migrants.

1.9.8 Khampa

Khampas are also considered as the migrants from Tibet who are very few in population. These are ranked at par with the Rajput communities. They believe in Buddhism.

1.9.9 Jad and Lamba

The Jads are also considered to be the original inhabitants of Tibet. Jads and Lambas used to visit Himachal Pradesh not to settle down here as a community but on adhoc basis for business purposes. They are Buddhist. They are in the Pangi area of Chamba.

1.9.10 Kinnauras

The kinnauras are primarily agriculturists with some subsidiary occupations like grazing, weaving, spinning etc. They belong to a mixed race. Those who are basically Hindus, they are Khashiyas. Indigenously, there were Khashiyas and Chamang. The present population also includes the descendents of Rajputs and Brahmins. The staple food of the kinner habitants is bras, barley, olga, shag dhankar, kodro and rad.[26] Further, a great majority of Kinnauras are now Buddhists in the northern half Chini division. The Kinnaura tribe has been mentioned in the Vedas, Puranas, the Indian Epics, the Theological literature of Jains and Buddhists etc. It is obvious that in Himachal Pradesh, the tribal communities are in the territories of upper mountainous ranges. These are in Kinnaur district, Lahaul- Spiti district and in some parts of Chamba and Kangra districts. However, in other districts of the State, there are few tribes. The district- wise population of Tribes in Himachal Pradesh is shown in the table 1.3. It is evident from the table that the population of Himachal Pradesh has grown up by 12.81 per cent in the decade of 2001 to 2011 and the population of Una, Kullu, Sirmaur and Solan has recorded more than its growth of the State. Similarly, the population of tribes has grown up by 60.32 per cent in 2011 and Una, Solan, Sirmaur, Shimla, Kangra and Hamirpur districts have recorded more decadal population growth of tribes in comparison to the growth of tribes in the State.

Table-1.3 : District-wise Population of Tribes in Himachal Pradesh

Districts	Population of Tribes			Decadal Growth	Total Population			Growth
	2001	2011	% of tribal population out of total population 2011		2001	2011	%	
Bilaspur	9,180 (3.7)	10,693 (2.7)	**2.79**	16.48	3,40,885 (5.6)	3,82,056 (5.6)	**100**	12.07
Chamba	1,17,569 (48.1)	1,35,500 (34.6)	**26.11**	15.25	4,60,887 (7.6)	5,18,884 (7.6)	**100**	12.6
Hamirpur	155 (0.1)	3044 (0.8)	**0.67**	1863.9	4,12,700 (6.8)	4,54,293 (6.6)	**100**	10.07
Kangra	1,597 (0.6)	84,564 (21.6)	**5.6**	5,195	13,39,030 (22.0)	15,072,23 (22)	**100**	12.56
Kinnaur	56,268 (23.0)	48,746 (12.4)	**57.82**	-13.36	78,334 (1.3)	84,298 (1.2)	**100**	7.6
Kullu	11,351 (4.6)	16,822 (4.3)	**3.85**	48.2	3,81,571 (6.3)	4,37,474 (6.4)	**100**	14.65
Lahaul-Spiti	24,238 (9.9)	25,707 (6.6)	**81.54**	6.06	33,224 (0.5)	31,528 (0.5)	**100**	-5.1
Mandi	10,564 (4.3)	12,787 (3.3)	**1.27**	21.04	9,01,344 (14.8)	9,99,518 14.6)	**100**	10.89
Shimla	4,112 (1.7)	8755 (2.2)	**1.07**	112.91	7,22,502 (11.9)	8,13,384 (11.86)	**100**	12.57
Sirmaur	5,960 (2.4)	11,262 (2.9)	**2.12**	88.95	4,58,593 (7.5)	5,30,164 (7.7)	**100**	15.60
Solan	3,542 (1.4)	25,645 (6.5)	**4.46**	624.02	5,00,597 (8.2)	5,76,670 (8.4)	**100**	15.19
Una	51 (0.02)	8601 (2.1)	**1.65**	16774	4,48,273 (7.4)	5,21,057 (7.6)	**100**	16.24
Total	2,44,587 (100)	3,92,126 (100)	**5.71**	60.32	60,77,900 (100)	68,56,509 (100)	**100**	12.81

Source: Statistical Outline of Himachal Pradesh, Sankhyakiya Pustika, Jan Jatiya Kshetra, Himachal Pradesh, Directorate of Statistics and Economics, Shimla-09.

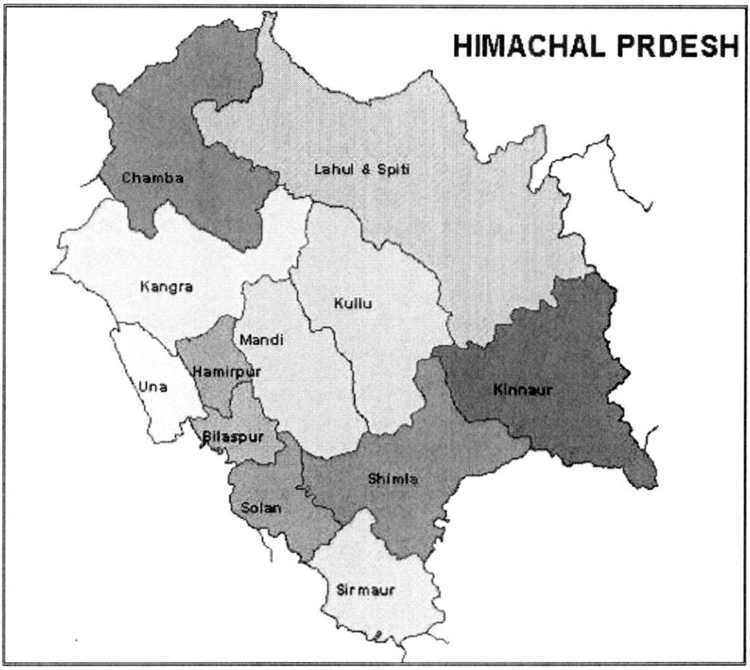

Map 1.2 : Himachal Pradesh

On the other side, the population of Kinnaur and Lahaul & Spiti districts has decreased as per the census 2011. A decline in population of tribal regions (Kinnaur -13.55% and Lahaul & Spiti -5.1%) leads to the conclusion that the people of tribal regions are migrating to other parts of the State as there has been unexpected growth of tribal population even in such regions which are not considered to have tribal communities.

1.10 Brief Explanation of the Study Area

The brief explanation of the districts viz. Kinnaur and district Lahaul & Spiti is as under:

1.10.1 Kinnaur District

Kinnaur is one of the districts of Himachal geographically considered as tribal region of the State. The inhabitants of Kinnaur are known as Kinnaura, Kinara, Kanawara, Kannaura or Kinnaurese. Recently it is known as Chini tehsil of Mhasu district which came into being as a self-governing district on May 1, 1960. According to 'Bhagwat Puran' Kinners trace their origin from the shadow of Lord Brahma. In mythological and legendry accounts, kinners are described as a distinct race of demigods, somewhere between human beings and gods.[27]

The names of the district were traditionally; Kanawar, Kunavur, Koonawur, Kanaur and Kanauring taken after the principal community Kanauras occupying the area. It is the north- eastern district of Himachal Pradesh, mountainous to an extra ordinary degree and lies on both the banks of the river Satluj. The people of Kinnaur formed the groups who during the period of cultural evolution, took refuge in accessible parts of the Country, lying in hills and forests, to escape extermination. They were cut-off from mobility of civilization and society and lived in isolation for centuries with their own belief, tradition and culture. Kinnaur comprises of main Trans- Sutlej valley and Sangla valley. The account of these ancient tribes is extensively found in the ancient literature like Vedas, Puranas, and Upanishads and in the account of classical writers both Indian and Greeks.[28]

Kinnaur has Uttar Kashi region of Uttaranchal and Rohru tehsil of Shimla district on the north. Its boundary lies with Spiti region on the west including the regions of Rampur and Kullu. It is marked by Sky- High Mountains, which are almost covered with snow most of the times. The district has beautiful valleys and climatically, it has long winter from October to May. The soil of the district contains minerals such as copper China clay, germ stones, mica, pyrites, silver etc. It has a typical flora and fauna. The socio-economic life of people of Kinnaur is quite different. People are peace loving and hard working. The Kinnauras have primarily been an agro-pastoral tribe. The traditional occupation of the Kinnauras had been agriculture, trade and sheep rearing but now a day's different kind of occupations such as weaving, spinning, grazing, carpentry, silver smithy etc. With the socio- economic changes in the region, a change has taken place in the life style of people of this district also. The people of this region have faith on the traditional systems, values and their gods and deities. The life style of the people is largely influenced by these systems and beliefs. Due to the development of infrastructure, facilities and literacy in the region, people have achieved good socio-economic status and their quality of lives has definitely changed. Yet, the prevailing traditional systems and beliefs are being given due recognition by them. The main places of the district are Chango, Chhitkul, Jangi, Kalpa, Kamru, Kanam, Kilba, Kothi, Leo, Lippa, Morang, Nichar, Nako, Namgya, Nesang, Puh, Rakchham, Ribba, Sangla, and Sapni.[29] The demographic status of Kinnaur is as shown below:

Table-1.4 : Demographic Status of Kinnaur District

Sr. No.	Particulars	Information
1.	Area	6401 Sq.Kms.
2	Head Quarter	Reckong Peo
3	Population (2011 Census)	84,298
4	Male Population (2011 Census)	46,364
5	Female Population (2011 Census)	37,934
6	Villages	660
7	Tehsils	6
8	Panchayats	65
9	Literacy rate (2011 Census)	80.77%
10	Male literacy rate (2011 Census)	88.37%
11	Female literacy rate (2011 Census)	71.34%
12	Population density (2011 Census)	13 per Sq. Km.
13	Agriculture Cultivated area	9407 Hectare
14	Horticulture cultivated area	9755 Hectare
15	Average rain	432.6 mm
16	Per capita land holdings	1.25 Hectare
17	Scheduled Tribe Population (2011 Census)	48,746
18	Number of Blocks	3
19	Health Institutions (Hospitals, CHCs, PHCs)	24

Source: Statistical Outline of Himachal Pradesh and Health at A Glance, Directorate of Statistics and Economics and Directorate of Health and Family Welfare, Govt. of Himachal Pradesh, Shimla-09.

1.10.2 Crops in Kinnaur

The Climate of Kinnaur is cold and dry and is ideally suited for the production of temperate and dry fruits. Apples, apricot, almond, walnut etc are found almost all over the district. The upper region of the district is famous for production of apple, chilgoza, almonds and walnut whereas, the lower region i.e. Sangla block and Nichar block are famous for production of apple, cherry, hazelnut, pears, peaches and grapes.

Map 1.3 : Kinnaur

Due to topographical, climatic and changing economic conditions and with exposure to new ideas and techniques, the emphasis of cropping in certain areas has started shifting from cereal crops to fruit crops in the district. The geography and the topography of the district inevitably determine the climate of the district which varies considerably with varying elevations and from the lower parts to the upper portions of the main Satluj valley by virtue of its elevation, the district may be said to have a temperate zone climate with a long winter from October to May, during which period snowfalls occur and there is a short summer from June to September. The transition periods from April to May and September to October correspond to the spring and autumn seasons of the temperate zone.[30]

1.10.3 Cropping Pattern of District Kinnaur

With the development of agriculture, which means land improvement, augmented facility improved input and credit supply, it is generally observed that the cropping pattern changed in favour of cash crops. "Until 1971-72, the economy of district Kinnaur was mostly non-commercial and underdeveloped in nature and hence, commercial crops were little in cropping. In Kinnaur district, about 90 percent area of total cropped area was under cereal crops. The area under cash crop like fruits, potato and vegetables was about 14 percent[31] in this district. During the decade of seventy to ninety (1970-90) the pattern of commercial crops has seen some changes as a lot of area has been shifted from non-commercial to commercial crops towards wheat, fruits, potato and vegetables. This changed trend towards commercialization of agriculture which has been more suitable. It is due to favourable agro-climate conditions that assured irrigation, better input supply road network etc. the percentage of area under fruits and cereals is highest in Kinnaur in 2015-16 is about 44.11 percent followed by, cereal crops 24.68 percent and 13.60 percent area under pulses in the district.[32] The change in cropping pattern thus suggests a movement in favour of commercial crops as against persistence of traditional agriculture.

1.10.4 Irrigation/Irrigated Intensity

Due to peculiar topography and the constant scarcity of rains have led people to improvise possibilities and methods of irrigating almost all their cultivated lands through the Kulh system. By and large, when water through Kulhs is available, all the lands receive their share, whereas, during the months when water is not so available, only such crops are grown, which do not need constant supply of water. In the district Kinnaur 51.04 percent of total cultivated area is under irrigation (2015-16)[33] and upper areas of Kinnaur is more cultivated, more irrigated and famous for chilgoza & dry fruits while lower areas of Kinnaur are better for growing apple crop.

1.10.5 Cropping Intensity

Kinnaur district is largely located in the dry zone where the temperature is very low throughout the year. The crops grown in the region take much time to mature as compared to other parts of the State. Most of the areas remain covered under snow for a long period and hence, the farmers grow only one crop. The intensity of cropping is 128.11 percent in 2015-16.[34]

1.10.6 Lahaul & Spiti

Lahaul & Spiti became a district of Himachal Pradesh in 1960. Alike Kinnaur, it is also considered as geographically tribal region of the State. The district in the Western Himalayas is situated between 31o 44′ 57" and 32o 59′ 57" North latitude and between 76o 46′ 29" and 78o 41′ 34" East latitude. It is separated in the North from Jammu & Kashmir, Tibet in the East and Kullu, Kinnaur in South-East and Chamba in the South-West and West. The sole access to Lahaul & Spiti lies over the 3,978 metres high Rohtang Pass. The two valleys Lahaul-Spiti have a tenuous link over the Kunzam Pass (4,520 meters). The two twin valleys, Lahaul & Spiti in the north eastern corner of Himachal Pradesh, protected by distance is a region of nature at its wildest which has lent it much enhancement. The threshold of Lahaul plateau is nourished by the Chandra and Bhaga rivers and surrounded by high mountains on all sides, the great Himalaya's to the North, the Pirpanjal to the south and the Spiti and Chandra watershed to the east. The languages spoken in Lahaul & Spiti are Bhoti, Manchat, Changsa and Gaheri.[35] The demographic status of Lahaul and Spiti district is depicted as follows:

Table-1.5 : Demographic Status of Lahaul & Spiti District

Sr. No.	Particulars	Information
1.	Area	13,835 Sq. K.M.
2.	H. Quarter	Keylong
3.	Population	31,528
4.	Male	16,455
5.	Female	15,073
6.	Village	521
7.	Tehsil	3
8.	Panchayats	41
9.	Literacy	77.24
10.	Male literacy	86.97
11.	Female literacy	66.50
12.	Population Density	2
13.	Agriculture Cultivated Area	3398
14.	Horticulture Cultivated Area	202
15.	Avg. Rain	496.6 MM
16.	Per Capita Land Holdings	1.56
17.	S.T.	25707
20.	Blocks	2

Source: Statistical Outline of Himachal Pradesh, Directorate of Economics and Statistics Kasumpti, Shimla-09, 2007-08 and census of India 2011.

Lahaul & Spiti is consisting of two districts of Lahaul & Spiti. Before the two districts were merged, Kardng was the capital of Lahaul, and Dharkar the capital of Spiti. The district is connected to Manali through the Rohtang Pass. Kunzam Pass is the entrance pass to the Spiti valley from Lahaul which is 21 Km. away from Chandra Tal. The Spiti ends at Samdho where the road enters Kinnaur and joins the National Highway No. 22.

1.10.7 Economy of Lahaul & Spiti

The primary source of economy is agriculture. Only 26 percent of the total land area is under cultivation. People of Lahaul-Spiti cultivate buck wheat, cauliflower, cabbage and cash crops like kuth, potato, hops, peas, mustard, raddish, trump, carrot, trench bean, beat root, tomatoes, soyabeen etc. Barley is the staple food of the people of this region. Lahaul-Spiti has earned the distinction of achieving the highest per hectare production of potatoes, relegating the Netherland, to second position.[36] The Lahaul valley figures in the record with potato fields located at the elevation ranging between 8,000 to 11,000 feet above the sea level.[37]

Chief medicinal herbs are species of 'Artimesin', 'Elpheelra', 'Acouitun', 'Podo phyllum', 'Karu', and 'Hyroscyamus niger', jelly of the fruit of Hippophae rhamnoides is recommended by Lamas in Lung complaints. 'Rattanjot' is found in Spiti valley. On the other side important forest products in Lahaul are Karu, Patish and Kala Zira. Cultivation of grass is the most remarkable feature of Lahaul. Lahaulis are forced to grow grass to save their live stock from starvation in the winter. A fruit-cum-demonstration farm at Tabo district encourages farmers to sow fruit plants like apricot, almond and apples. The area being provided improved saplings under 50 percent subsidies by the horticulture department.[38]

Map 1.4 : Lahaul & Spiti

The climate in the district is quite variable as the temperature goes below minus 20 degree Celsius during winter and 26 degree in summer and as such, it is temperate. The winter season is from the mid of November to March and is followed by spring which lasts for a month or so and is then followed by summer of 4 months and finally there is autumn for 6 weeks in October. Summers of the valley are cool and pleasant with green grass and alpine flowers and variety of crops. There is no monsoon in Lahaul and this enables climbers and trekkers to enjoy a long and unbroken season in pre perpetual sun shine and dry crisp air of Lahaul and explore the wilderness and grandeur of the inner Himalayas.[39]

1.10.8 Irrigation

Resources of irrigation in the district are kulhs (small water cannels) drawn from streams/khads. All the irrigation cannels could not run satisfactorily due to non-availability of sufficient water and scanty snowfall during the winter months. Rain is almost unknown, falling erratically and whimsically live angel's visits and even then so untimely and sparingly as to be a little benefit of land except to subside the clouds of dust. Average rainfall is 496.6 mm per annum. The monsoon rains reach the form of a misty drizzle. The only season in which moisture is obtained, is precisely that when no vegetation can be produced, namely in the winter months, when snowfall is both heavy and frequent and continues often, more or less from September till April. Snow does not lie permanently at lower elevations then 5334 m except in a few crannies. Glaciers are also not very large[40].

1.10.9 Cropping Pattern in Lahaul & Spiti

Lahaul & Spiti is the district which is pre dominantly engaged in agriculture and very less area 5.74 percent area is under fruits and vegetables in 2015-16[41]. Apple, plum, apricot, etc. are the horticulture crops which are being produced in some parts of the district. The areas for production of crops is limited due to steep valley for cultivation of crops and as such agricultural is the predominant holdings of buck wheat and pulses, peas, oil seed etc. with the opening of the vehicular roads and awareness, people have shifted from cereal crops to commercial crops like seed potatoes. The cropping intensity in Lahaul & Spiti district is 103.5 and irrigation intensity is about104 percent. The percentage of area under pulses is 50.63 percent followed by, cereal crops 16.69 percent in 2015-16.[42]

Lahaul valley produces seed potato which is popular throughout the Country. Before the introduction of seed potatoes, Kuth was used to be the principal commercial crop in the valley for which a research station was setup at Keylong in 1960; Vegetables have also been introduced in the valley. Hops are also grown in some parts a cash crop.

SUMMARY

India covers high hills, mountains, deserts, seas and plains etc. Majority of the population resides in rural areas and their source of live hood is agriculture and horticulture. With a view to encourage agriculture, land reform were made to revamp the institutional framework by redistributing land in favour of the poor, providing security of tenure, regularity of rents on land and consolidating small and fragmented holdings.

The crops are categorized on the physical and economic basis consisting of Kharif, Rabi, food crops, oilseeds, fiber crops, plantation crops and horticultural crops. During the period of green revolution in the late sixties and early seventies, there is a continuous surge for diversified agriculture on techno- economic considerations. Further, the topographical conditions have influenced production due to which, there is diversity in quality of production of crops and their demand in respect of changes in topography or regions , India has diversity in terms of communities including tribes identified on the basis of geographical, economical, religion, linguistic, cultural and topographical conditions. To ensure accurate and meaningful classification of Indian tribes, a Committee was constituted by the Government of India under the aegis of "The Indian Conference of Social Work" to look into the matter which suggested four classifications of tribes, viz tribal community, semi-tribal community, accumulated tribal community and totally assimilated tribes. Himachali tribes are one amongst them.

The Himachali tribes are basically categorised on the basis of topography living in border of Indian Territory which is close to China and Tibet. The tribes which are residing in Himachal Pradesh are; Gaddis, Gujjars, Lahaulis, Spitians, Pangwals, Bodh, The Swangla Tribe, Khampa, Jad, Lamba and Kinnauras. Kinnauras are in Kinnaur district which came into being as an independent district on May 1st, 1960 earlier known as Chini Tehsil of Mahasu. It is surrounded with the borders of other countries and hence, comprises a mixed culture. The people of the district are living for long, in isolation with their own belief, tradition and culture. It is only due to such faith and belief that the traditional system of livelihood, life style and treatment is in existence in the area. The main occupation of the people of Kinnaur is agriculture and horticulture as well as rearing of cattle in addition with the other occupation like weaving, spinning, grazing, carpentry, silver smithy etc. The upper region of the district is famous for production of apple, chilgoza, almonds and walnut and lower region for apple, cherry, hazelnut, pears, peaches and grapes.

Located in the north-eastern region of Himachal Pradesh, head quartered at Keylong, the primary source of economy of the Lahaul Spiti district is agriculture. The people of the district cultivate buck wheat, cauliflower, hops, cabbage, kuth, potatoes and peas etc. The main source of irrigation in both the tribal districts is kulh which is drawn from streams/khads.

Despite of a very small growth in the irrigation system through Kulhs, the high crop intensity affects high irrigation demand through kulhs in these districts as there is lack of viable irrigation system and low rain-receiving. There is great demand of the crops of tribal regions which is due to the feature of qualitative generic crops of these areas.

Endnotes

1. Census of India 2011.
2. V.S. Vyas, India's Agrarian Structure Economic Policies and Sustainable Development, Delhi: Academic Foundation, 2003, pp. 257-273.
3. Ibid., p.2.
4. Chandra Shekhra Prasad, Agriculture and Rural Development in India Since 1947, Delhi : New Century Publications, 2009, p. 12.
5. Ibid.,p.13.
6. Ibid.
7. Husain M., Systematic Agricultural Geography, Jaipur: Rawat Publications, 1996, pp. 222-223.
8. J.T. Coppock , "The Geography of Agriculture", Journal of Agriculture Economics, Volume 19, Issue 2, May 1968, pp. 153-175.
9. Census of India, 2011.
10. http://www.ecoindia.com/tribes/p. 1, accessed on 2/07/2015.
11. Ministry of Tribal Affairs Statistical Division Government of India, New Delhi: 2013, p. 26.
12. Ibid., p. 26.
13. Ibid.
14. Ministry of Tribal Affairs Statistical Division Government of India, op. cit., 2013, p. 26.
15. Census of India, 2011.
16. Majumdar, D.N., The Affairs of a Tribe: A Study in Tribal Dynamic, Lucknow: University Publishers, 2002, pp. 1-3.
17. Census of India, 2011.
18. Census of India 2011.
19. http://mrunal.org/2012/07/culture-tribes, p. 1, accessed on 1/08/2015.
20. Brief Facts - Himachal Pradesh (2011), Economics and Statistics Department, Himachal Pradesh, Shimla-9, p.vi.
21. Economic Survey of Himachal Pradesh, 2016-2017, p.42.
22. Ibid.
23. Ibid.
24. Ibid.,p. 56.
25. Ibid.
26. Rajender Attri, Himachal Pradesh: A Himalyan Dreamland, Shimla: Sarla Publications, 2016, p.66.

27. Jag Mohan Balokhra, The Wonderland – Himachal Pradesh, New Delhi: H.G. Publications, 2016, p. 97.

28. Ibid., p. 98.

29. Ibid., p. 552.

30. Mamgain, M.D., District Gazetteers: Kinnaur, Chandigarh:Punjab Press 163-A , 1975, pp. 34-35.

31. Verma, and Sharmaet.al, Tribal Development; Appraisal and Alternatives, New Delhi: Indus Publishing Co., 1998, p. 207.

32. Annual Season and Crop Report, Directorate of Land Record, Kasumpti Shimla Himachal Pradesh-09.

33. State Statistical Abstract of Himachal Pradesh, Department of Economics and Statistics Kasumpti Shimla-09, p. 21.

34. Annual Season and Crop Report, Directorate of Land Record, Ksumpti Shimla Himachal Pradesh-09.

35. Jag Mohan Balokhra, op. cit., p.396.

36. Jag Mohan Balokhra , op. cit., p. 616.

37. Ibid.

38. Ibid., pp. 616-617.

39. Sharma, Manorma, Tribal Melodies of Himachal Pradesh: Lahaul Valley, New Delhi:A.P.H. Publishing Corporation, 1998, pp.15-16.

40. Mamgain, M.D., District Gazetteers: Kinnaur, Chandigarh: Punjab Press 163-A,1975, pp. 34-35.

41. Annual Season and Crop Report, Directorate of Land Record, Kasumpti Shimla Himachal Pradesh-09.

42. Ibid.

2

Review of Literature

Abundance of literature is available on different aspects of agricultural economy. The scholars have studied the implications of different crops in the socio-economic set-up of the households, the community and the nation as well. Authors have tried to diagnose the obstructions and barriers paving the way of fast growth in agricultural sector and consequently unscientific cropping pattern which is not much instrumental in the development. Researchers have recommended measures to strengthen agricultural economy. However, the problem under research is still not being addressed substantially with reference to the tribal regions. To justify and to know about the causes responsible for it, attempt has been made in this chapter to review the existing available relevant literature.

2.1 Review of Literature

The existing related studies are reviewed as below:

Shah, (1948)[1] in **"Crops-Planning & Production"**, concluded that without a radical reconditioning and reorganization, there is little hope of any plan for the improvement of crops yields in India. According to him, without such a basic reorganization, there would be no chance of avoiding the greatest single handicap of the Indian farmer, viz., the excessive fragmentation and subdivision of his land. Thus, the author suggests that the area available can, and must be improved in quality so that improvement is reflected in the better nutritive value and larger yield of the crops, should be improved in terms of discovering of developing proper seeds suited to given conditions of soil and moreover, co-operative organization is required for profits in this behalf.

Jinha's paper, **(1962)**[2] **"Agriculture in the Hill Region of North India"**, elucidates that in India, farming gives a very small margin of income to the farmers particularly in hill regions of North India. He feels that the prospects of farm returns often hinge in natural factors, which are beyond the control of the farmers and that these factors may be; storms, drought, high winds, insects attract etc. According to him, the technical advances have greatly widened the scope of human action against natural hazards. So to uplift agriculture, the main emphasis has to be on the adoption of improved seeds and fertilizers, modern implements and the scientific methods of cultivation, for fighting pests and diseases.

Bradfield's (1964)[3] study, **"The Role of Educated People in Agricultural Development"**, focuses that in most developing countries, the number of men trained in the agricultural sciences is inadequate. Thus, limited human and physical resources of the new nations should be utilized in establishing a limited number of first–class institutions. Further, the services of large number of capable high-school, college, and university teachers who reach the mandatory retirement age each year, but who are in good health and wish to continue to serve mankind, should be utilized as a "Senior Peace Corps" to teach the teachers of science and moreover, emphasis needs to be drawn to improve quality of training particularly to motivate towards agriculture.

Frazier and Peterson's, paper **(1964)**[4] **"Plant Agriculture in the Emerging Nations"**, states that plant agriculture in the emerging nations is advancing rapidly, but is barely staying ahead of increasing population. According to the authors, average world production and population figures are somewhat misleading owing to gross inequality in distribution of food and population. It has been stated that a relatively short time is required to increase productivity by bringing new technology to bear in developing areas. Although he feels that known technology is shown to be capable of impressive production increase, a changed philosophy concerning agricultural research and education is necessary for a permanent solution of the production problem in the emerging nations.

Regarding agriculture institutions, **Hill (1964)**[5] reveals in his study, **"Developing Agricultural Institutions in Underdeveloped Countries"**, that development of an effective agricultural extension service is of major importance to a developing country and it must be based on adequate research and experimentation. According to the author, if a developing country wishes substantially to increase production by shifting from a traditional to a modern agriculture, it must be prepared to make large investments; public and private, in education, research, extension, transportation, storage, processing, plants, marketing facilities, and credit facilities and heavy investment as part of a program of land reforms and outside assistance should be most effective, organized on a long term basis and should be continued at or near the established level to enable the developing countries to "take off" on their own.

Kellogg, (1964)[6] has highlighted in his paper, **"Interactions and Agricultural Research"**, that interdisciplinary research to learn the interaction among farm practices and the application of combination in accordance to the local kinds of soil is characterized in modern agriculture in the advanced countries. The author opines that the principle of interaction applies in planning a management system for a field or for a farm so research and education is required to develop the basis for the efficient agriculture, which modern science and technology makes possible in newly emerging countries.

Long, (1964)[7] reveals in his study, **"Institutional Factors Limiting Progress in the Less Developed Countries"**, that the agricultural scientists and administrators in the United States advise on technology, and services in the developing countries to the effectiveness of the institutions without understanding the changing role which the institutions play in the country they serve towards development.

In **Phillip's, (1964)**[8] work, **"Animal Agriculture in the Emerging Nations"**, the author opined that development of crop rotation systems in intensively cultivated areas can contribute to feed supplies for animal kept as adjuncts to plant agriculture. So, development of improved transportation, processing and marketing facilities is needed in order to provide adequate links between producers and consumers with in the emerging countries or between produces and export facilities.

Jakhade, (1965)[9] in his study, **"Food Grain Marketing Zone in India"**, feels that the formation of institutional structures is a long term process, and changes if any, to be made, must be throughout and must lead to the attainment of the socio- economic development. So the author suggests that adhoc changes at frequent intervals need to be avoided and the new institutional set up should be steadily built up on strong foundations.

Evans, (1966)[10] opined in his study, **"The Apple Processing Industry"**, that apple growers must be informed about the relative net return from each processing firm and always be alert to switch supplies to the processors paying the highest net return, thereby supporting and maintaining strong cooperative processors.

Gupta, (1966)[11] comments in **"Some Aspects of Input-Output Relationship in Indian Agriculture"**, that agriculture in India is now on the threshold of entering into a stage of development characterized by a shift from static technology embracing land and labour as major inputs to a modern technology in which capital, equipment and purchased inputs occupy the larger shape. But to realize the output potential of the new technology quickly and to fuller extent, farmers will have to be made aware of new horizon. According to the author, the diffusion of new technology may, however be halted by the conditions of tenancy in the rural areas. He states that under static conditions, productivity of a tenant-operated farm may be, in many cases, higher than that of the owned-operated farms. But when development forces start working, tenancy will pose a barrier to output growth. So he advocates that for the successful diffusion of the new technology, institutional reforms are necessary and expansion of material resources, spread of education and modification of the tenure system must go hand to hand for the realization of the objective of higher productivity.

The research of **Mujumdar, (1966)**[12] **"Agricultural Growth in A Labour** Surplus **Economy"**, concludes that economic development in India may not be able to bring about any labour transfer from the agricultural sector to the non-agricultural sector for a considerable length of time and that the persistence of population pressure on agriculture, say for the next three decades or so, has certain important implications for agricultural growth like the pattern of agricultural growth will have to broadly follow the Japanese rather than the West European or American pattern in the sense that growth has to be ushered in the framework of small-scale family farming and by methods which permit a fuller use of the surplus labour and thus, rural economy has to learn to live with small and underemployed farmers.

Sangwan, (1966)[13] in his study, **"Changing Indian Agriculture-Epitomised Version of Left-Over Problems"**, feels that some of the vital issues and complex factors which normally stand in the way of agricultural production program need to be solved as and when they occur or inhibit and to cover up and solve these issues, there is a need of funds and a genuine, sympathetic and systematic human approach to solve them. Stress has been laid up on digging of more common field wells, bounding the fields, levelling the slopes and filling-up of gullies which could possibly help to expand agricultural production with little investment and technical knowledge. Further that the basic role of concerned agencies and Government is to know the farmer, his practical day-to-day field problems and for that matter, to extend correct guidance to farmers and to provide the necessary techno-economic and financial help.

Shivamaggi, (1966)[14] reveals in **"Impact of Food Aid on Agricultural Development"**, that the net effect of the Foreign Food Surplus Aid to India has been favourable from the point of India's overall economic development and the impact on developmental efforts in the agricultural sector can be maximized by making the Aid distinctly development-oriented in the sense of providing additional food grains for strengthening the agriculture base.

Ellott, (1967)[15] has lamented in **"Role of Agriculture"**, that except in very small number of 'oil economies' where the part played by agriculture is smaller, the mutual interdependence of the primary and secondary sectors in the process of development cannot be over-emphasized. In each stage of the argument, the author stressed that the way ahead seems to lie in the growth of productivity of the agricultural sector, only so can food be released to the industrial sector in adequate quantities adding to the right quality and in sufficient number of labour be transferred with adequate capital be raised, the natural linkages be maximized, and the balance of payment problems be minimized and hence, it would be easy to dismiss this as special pleading. The author concluded that there are no cases of successful development of a major country in which, rise in agricultural productivity did not precede or accompany industrial development.

Ray, (1967)[16] remarked in his book, "**Agricultural insurance"**, that a successful implementation of an international scheme for crop reinsurance would require the building-up of a substantial reserve to be used when aggregate identity period to the member countries in any year, exceeds the premium received from them or for an emergency, calls from more member countries. According to him, the maintenance of reinsurance reserve may be in kind or partly in cash as a measure of protection against large-scale deterioration in quality or damage by pets during storage or to purchase new stocks if necessary. It has been admitted that reserve can also be used as a measure of protection against excessive physical loss of insured crops.

Surridge, (1967)[17] has revealed in **"Farmers Marketing Organizations"**, that unless the new crop or new method has been actually seen, it is not likely to be adopted and if it calls for fertilizers, insecticides, selected seeds, or new implements, no progress will be made unless these objects are readily available at reasonable prices and if there is addition to these factors with a stimulus provided by a department of government whose officers are accepted as guides, philosophers and friends of the farming community, progress can be achieved.

Desai, (1969)[18] has concluded in **"Our Food Problem"**, that the problem of food in India has different dimensions. The author states that availability of food at the outset is low in quantity whereas, dietary and the defective distinction system and political pulls have enhanced the crisis as well as prices and that the food problem in India is mainly due to the slow growth of food production, low yield, malnutrition, under-nourishment, controlled distribution, wastages, food habits, rising prices and most important is the absence of a National Food Policy. Moreover, the author suggests that steps should be taken to accelerate food production by modernizing farming and by intensive use of irrigation and for this sector specific education has been felt to play a vital role to awaken people regarding their food habits.

Deshpande, (1969)[19] in his study, **"Low Returns to Cultivators"**, reveals that agriculture is the major industry in India with nearly 70 percent of the population engaged in it, but farmers get very low price for their produce. This causes a great deterrent to the sincere efforts of the farmers for increased food production. According to the author, it will go a long way in meeting the demands of the farmers all over the Country for getting the minimum, fair, remunerative and incentive prices for their agricultural produce and will give them a positive encouragement to put in their best efforts and invest more in the land for increased agricultural production. Hence, the author suggests that Co-operative credit at reasonably low rates of interest, co-operative processing, grading, marketing and buying should be extended to greatly help the farmers to augment the returns from land. Only then, all these factors will not only help to improve the economic condition of the Indian farmers and raise their standard of living in the years to come but will also solve the Country's serious food problem.

Shastri, (1969)[20] in **"Factor Influencing Cropping Pattern"**, states that price incentives for increase in production, might not hold good as a general rule as the cultivators are aware of the remunerativeness of cash crops, their decisions do not always conform to economic logic. Rather external forces of irrigation or intense urban influence, act upon their decision about price determination. It is felt that the existing price situation in the market favours cash crops and therefore, the cultivators find it distinctly advantageous to grow more of such crops. Again such features have alarming possibilities in the sense that it may lead to indiscriminate expansion of the areas under cash crops. So it is necessary to establish and maintain parity between the prices of grain and cash crops so that they retain the complementary relationship and do not become competitive for the use of the land as suggested by the author.

Jodha and Vyas, (1969)[21] reveal in **"Condition of Stability and Growth in Arid Agriculture"**, that in the arid region where water is needed most, it is difficult to arrange for water resources which are extremely limited and in the absence of irrigation facilities, the only alternative for stability and growth of agriculture in the dry region is the adaptation of farming system to arid environment. In this regard, the author feels that, there is need of integrated approach for stability and growth of desert agriculture, where the measures like exploration and exploitation of ground water resources, adoption of conservation measures, reorganization of crop farming, revitalization of livestock farming through proper facilities for drinking water, pasture regeneration and regular and adequate marketing facilities would play their respective roles.

Singh, (1973)[22] has suggested in **"Key Communicators of Agricultural Innovation"**, that since a long time ago, the Indian farmer is basically traditional and the efforts to change his attitude, skill, behaviour or practice should be transmitted into his social system through the soft spot (whom the farmers have more faith and confidence as compared to any outsider). Further, he states that and no one can be more interested in increasing production than the farmer what he needs is motivation and guidance, hence the significance of locating those sources of human stimuli and finally to activate them in the desired direction.

While comparing the scope of horticulture in the developed and developing countries, **Singh and Harbans, (1975)**[23] have pointed out the problems in their study **"Development of Horticulture in Hill Regions of India".** The major problems sorted out by them are insufficient orchard management, delineation of area, picking and packing materials and methods etc.

Nadda et. al, (1978)[24] in their study, **"Optimising Crop Production Patterns in Different Agro-Climatic Zones of Himachal Pradesh",** have focused on the optimizing crop production in different agro climatic zones of Himachal Pradesh. The authors have used linear programming and stated that the existing cropping pattern found to be diversified and sub optimal in the low and mid hill zones. They have suggested that the normative cropping pattern should have fewer crops, indicating a tendency towards specialised farming. The study also reveals surplus labour force engaged in the study area.

Tewari and Awasthi, (1978)[25] have carried out a study on the **"Importance of Horticulture in Economic Development of Kangra District".** The study concluded that fruit plantation is more economical than cultivation of field crops which would not only help the farmers in improving economic standard but also to conserve the soil. However, it is pointed out that due to variations in climate conditions of the district, fruit production varies widely.

Jodha, (1979)[26] highlighted in her paper, **"Inter-cropping in Traditional Farming Systems",** the superiority of mixed inter-cropping over sole cropping in terms of higher gross returns per hectare as well as per unit of peak period labour use. The author revealed its potential for greater employment. She further stated that inter cropping is largely a system of small and un-irrigated farms and any breakthrough in inter cropping technology will help poor farmers more than the rich.

Singh and Saraswat, (1984)[27] have stated in the article **"Impact of Irrigation on Cropping Pattern and Farm Income under Optimal Solution",** that the existing cropping patterns in the Valleys of Himachal Pradesh are sub-optimal, indicating thereby that even without bringing additional lands under cultivation, agricultural production can be substantially increased by adopting optimum crop plans with the existing resource base and irrigational facilities.

Randev, (1986)[28] in his study entitled **"Economics of Horticultural Crops in Tribal Areas of Himachal Pradesh"**, has focused on the economics of production of apple and almond in Kinnaur district. The author has select multistage random sampling for getting information, he applied tools and techniques like Payback period, Net present value, Internal rate of return, Benefit cost ratio and Annuity value method to analyze the data. He has revealed the relationship between the output of two fruits and various inputs used and concluded that area under fruit crops is declining and orchards are increasing.

Sharma, (1987)[29] in his research, **"The Economy of Himachal Pradesh"**, has analyzed the changes in the cropping pattern during the period 1950-51 to 1982-83. The author reveals that there is hardly any change in the cropping pattern of Himachal Pradesh during the entire period. According to the author, the share of land allocated to the cereals and non cereals crops remains by the large unchanged and the share of area under wheat has increased from one third to nearly two fifth of total area sown during the period 1950-51 to 1982-83 as a result of the adoption of new form technology. Further, the author finds a noticeable change in the cropping pattern of Himachal Pradesh, with in the non cereal category, i.e. the rise in share of area under fruits of all kinds. The study concluded that Himachal Pradesh has a large potential for the production of fruits of different categories, but the fruits crops still enjoy a low weight age in the total area sown.

Nagaraji, (1989)[30] has mentioned in **"Effect of Crop Mixtures on Income and Employement. A Case study of Anantapur District"**, that crop mixtures not only give relatively higher monitory return but also provide more opportunities of employment. According to the author the system of crop mixtures harmonies the goals of increasing employment associated with an increase in output. He concluded that reorientation of cropping pattern in favour of crop mixtures in a long way in the agro-economic development of farm households in rain fed areas, where climate decides the crop and weather decides yield.

Sharma et.al, (1991)[31] in their research entitled **"Emerging Farming Systems in Himachal Pradesh: key issues in sustainability"**, focused on heavy interdependence and strong linkages among different sub-systems of farming as well as with common property resources. According to the authors, integrated planning for sustainable farming systems is essential for development. They used the input-output matrix approach to quantify the interlink ages in various farming sub-systems in the State. The authors have suggested that suitable policy measures like integrated planning, ecologically sound management of land resources, substitution of wood based material, promotion of nonfarm enterprises and efficient marketing structure would go a long way in making the various farming system sustainable.

Bhati et. al, (1992)[32] cautioned on ecological influences of high yield crops in high and mid hill zones in their research **"Diversity of Mountain Farming System in Himachal Pradesh. Farmers Strategies for Natural Resources Use"**, by stating that it may be harmful for sustained agricultural growth and therefore the authors have recommended that there is a need to protect natural resources specially forests which are the generators of climate. According to the authors, it is a matter of sorrow that Himachal Pradesh has lost its huge forest wealth in the shape of deforestation in large scale.

Sharma et. al, (1992)[33] in **"Impact of Irrigation on Socio-economic Structure of Farm Families in Himachal Pradesh"**, focused on the impact of irrigation on the vegetables based and cereal based crops. The authors have found that in vegetable based farming, a net return on per hectare of cultivated land was high as compared to cereals based farming of the State. They have concluded that irrigated land gives more output in terms of vegetables as compared to cereals, and the positive impact of irrigation is found in socio-economic structure of the farm families in the State.

Vayas, V.S., (2003)[34] in the book **"India's Agrarian Structure, Economic Policies and Sustainable Development"**, viewed that participatory management is the king-pin in the delivery of the major goals of agricultural policies like to preserve ecological balance, improving the incomes and living standards of rural producers, ensuring food and nutritional security for the population. However, participatory management which is the king-pin in the delivery of these programmes and a prerequisite to genuine people's participation is an institutional underpinning. To him the capable of delivering economic goods and services in an equitable manner would possible, provided the gross inequities in the ownership of assets, particularly with a large section being asset less to be minimized.

Archana Mathur et. al., (2006)[35] pointed out in the paper **"Status of Agriculture in India Trends and Prospects"**, that the role of public investment /government expenditure on agriculture as being the crucial determinant in stepping up the rate of growth of agricultural production. Given other factors a constant increase in public investment to 15 per cent per annum should lead to agricultural growth of 4 per cent, which is concomitant with the project the projected growth rate in the Eleventh Plan. They concluded that enhanced government expenditure particularly on investment in rural infrastructure comprising irrigation and water management, processing, storage and marketing, timely supplies of improved inputs, credit, research and extension services and the upward trend in this direction is required to continue.

Gupta, (2008)[36] in his edited book on **"Water Crisis in India"**, pointed **out** that management of the water resources for diverse uses should incorporate a participatory approach by involving not only the various governmental agencies but also the users and other stakeholders, in an effective and decisive manner, in various aspects of planning, design, development and management of the water resources schemes. He argues that necessary legal and institutional changes should be made at various levels for the purpose. Water Users' Associations and the local bodies such as municipalities and gram panchayats should particularly be involved in the operation, maintenance and management of water infrastructures/facilities at appropriate levels progressively, with a view to eventually transfer the management of such facilities to the user groups / local bodies. He also mentioned that conservation of water consciousness should be promoted through education, regulation, incentives and disincentives.

Ahmadi et. al, (2009)[37] in their study entitled **"Development of Management Schemes in Irrigation Planning: Economic and Crop Pattern Consideration"**, focused on development of an optimization model for determination of optimal crop patterns and water allocations. The authors' have studied mainly on maximizing net income with a conjunctive use of surface and groundwater, considering the effects of a marginal water deficit in the reduction of crop production. The authors are developed two scenarios for the evaluation of regional policies on crop patterns in the study areas, the scenarios are compared based on the system performances indices including reliability, resiliency and vulnerability. They found that the scenario A provides more net benefits than the constrained model by up to 50%. In Scenario B, the areas of non-economical crops increase because of some socio-political considerations. Also, the possibility of deficit irrigation application in the study region is evaluated. The authors concluded that because the region is under water stress under the existing condition, reducing crop coverage will increase net income. They also suggested that although the economic analysis shows that reducing the cultivated area could boost net income, social and cultural adverse consequences could follow.

Baba, (2010)[38] has revealed in his study, **"Substantial Hill Agricultural Practices through Watershed Development",** that increasing water security is a serious threat arising from climate change and the Himalayas are facing its brunt through glacier retreat. The author has emphasized on maintaining, operating and governing watershed on a substantial basis. Further, it is stated that watershed has been needed to be connected with effective market linkages in order to get good returns out of the produce from these units which in turn, will strengthen the belief and importance of such programs as well as reinvestment by the community people or beneficiaries in such interventions. According to the author, separate policy and guidelines for water shed development programs need to be developed at National Level for hill states looking at the specific nature of the problems confronted by these states.

Dharmalingam and Periasamy, (2010)[39] in their article **"Erratic Monsoon and Indian Economy",** pointed out that erratic monsoon has impacted in Indian Economy in the form of distress to farmers and their families, commodity trading and price movement and food inflation. The important suggestion advocated by them is promote through Gram Sabhas community food and water security systems. They should involve establishing at the village level seed, grain and water banks. Seed banks will help to introduce alternative cropping strategies and contingency plans to suit different rainfall patterns. Also they have hoped that the recommendations of the Punchhi Commission would enable the central government to take proactive decisions on the issue facing the water sector.

Thakur, (2010)[40] observed in his study, **"Impact of Investment on Agricultural Growth and Rural Development in Himachal Pradesh: Dynamics of Public and Private Investment",** that growth rate of public investment has declined over the years in Himachal Pradesh, which needs to be reversed. The author stated that investment in agricultural technology; development and dissemination of inform action, rural infrastructure, irrigation, rural development, market development, soil and water conservation and other social overheads amounts to a "win-win" strategy for reducing rural poverty directly as well as through creation of avenues of employment and higher rural wages. The author suggested that private placement in agriculture must also be encouraged by providing the necessary support like credit, cheap power, tube well subsidy, etc. and investment needs to be encouraged. He further suggested that whatever subsidies are to be provided should be targeted to the poor and backward regions, where productivity is lower and farmers are unable to invest more in agriculture.

Pratap, (2011)[41] has stated in **"Hill Agriculture: Challenges and Opportunities"**, that the substantiality prospects for mountain agriculture remain bleak unless the main stream perceptions about the problems are not changed. So the hill prospective based development strategies are essential for formulating farmer responsive plans, giving due consideration to the nature of marginality, fragility, diversity and niches of each area. According to him, it will not only help ameliorate the impact of the marginalization of hill communities but also help in achieving social equity by building on the comparative advantages of key land resources.

Khan and Islam, (2011)[42] in their research **"Impacts of Mini Dams on Socioeconomic Development of Farmers of Rain fed Region"**, have thrown light on the impact of construction of dams on the socioeconomic development of poor farmers of arid rural areas. According to the authors, the impact of Irrigation from mini dams is creating employment opportunities, to the poor farmers. The authors, revealed that irrigation facility has not only raised the income of farm owners but has also helped directly in alleviating poverty by employment generation, besides giving indirect job to temporary workers and other professionals such as electricians, construction labourers. The authors have concluded that the farmers have gained more crop production and good economic condition after the construction of dams. Dams under study have been proved successful in providing benefits for farmers, which is apparent from tremendous increase of monetary income and satisfaction level of the farmers.

Kannan and Sundaram, (2011)[43] in their study, **"Analysis of Trends in India's Agricultural Growth"**, have thrown light on the important variables like area, production, input use and value of output. According to authors the cropping pattern in India has undergone significant changes with a significant shift from the cultivation of food crops to commercial crops. The authors focused on various important factors like use of modern varieties, irrigation and fertilisers which is the important aspect of higher growth in crop production in the Country. They have used crop output growth model to examine the determinants of aggregate growth of crop output at the national level. The authors have found that the crop output has enhanced capital formation, better irrigation facilities, normal rainfall and improved fertiliser consumption to improve crop output in the Country.

Swamy, (2011)[44] observed in **"Tribal Land Question and Land Reforms in Kerala"**, that the exclusion of 'adivasis' in India in terms of land rights remains a reality in contemporary India, and their rights to productive resources have generally been left unattained by the State Government. The author highlighted that Government has not taken any significant effort to grant land rights to landless tribal households and the shift from food to cash crops and from indigenous to hybrid seeds have also undermined the livelihood of these people which must be taken care of by the Government.

Uma, (2011)[45] reveals in her study, **"Land Reform a Panacea for Agricultural Development"**, that agriculture is mainly dependent on two sets of factors – technology and institutional changes which include the redistribution of land ownership in favour of cultivating classes or rich to the poor. The author states that the Land Acquisition Bill brought by the Government can be used to stop exploitation of tribal and marginal farmers and stressed to raise rate of literacy particularly female literacy at village level institutions which can be used to raise awareness about the bill and other programs of the Government so that farmers are better informed.

Wani, (2011)[46] has observed in **"Hill Agriculture in India: Problems and Prospects of Mountain Agriculture"**, that hill agriculture is gradually diversifying in favour of fruits and vegetables. It has been felt that hill states have potential for production of vegetables in off-season that have higher demand in neighbouring plains when there is scarcity of supply, so innovation in the form of hill specific tools and dissemination of organic technologies could encourage this enterprises as a better livelihood opportunity.

Gopinath and Bhat, (2012)[47] in their research paper, **"Impact of Climate Change on Rain fed Agriculture in India: A Case Study of**

Dharwad", have focused on the occurrence of drought and its impact on the yield of rain fed crops. The authors have revealed that farmers' perception on the impact of climate change on the crops grown in rain fed condition has reduced yield and net revenue. They are of the view that the farmers have adopted the technological coping mechanisms on both positive and negative sides through shifting to other professions. The authors concluded that the small and medium rain fed farmers were highly vulnerable to climate change and to a larger extent the small and medium rain fed farmers adopted coping mechanisms for climate change compared to large farmers. The authors suggest that as the impact of climate change is intensifying day by day, it should be addressed through policy perspective at the earliest to avoid short term effect such as yield and income loss and long-term effects such as quitting agricultural profession by the rain fed farmers.

Kalaiselvi's, (2012)[48] work, **"Pattern of Crop Diversification in Indian Scenario",** reveals that the, patterns of crop diversification of modern agricultural technology, especially during the period of the Green Revolution in the late sixties and early seventies, is a continuous surge for diversified agriculture in terms of crops, primarily on economic considerations. In his study, he identify crop diversification in the Indian prospective and also examined the pattern of crop diversification in India .The study suggests that for achieving the gains of diversification of farming, there is an urgent need for further strengthening the required infrastructure pertaining to input supply system, marketing system and the existing research and extension programmers to increase the adoption of advanced production technologies. Finally the study concludes that there is a mixed picture regarding the typology of diversification within the states. Some states exhibit more diversification and there is no direct link between the number of crops and spread in the cropping pattern.

Kumari, et. al, (2012)[49] have thrown light on the areas of water, land use Pattern, crop productivity and devastating effects of climate change in Himachal Pradesh under different agro climatic zones. In their research **"Climate Change An-Impact Study in Himachal Pradesh",** the authors have discussed the four different climatic zones of Himachal Pradesh in terms of the rainfall, precipitation, land use and crop productivity. According to the authors, water level and flow of Nallahs, rivers etc has declined due to rise in temperature during summer season and there is less precipitation during the winter season thereby reducing the moisture content of soil affecting the delay in sowing of crops. The authors have also revealed that the apple growing belt in low lying areas has become extremely marginal therefore shifting trends have been observed for diversification with other fruit crops like kiwi and pomegranate and vegetable seed production. Further, according to them, the snowline has also been shifted upward to higher altitude. Thus the quality production of apple has been shifted to higher altitude including dry temperate zone of Kinnaur and Spiti area of Lahaul and Spiti district. The shift in scenario of farming community in cultivating crops due to direct impact on hydrological services is outlining changes in environment which has led to the adaptation strategies of the species as bio-indicators of climate change.

Shinde et. al, (2012)[50] have revealed in their study **"Impact of Water Percolation Tank on Changing Cropping Pattern"**, that irrigated cropping and sources of irrigation have changed. The authors have concluded that after the water percolation in Rampur village the cropping pattern has changed drastically and farmers have turned from cereals to cash crops. This indicates that there is positive and direct impact of water percolation on cropping pattern changes.

Barla, (2013)[51] has mentioned in **"The Impact of New Agricultural Technology on Tribal Farming: A Study of Ranchi District of Jharkhand State"**, that the major tribal groups in Jharkhand are dependent on agriculture for their livelihood. According to the author, the new agricultural technology can improve the production and productivity of agricultural sector in tribal region and can cause the improvement in economic condition of the people. The author reveals that the spread of information regarding New Agricultural Technology, improvement in irrigation facility, support from block, bank or NGO, easy availability of HYV seeds and fertilizers are some of the factors, which have helped in adoption, and spread of New Agricultural Technology in this region. She also found that the factors restricted of its spread i.e. ignorance of the farmers, lack of irrigation facility, poor credit supports etc. Hence she concludes that the nature and magnitude of impact, varies from region to region and therefore, needs to be explored. She also suggest that government should come forward to help this.

Arif et. al, (2013)[52] **have concluded in** "Changing Land Use and Cropping **Pattern in Budgam District of Jammu and Kashmir-A**

Spatio-temporal Analysis", that land is the basic natural resource which provides source of our food, shelter and clothing. According to the authors' an assessment of the land resources, their extent, distribution and utilization are of prime importance for rational exploitation and sustainable development. The authors have focused on land-use and cropping pattern in District Budgam of Kashmir valley mostly dominated by agricultural occupation. They have adopted secondary sources for their research work; a multi-temporal analysis was carried out in order to analyze the extent as well as direction of change. In their analyses they found major change, from shifting of agricultural crops to horticultural crops which is economically beneficial for the farmers of that region.

Maruti, et. al, (2013)[53] have revealed in **"Indian Agriculture-Status, Importance and Role in Indian Economy"**, that agriculture sector provides approximately 52 percent of the total number of jobs available in India and contributes around 18.1 percent to the GDP. According to the authors, agriculture is the only means of living for almost two-third, of the employed class in India. The authors concluded that agriculture has benefited in terms of improved farming techniques but the growth is not equitable, as land use is changing in rural areas as farmers are getting good value for their holdings. They have suggested to stop the migration of urban areas, wholesale prices be primarily used to monitor the weekly price movements, and the number of essential commodities to be reduced to absolute minimum, especially the non-food crops.

Uma et. al, (2013)[54] in their study **"Changing cropping pattern: A Boon or** a **Bane to Food Security"**, revealed that most of the agricultural labourers are showing less interest in producing food crops and are changing their cropping pattern to commercial crops. The authors also find that all marginal farmers are slowly depending on other sector for higher wages without fully neglecting the agriculture. The authors' reveal that instead of changing the cropping pattern and continued their agriculture activity with other family members and relatives they are changing cropping from food crops to commercial crops. They conclude that changing in cropping pattern has posed a threat to the overall production of food crops and directly adverse effect on countries food production and food security. The authors also suggest that if every farmer thinks that changing the food crops to commercial crop will bring more income, there will be no one to produce needed amount of food crops in the country.

Zivanomoyo and Mukarati, (2013)[55] have focused on the impacts of climate change on the agrarian economies in their paper **"Determinants of Choice of Crop Verity as Climate Change Adaptation Option in Arid Regions of Zimbabwe".** According to the authors, climate change affects agriculture and food production in complex ways. Changes in agro ecological conditions get manifested in the overall production of the food and thus, the distribution of income. Agricultural production has been stated to be declined due to change in the climate across the world especially in the developing region. Besides this, the authors have highlighted upon the significance of crop diversification techniques and provision of minimum credit facility to the farmers to face the challenges resulting out of climate change.

Madhu and Uma, (2014)[56] have thrown light on the effects of Rural-Urban migration in terms of rapid process of urbanisation in their paper, **"A Study on the Changing Cropping Pattern and Internal Migration Issues and Challenges".** They examined a very relevant issue that Indian agriculture is grappling with considering Urbanisation and Rural-Urban migration as an unavoidable process of development. They have established the fact that the process of migration is benefiting more the poorer section of Rural India which includes land less labourers involved in farming as working under urban settings provides them a more stable and increased amount of income. The authors point out that the negative aspect of this migration in terms of growing problem of unavailability of agricultural labour in Rural India. They find that males are migrating from rural areas affecting cropping pattern but it has improved the economic status of the families of these migrants. They argue that agricultural activities and the opportunities of the urbanisation can go hand in hand. It is concluded that internal migration has somewhere attempted to reduce the excessive burden on the agricultural land but the lack of technological know-how among the farming section is unable to convert change in to the transformation of rural India.

Mahato's, (2014)[57] study, **"Climate Change and Its Impact on Agriculture",** focuses that the global climate changes in the long run and its impact on agriculture in terms of productivity, growth rates, photosynthesis and transpiration rates, moisture availability etc. According to the author, climate change is likely to directly influence food production across the globe and the consequences of agriculture's contribution to climate change, as well as climate change's negative impact on agriculture, are severe which is projected to have a great impact on food production and may threaten the food security and hence, require special agricultural measures to combat with. The author analyses that net impact of food security will depend on the exposure to global environmental change and the capacity to cope with and recover from global environmental change. The author concludes that coping with the impact of climate change on agriculture will require careful management of resources like soil, water and biodiversity. He also suggest that to cope with the impact of climate change on agriculture and food production, India will need to act at the global, regional, national and local levels.

Prabha, (2014)[58] in her research, **"Impact of Farm Ponds on Cropping Pattern",** focused on changes in cropping pattern before and after farm ponds. The author reveals that farm ponds are vital to increase ground water level, to increase storage of rain water, to improve recharge of bore wells, to provide water facility for crops during crucial period, to facilitate rising of ID crops, to provide drinking water for cattle, and to provide wage employment to agricultural labour. The author studied the socio-economic status of farmers before and after the construction of farm ponds and found that cropping pattern has changed as before farm Ponds, only Vegetables were planted, but later on, the cropping pattern changed.

Patil et. al, (2014)[59] in their research, **"Comparative Analysis of Cropping Pattern and Socio- Economic Status of Fisherman and Farmers",** have identified that cropping pattern was tremendously changed as compared before construction of wetlands. The cropping pattern plays an important role in socio - economic development that is directly dependent on either rainwater or irrigation system. The authors' main focus of the study is the economic and social development of local people after and before construction of dams and compares it with previous situations. They have found that farmers are shifted from traditional cropping pattern to advanced cropping pattern by cultivating cash crops. The study revealed that both the farmers and fisherman got socio-economically strengthened after construction of wetlands. The authors have concluded that the cropping pattern was tremendously changed as compared before construction of wetlands. It is considerably strengthened by the means of economic as well as social development.

Patil, (2014)[60] has envisaged in **"Displacement and Rehabilitation : A Study of Change in Agricultural Practices of Dudhgangha Dam**

Affected People in Kolahpur District", that change in agricultural practices rehabilitated people due to displacement of Dudhaganga dam in Kolapur district of Maharastra. The study reveals that the construction of dam is responsible for the displacement of natives and rehabilitated in new environment. Therefore, change in agricultural practices is common among rehabilitated families, cultivation of land is divided in own land cultivation and land leased out cultivation, and consequently after rehabilitation, people have turned cash crops from food crops. The author advocates that the socio - economic development of farmers depends upon agricultural practices and development and the Kolhapur is one of the socio - economically developed districts of Maharashtra.

Aggarwal and Moudgil, (2015)[61] have concluded in their study, **"Structural Change and Growth of Agriculture in Haryana",** that cropping intensity, irrigation intensity and crop yield and density of tractors had increased since green revolution but the contribution of agriculture to Haryana's GDP declined over the years. The authors have suggested that Govt. should make efforts for agriculture development.

Akhter and Acharya, (2015)[62] in their study **"Changes in Cropping Pattern in Jammu and Kashmir",** have revealed that the cropping pattern of Jammu and Kashmir was based on the traditional system of the subsistence farming without any surplus. The author's have focused on the changes in the cropping pattern in Jammu and Kashmir. The authors found that with the advent of New Agricultural Strategy, there emerged the complementary relationship between the commercialization and cropping pattern of the state. The authors have applied Regression analysis in order to see causal relationship between area and production. The study also reveals that the crop sector of Jammu and Kashmir agriculture at an aggregate level is gradually diversifying in favour of high-value crops. The authors found that the Jammu division is witnessing a specialization in food-grain crops, while Kashmir division is depicting a trend towards diversification. The farmers are gradually diversifying to commercial crops for the sake of higher earnings.

Chinky, (2015)[63] in her study, **"Changes in Cropping Pattern and Crop Diversification in Jammu and Kashmir",** has revealed that the cropping pattern of Jammu and Kashmir was based on the traditional system of the subsistence farming without any surplus. According to the author, the real difficulty in adopting a better cropping pattern is that farmers may not have adequate amount of capital to invest in new techniques. The author has focuses on the changes in cropping pattern in Jammu and Kashmir. According to the author, the farmers are gradually diversifying to commercial crops for the sake of higher earnings. She found that the state farmers should appreciate the importance of horticulture sector include fruits, vegetables, floriculture to improving the productivity of land, generate employment and improve their economic conditions.

Kumar et. al, (2015)[64] in their research, **"Kala Matar: an Indigenous Legume Crop of Spiti Vally in The Trans Himalyan Cold Desert of India Facing Threat of Extinction"**, have identified that Kala Matar or so called black pea is a traditional legume crop grown by the tribal community of snow bound Spiti valley in Himachal Pradesh, India. But the authors found that with the transition of the Spitian economy from a subsistence based to cash based one; this traditional crop has gradually been replaced by market friendly crops. The authors reveal that due to the lack of any economic value attached to the black pea, it has now been replaced by the green pea which also has a good market value. They conclude that as a result of this, the black pea now faces the threat of extinction. The authors suggest that there is a need of conservation of this highly nutritious crop which has now become underutilized in spite having very good source of cholesterol-lowering fibre and excellent amount of five important minerals, three B-vitamins, and protein—all with virtually no fat.

Singh, (2015)[65] in his study, **"Analysis of Spatial Temporal Changes in Cropping Pattern and Cropping Intensity in Agriculture of Haryana"**, found that highest cropping area is covered by wheat and rice respectively. In contrast, maize, jowar and barley have covered lowest cropping area. Further, the author has revealed that the cropping intensity of Haryana has increased over the years. All districts have achieved above average cropping intensity except very few districts.

Ahlawat & Renu, (2016)[66] in their study **"Regional Disparity in Cropping Intensity and Relative Impact of Irrigation in Haryana"**, reveal that, higher cropping intensity indicates that maximum area is cropped more than once. The authors focus on the district -wise performance in intensity of cropping in Haryana. They used secondary sources of data for study of the impact of irrigation on cropping intensity. They have applied average; variance and simple linear regression for analysis of data. The authors found variations among the districts in terms of cropping intensity and found that Panipat and Karnal districts were best performers in intensifying crops while Gurgaon, Jhajjar and Rewari were the poor ones. Further, according to them, moderate performance was observed in Fatehabad and Sirsa districts. Authors concluded that variations were due to differences in rainfall, resources for irrigation and use of modern agricultural techniques. They suggested that improved irrigation facilities will enhance the cropping intensity as well.

Khot and Talwar, (2017)[67] in their study **"Scenario of Cropping Pattern and Crop Diversification: A Study of Gokak Taluk in Belgaum District, Karnataka, India",** have revealed that cropping pattern has important implications for the growth of agriculture in general and food security and livelihood of millions of farmers in particular in India. According to the authors' the cropping pattern has affected by agro-ecological conditions and different socio-economic and institutional factors. The authors have focused on the production risk arises from diseases of crops, pests, weather-related conditions like rainfall, flood and drought and price risk arises due to fluctuations in price of the produce that may be caused by changes in demand as well as supply conditions. The Authors' have found that the contract farming may help farmers mitigate price risk by offering an assured market of their produce and also inputs of production, crop insurance may be quite useful in minimizing production risk arising out of weather shocks. And also the farmers try to cope with risks in their own capacities by making adjustments in the cropping pattern across crops as well as seasons.

2.1.1 Research Gap

After taking a stock of available literature mentioned above, it is found that researches on cropping pattern have been done.

As Long (1964), Frazier & Peterson (1964), Kelogg (1964), Sangwan (1966), Gupta (1966), Jodha (1979) and Uma (2011) have focused on the role of technology in bringing changes in the cropping pattern. Their studies revealed that a relatively short time is required to increase productivity by bringing new technology and services in the developing countries. However, Jinha (1962), Tewari & Awasti (1978), Baba (2010), Khan & Islam (2011), Gopinath and Bhat (2012),

Zivanmayo & Mukarati (2013), and Mahato (2014) have focused that there is influence of natural factors on productivity such as storms, drought, high winds, glacier, insects attack and irrigation etc. which are beyond the control of farmers.

Further, Deshpande (1969), Sharma (1987), Randev (1986) and Khanan & Sundram (2011) have emphasized on shifting of fruit crops to commercial crops. There are researches on increasing productivity by bringing new technology and services, use of natural resources and shifting of fruit crops to commercial crops but still the researches confine not only to these considerations. But are generalised for all without taking the topographical and other considerations into account like tribal areas of Himachal Pradesh.

Moreover, Maruti (2013), Atif and Kumari (2013) have focused on the land use pattern, crop productivity and divesting effects of climate change on crop production. Further, Shindhe (2012), revealed that there is positive and direct impact of water percolation on cropping pattern changes. Unlike many of the earlier studies, in this paper, computation of crop diversification at the State as well as district level, has also been provided. Along with this, district wise share of each crop for the four time periods has also been calculated which makes the study more meaningful.

One of renowned scholars, Thakur (2010) has emphasized on the encouragement of providing the necessary support for privatisation in agriculture in terms of credit facility, cheap power, use of tube well and agricultural subsidy etc. Despite of extensive scholarly efforts, it is evident that crop intensity and outturn have not been considered the criteria in relation to topographical conditions and economic considerations by the researchers so far. Further, in topographically hard areas having high level of land fertility, emphasis has not been drawn by the scholars on factors influencing cropping pattern and development.

In this backdrop, the present study is one among the many bricks to bridge the gap between research needs and research efforts made so far. Though the study is confined to the two districts of Himachal Pradesh, it obviously has the relevance and significance of knowing about the pattern of crop production and its impact of socio-economic development of tribal areas.

2.1.2 Research Methodology

Descriptive Survey method of research is used for the collection of data. Opinion of 300 household respondents are selected as per the population ratio of both the districts. The respondents have been taken from each village as per the population ratio of each block of the districts. The research also contains information through secondary sources.

2.1.3 Objectives of the Research

Following are the objectives of the research:

- To analyze the trend of crop intensity and outturn of different crops in tribal areas of Himachal Pradesh.
- To empirically examine the factors affecting cropping pattern of Tribal Areas.
- To examine employment in context to cropping pattern and socio economic development of tribal communities.
- To empirically examine the dependency of tribal population on their cropping pattern.

Endnotes

1. K.T. Shah, Crops-Planning and Production, Bombay: Vora & Co. Publishers Pvt. Ltd., 1948, pp. 195-201.
2. Padam Singh, Agriculture in the Hill Regions of North India, New Delhi: Directorate of Extension, Ministry of Food and Agriculture, 1962, pp. 121-122.
3. Richard Bradfield, "The Role of Educated People in Agricultural Development", Albert H. Moseman (ed.), Agricultural Science for the Developing Nations, Delhi: Radhika Krishan Prakashan, 1964, pp. 112-113.
4. R.D. Fraizer and J.B. Peterson, "Plant Agriculture in the Emerging Nations", Albert H. Moseman (ed.), Agricultural Science for the Developing Nations, Delhi: Radhika Krishan Prakashan, 1964, p. 49.
5. F.F. Hill "Developing Agricultural Institutions in Underdeveloped Countries", Albert H. Moseman (ed.), Agricultural Science for the Developing Nations, Radhika Krishan Prakashan Delhi, 1964, pp. 160-161.
6. Kellog, Charles E., Interactions and Agricultural Research, Albert H. Moseman (ed.), Agricultural Science for the Developing Nations, Delhi: Radhika Krishan Prakashan, 1964, p. 91.

7. J. Erven Long, "Institutional factors Limiting Progress in the Less Developed Countries", in Albert H. Moseman (ed.), Agricultural Science for the Developing Nations, Delhi: Radhika Krishan Prakashan, 1964, pp.12-13.

8. Ralph W. Philips, "Animal Agriculture in the Emerging Nations", Albert H. Moseman (ed.), Agricultural Science for the Developing Nations, Delhi: Radhika Krishan Prakashan, 1964, pp. 31-32.

9. V.M. Jakhade, Food Grain Marketing Zone in India, Mirchandani, R.T. and Hiranandani, G. J. (ed.) Marketing of Agricultural Commodities, Bombay: The Indian Societies of Agricultural Economics, 1965, pp. 41-48.

10. Evans C. Homer, "The Apple Processing Industry" Fraizer, R.D. (ed.), Market Structure of the Agricultural Industries, USA.: The Iowa State University press Ames, 1966, p. 190.

11. Amiya K. Gupta, "Some Aspects of Input- Output Relationship in Indian Agriculture", Jain, S.C. (ed.) Changing Indian Agriculture, Bombay: Vora & Co. Pvt. Ltd., 1966, pp. 30-43.

12. N.A. Majumdar, Agricultural growth in A Labour Surplus Economy, Jain, S.C. (ed.), Changing Indian Agriculture, Bombay: Vora & Co. Pvt. Ltd. 1966, pp. 16-28.

13. Sangwan, P.S., Changing Indian Agriculture-Epitomised version of Left-Over Problems, Jain, S.C. (ed.) Chnging Indin Agriculture, Bombay: Vora & Co. Pvt. Ltd., 1966, pp. 7-15.

14. Shivamaggi, H.B., "Impact of food Aid on Agricultural Development, Jain, S.C. (ed.) Changing Indian Agriculture, Bombay: Vora & Co. Pvt. Ltd. 1966, pp. 84-98.

15. C.M. Ellot, "Role of Agriculture", Warley, K. (ed.) Agricultural Producers and their Markets, U.K.: Basil Blackwell Oxford, 1967, pp. 41-49.

16. P.K. Ray, Agricultural Insurance, London: Peegamin Press Ltd., 1967, pp. 279-281.

17. B.J. Surridge, "Farmers Marketing Organizations", Warley, K. (ed.), Agricultural Producers and their Markets, U.K.: Basil Blackwell Oxford, 1967, pp. 99-104.

18. N.S. Jhodha, and V.S. Vyas, Condition of Stability and Growth in Arid Agriculture, Anand Press Gamdi Gujrat: Agro Economic Research Centre, 1969, pp. 111-117.

19. A.R. Desai and V.R. Mutalik, "Our food Problem", V.R. Mutalik (ed.), The Strategy of food and Agriculture in India, Bombay: Western Printers and Publishers, 1969, pp. 15-37.

20. B.R. Deshpande, Low Returns to Cultivators, V.R. Mutalik (ed.),The Strategy of food and Agriculture in India Bombay: Western Printers and Publishers, 1969, pp. 93-104.
21. C.P. Shastri, Factor influencing Cropping Pattern, V.R. Mutalik (ed.), The Strategy of food and Agriculture in India, Bombay: Western Printers and Publishers, 1969, pp. 174-187.
22. Y.P. Singh, Key Communicators of Agricultural Innovation, Agra: Satish Book Enterprise, 1973, pp. 32-33.
23. Harbans Singh, Development of Horticulture in Hill Regions of India. Paper presented in a seminar held at Vigyan Bhavan, New Delhi: On Development of Hilly Areas Problems and Potential, 1975, pp. 25-28.
24. A.L. Nadda and L.R. Sharma et al., "Optimising Crop Production Patterns in Different Agro-Climatic Zones of Himachal Pradesh", Indian Journal of Agricultural Economics, Vol. No. XXXIII (4), 1978, pp. 22-28.
25. S.C. Tewari, and O.P. Awasthi, Analysis of Integrated Resource Inventory and Inventory of Resource, Kangra District, Himachal Pradesh. Palampur: Himachal Pradesh Krishi Vidyalaya, 1978, p. 15.
26. N.S. Jodha, Inter-Cropping in Traditional Farming Systems, Economic Progress Report-3. ICRISAT, Patancheru, AP, India, 1979.
27. D.V. Singh and S.P. Saraswat "Impact of Irrigation on Cropping Pattern and Farm Income under Optimal Solution", Indian Journal of Agricultural Economics, Vol. 39, No. 3, 1984, pp. 540-541.
28. A.K. Randev Economic of Horticultural Crops in Tribal areas of Himachal Pradesh: A Case Study of Kinnaur District, Palampur: Unpublished Ph.D. Thesis, Department of Agriculture Economics, Himachal Pradesh Krishi Vishva Vidyalaya 1986, pp. 28.
29. L.R. Sharma, The Economy of Himachal Pradesh, New Delhi: Mittal Publications, 1987, pp. 95.
30. Nagaraji, "Effect of Crop Mixtures on Income and Employment-Case Study of Anantapur District", Agricultural Situation in India, Vol. XVII, No. 11, 1989, pp. 957-963.
31. L.R. Sharma and J.P Bhati et al., "Emerging Farming Systems in Himachal Pradesh: Key Issues in Sustainability" Indian Journal of Agriculture Economics, Vol. No. XXVII (3) 1991, pp. 422-427.
32. J.R. Bhati et al., "Diversity of Mountain Farming System in Himachal Pradesh", N.S. Jodha et al. (ed.), Sustainable Mountain Agriculture, New Delhi: IBH Publishing Co. 1992, pp. 497-515.
33. M.L. Sharma and Ranveer Singh et al., Impact of Irrigation on Socio Economic Farm Families of Himachal Pradesh. Shimla: Agro-Economic Reasearch Centre H.P.U, 1992.

34. V.S. Vayas, India's Agrarian Structure, Economic Policies and Sustainable Development, New Delhi: Academic Foundation, 2003, p. 24.

35. S. Archana Mathur and Surajit Das, "Subhalakshmi Sircar, Status of Agriculture in India Trends and Prospects", Economic and Political Weekly, Vol. XLI, No. 52, December 30, 2006, pp. 5337-5344.

36. K.R. Gupta, Water Crisis in India, New Delhi: Atlantic Publishers & Distributors Ltd., 2008, pp. 195-197.

37. M. Karamouzi et al., Development of Management Schemes in Irrigation Planning: Economic and Crop Pattern Consideration Transaction A: Civil Engineering Vol. 16, No. 6, December 2009, pp. 457-466.

38. S.H. Baba, "Substantial Hill Agricultural Practices through Watershed Development", Agricultural Economics, 2010, pp. 364-365.

39. G. Periasamy, "Erratic Monsoon and Indian Economy", Southern Economist, Volume 48, Number 18, January 15, 2010, pp. 8-10.

40. D.R. Thakur, Impact of Investment on Agricultural Growth and Rural Development in Himachal Pradesh: Dynamics of Public and Private Investment, Agricultural Economics, 2010, pp. 154-155.

41. Tej Pratap, "Hill Agriculture: Challenges and Opportunities", Agricultural Economics, 2011, pp. 48-50.

42. Muhammad Tariq Khan, "Muhammad Islam Thair Hussain, Impact of Mini Dams on Socio-Economic Development of Farmers of Rainfed Region", Journal of Agriculture of Social Sciences. 2011, pp. 124-130.

43. Elumalai Kannan and Sujata Sundaram, "Analysis of Trends in India's Agricultural Growth", The Institute for Social and Economic Change, Bangalore, 2011, pp. 1-21.

44. Raju Narayan Swamy, "Tribal Land Question and land Reforms in Kerala", Yojna, 2011, pp. 42-46.

45. H.R. Uma, Land Reform a Panacea for Agricultural Development, Yojna, 2011, pp. 52-54.

46. M.H. Wani, "Hill Agriculture in India: Problems and Prospects of Mountain Agriculture", Agricultural Economics, 2011, pp. 64-66.

47. V. Asha Latha K. et al., "Impact of Climate Change on Rainfed Agriculture in India: A Case Study of Dharwad", International Journal of Environmental Science and Development, Vol. 3, Issue No. 4, August, 2012, pp. 368-371.

48. V. Kalaiselvi, Pattern of Crop Diversification in Indian Scenario, Scholars Library Annals of Biological Reasearch, 2012, pp. 1914-1918.

49. Anita Kumari, P. Kaushal, J.K. Dubhey and D.K. Sharma, "Climate Change- An Impact Study in Himachal Pradesh", International Journal of Farm Sciences, Vol. 2, No. 2, 2012, pp. 95-101.

50. R.B. Patil et al., "Impact of Water Percolation Tank on Changing Cropping Pattern: A Case Study of Rampur Village, Tal.-Jath Dist: Sangli, Maharashtra", Online International Interdisciplinary Research Journal, Volume-II, No. VI, Dec. 2012. pp. 94-103.

51. Barla Marcus, "The Impact of New Agricultural Technology on Tribal Farming: A Study of Ranchi District of Jharkhand State", Journal of Economic & Social Development, Vol-IX, No.1, 2013, pp. 121-131.

52. Arif H. Shah and Hakim F. Ahmad et al., "Changing Land Use and Cropping Pattern in Budgam District of Jammu and Kashmir-A Spatio-Temporal Analysis", International Journal of Scientific & Engineering Research, Volume 4, No. 2, February, 2013, pp. 1-9.

53. Arjun Kekane, Maruti, "Indian Agriculture-Status, Importance and Role in Indian Economy" International Journal of Agriculture and Food Science Technology, Volume 4, No. 4, 2013, pp. 343-346.

54. Uma, H.R. Madhu and G.R. Pushpa, Nanaiah K., "Changing Cropping Pattern: A Boon or a Bane to Food Security", International Journal of Humanities and Social Science Invention, Volume 2, No. 8, August 2013, pp. 7-11.

55. James Zivanomoya and Julius Mukarati, "Determinants of Choice of Crop Variety as Climate Change Adaptation in Arid Regions of Zimbabwe", Russian journal of Agricultural and socio-economic Sciences, Volume 3, No. 15, 2013, pp. 54-62.

56. Madhu G.R., Uma H.R., "A study on the Changing Cropping Pattern and Internal Migration Issues and Challenges", International Journal of Applied Research, Volume 4, No. 6, June 2014, pp. 119-122.

57. Anupama Mahato, "Climate Change and its Impact on Agriculture" International Journal of Scientific and Research Publications, Vol. 4, No. 4, April 2014, pp. 1-6.

58. Lakshmi Prabha U., "Impact of Farm Ponds on Cropping Pattern- A Case Study on Vembedu Village in Tamilnadu", International Journal of Innovative Research in Advanced Engineering, Vol. 1, No. 4, May 2014, pp. 50-52.

59. Sachin Kumar, Patil, S.S. and T.V. Sathe, "Comparative Analysis of Cropping Pattern and Socio-Economic status of Fisherman and Farmers", International Journal of Science, Environment and Technology, Vol. 3, No 5, 2014, pp. 1882-1892.

60. R.B. Patil, Displacement and Rehabilitation A Study of Change in Agricultural Practices of Dudhgangha Dam Affected People in Kolapur District (MH). Research Directions Vol. 1, No. 10, April, 2014, pp. 1-8.

61. Aggarwal, P.K. and Moudgil, A., "Structural Change and Growth of Agriculture in Haryana", International Journal of Applied Research, Vol. 1, No. 13, 2015, pp. 133-139.

62. Rubeenah Akhter and Rekha Acharya, "Changes in Cropping Pattern in Jammu and Kashmir" International Journal of Advanced Research in Education & Technology, Vol. 2, Issue 4 (Oct. - Dec. 2015), pp. 88-91.

63. Chinky Sangral, "Changes in Cropping Pattern and Crop Diversification in Jammu and Kashmir" IOSR Journal of Humanities and Social Science, Vol. 20, No. 4, April, 2015, pp. 07-09.

64. Naveen Kumar et al., "Kala Matar: an Indigenous Legume Crop of Spiti Valley in The Trans Himalyan Cold Desert of India Facing Threat of Extinction" International Journal of Current Research in Life Sciences, Vol. 4, No. 08, August 2015, pp. 346-348.

65. R. Singh, "Analysis of Spatial-Temporal Changes in Cropping Pattern and Cropping Intensity in Agriculture of Haryana", Online International Interdisciplinary Research Journal, Vol. 5, No. 6, 2015, pp. 96-104.

66. Vanita Ahlawat and Renu, "Regional Disparity in Cropping Intensity and Relative Impact of Irrigation in Haryana" IOSR Journal of Business and Management, Volume 18, Issue 9, September, 2016, pp. 41-45.

67. Vishwanath A. Khot and Talwar Sabanna, (2017) "Scenario of Cropping Pattern and Crop Diversification: A Study of Gokak Taluk in Belgaum District, Karnataka, India". International Journal of Research in Management, Economics and Commerce, Volume 07, Issue 04, April 2017, pp. 20-24.

3

Outturn of Cash Crops in Himachal Pradesh with Reference to Kinnaur and Lahaul and Spiti

As stated in Chapter-I, Himachal Pradesh has a huge diversity in terms of geographical distribution and use of land for production of crops. Multiplicity of factors are responsible for such a diversity including topographical conditions, fertility, irrigation facility and transport etc. Further, occupational shifting has also influenced the pattern of cropping particularly in the tribal regions. It is pertinent to understand that all such factors are responsible for crop outturn and intensity and as such, are responsible for attention of people towards their involvement in opting agriculture and horticulture as the major occupations. This chapter endows to analyze outturn of cash crops in Himachal Pradesh with reference to Kinnaur and Lahaul & Spiti.

3.1 Land-Use -Wise Geographical Area of Himachal Pradesh

The total geographical area of Himachal Pradesh is classified as Forests (under any legal enactment dealing with forests, whether state owned or private), Barren & Uncultivated lands (mountains, desert etc.), Land put to non-agricultural uses (lands occupied by buildings, roads and railways or under water), Permanent pastures and Grazing lands (it includes all grazing land whether they are permanent pastures and meadows or not), Land under miscellaneous tree crops and Groves not included in area sown, Cultivated waste (it includes land available for cultivation), Other fallow land, Current fallows, Net Area Sown (under crops and orchards) and Land unutilised. The land use-wise geographical area of Himachal Pradesh is depicted in table 3.1.

Table-3.1 : Land-Use –Wise Geographical Area of Himachal Pradesh

(in hectares)

	HIMACHAL PRADESH												
Year	Forest	B.U.L	L.P.N.A	P.P. & GL	L.U. Mis	C.W.	OFL	CF	NAS	TUA	Growth	Land not Utilised	Total Geographical Area
1998-99	1043178 (100)	14778 (100)	201744 (100)	1198300 (100)	46242 (100)	119647 (100)	21018 (100)	50232 (100)	571744 (100)	3399887 (61.07) (100)		2167413 38.93	55,67,300 (100)
1999-2000	1049039 (100)	149388 (100)	198669 (100)	1193602 (100)	48634 (100)	118126 (100)	20695 (100)	55938 (100)	568338 (100)	3402429 (61.12) (100)	0.07	2164871 (38.88)	55,67,300 (100)
2000-01	1056143 (100)	138853 (100)	192088 (100)	1203531 (100)	45908 (100)	123500 (100)	25816 (100)	52622 (100)	557742 (100)	3396203 (61.01) (100)	(0.18)	2171097 38.99	55,67,300 (100)
2001-02	1084633 (100)	715578 (100)	226446 (100)	1290727 (100)	97751 (100)	106150 (100)	21663 (100)	50781 (100)	567534 (100)	4161263 (77.75) (100)	22.53	1406037 25.25	55,67,300 (100)
2002-03	1086548 (100)	775896 (100)	224791 (100)	1340222 (100)	97527 (100)	103942 (100)	22706 (100)	5410 (100)	560154 (100)	4267196 (76.65) (100)	2.55	1300104 23.35	55,67,300 (100)
2003-04	1092384 (100)	905730 (100)	233110 (100)	1491072 (100)	67053 (100)	107393 (100)	27606 (100)	56905 (100)	549419 (100)	4530672 (81.39) (100)	6.17	1036628 18.61	55,67,300 (100)
2004-05	1094209 (100)	856911 (100)	302194 (100)	1471536 (100)	64161 (100)	119413 (100)	15714 (100)	56233 (100)	551457 (100)	4531828 (81.41) (100)	0.03	1035472 (18.59)	55,67,300 (100)
2005-06	1093545 (100)	807217 (100)	313729 (100)	1529243 (100)	56834 (100)	124458 (100)	13497 (100)	54165 (100)	554592 (100)	4547280 (81.68) (100)	0.34	1020020 (18.32)	55,67,300 (100)
2006-07	1098661 (100)	806574 (100)	317469 (100)	1518688 (100)	60230 (100)	122114 (100)	13093 (100)	56287 (100)	549643 (100)	4542759 (81.6) (100)	(0.10)	1024541 18.40	55,67,300 (100)
2007-08	1099447 (100)	806258 (100)	319206 (100)	1518025 (100)	57957 (100)	122221 (100)	15143 (100)	60314 (100)	544575 (100)	4543146 (81.61) (100)	0.01	1024154 (18.39)	55,67,300 (100)

2008-09	1099055 (100)	672512 (100)	453498 (100)	1515011 (100)	62490 (100)	128411 (100)	16537 (100)	56124 (100)	540518 (100)	4544156 (81.62) (100)	0.02	1023144 (18.38)	55,67,300 (100)
2009-10	1101013 (100)	671991 (100)	458176 (100)	1500517 (100)	68665 (100)	127404 (100)	14091 (100)	60432 (100)	542550 (100)	4544839 (81.62) (100)	0.02	1022461 (18.38)	55,67,300 (100)
2010-11	1100853 (100)	656079 (100)	473316 (100)	1495863 (100)	65433 (100)	138029 (100)	13435 (100)	62801 (100)	539020 (100)	4544829 (81.64) (100)	(0.00)	1022471 (18.36)	55,67,300 (100)
2011-12	1101046 (100)	657967 (100)	473407 (100)	1491158 (100)	65840 (100)	136625 (100)	14577 (100)	63517 (100)	540820 (100)	4544957 (81.64) (100)	0.00	1022343 (18.36)	55,67,300 (100)
2012-13	1102960 (100)	655820 (100)	466961 (100)	1499889 (100)	67513 (100)	136434 (100)	17579 (100)	60194 (100)	542199 (100)	4549549 (81.72) (100)	0.10	1017751 (18.28)	55,67,300 (100)
2013-14	1103036 (100)	653928 (100)	467829 (100)	1503317 (100)	67791 (100)	135079 (100)	19875 (100)	59294 (100)	539462 (100)	4549611 (81.73) (100)	0.00	1017689 (18.27)	55,67,300 (100)
2014-15	1105997 (100)	783404 (100)	348649 (100)	1503833 (100)	68391 (100)	128224 (100)	22109 (100)	59991 (100)	538412 (100)	4559010 (81.89) (100)	0.20	1008290 (18.11)	55,67,300 (100)
2015-2016	1125742 (100)	778525 (100)	352667 (100)	1507522 (100)	64905 (100)	124121 (100)	21294 (100)	57497 (100)	543365 (100)	4575638 (82.19) (100)	0.36	991662 (17.81)	55,67,300 (100)
C.G											**1.88**		
MEAN	**1090971.61**	**746959.33**	**334663.83**	**1431780.89**	**65184.72**	**123405.05**	**18691.56**	**54374.28**	**55008.77**	**4318625.11**		**22476149**	
SD	**21080.69**	**83000.94**	**104408.32**	**123948.24**	**13941.96**	**10159.01**	**4444.69**	**12777.87**	**10935.62**	**436568.53**			
CV	**1.93**	**11.11**	**31.19**	**8.65**	**21.38**	**8.23**	**23.77**	**23.49**	**1.98**	**10.1**			

Source: Annual Season Crop Report, Directorate of Land Records, Kasumpti, Shimla-9,1998-99 to 2015-16.

Land-Use – Wise Geographical Area of Kinnaur

(in hectares)

KINNAUR													
Year	**Forest**	**B.U.L**	**L.P.N.A**	**P.P& GL**	**L.U Mis**	**C.W.**	**OFL**	**CF**	**NAS**	**TUA**	**Growth**	**Land not Utilised**	**TGA**
1998-99	26583 (2.55)	34009 (23.01)	9392 (4.66)	161249 (13.46)	83 (0.18)	6365 (5.31)	303 (1.44)	1611 (3.21)	7513 (1.31)	247098(38.31) (7.27)		393002 (61.39)	640100 (100)
1999-2000	27206 (2.59)	34033 (22.78)	9370 (4.72)	160619 (13.46)	83 (0.17)	6333 (5.36)	318 (1.54)	1529 (2.73)	7607 (1.34)	247098(38.61) (7.26)	-	393002 (61.39)	640100 (100)
2000-01	31950 (3.03)	26538 (19.11)	8675 (4.52)	166544 (13.84)	93 (0.2)	6247 (5.06)	206 (0.8)	1630 (3.1)	7449 (1.34)	249332(38.96) (7.34)	0.90	390768 (61.04)	640100 (100)
2001-02	37880 (3.49)	26614 (3.72)	51183 (22.6)	190684 (14.77)	737 (0.75)	6440 (6.07)	115 (0.53)	1714 (3.38)	7537 (1.33)	322904(50.55) (7.76)	29.51	317196 (49.55)	640100 (100)
2002-03	39163 (3.6)	90645 (11.68)	51203 (22.78)	218040 (16.27)	852 (0.87)	6226 (5.99)	114 (0.5)	1596 (2.88)	7602 (1.36)	415441(64.91) (9.74)	28.66	224659 (35.09)	640100 (100)
2003-04	39163 (3.59)	179407 (19.81)	70408 (30.20)	321950 (21.59)	55 (0.08)	3312 (3.08)	316 (1.14)	1614 (2.84)	7517 (1.37)	623742(97.45) (13.77)	50.14	16358 (2.55)	640100 (100)
2004-05	36609 (3.35)	142267 (16.6)	113414 (37.53)	318352 (21.63)	79 (0.12)	3487 (2.92)	127 (0.81)	1601 (2.85)	7806 (1.42)	623742(97.45) (13.76)	-	16358 (2.55)	640100 (100)
2005-06	37172 (3.4)	134449 (16.66)	121053 (38.59)	318027 (20.8)	60 (0.11)	3649 (2.93)	112 (0.83)	1634 (3.02)	7586 (1.37)	623742(97.45) (13.72)	-	16358 (2.55)	640100 (100)
2006-07	36904 (3.36)	130887 (16.23)	124635 (39.26)	318131 (20.95)	76 (0.13)	3670 (3.01)	108 (0.82)	1751 (3.11)	7580 (1.38)	623742(97.45) (13.73)	-	16358 (2.55)	640100 (100)
2007-08	37359 (3.4)	130919 (16.24)	124544 (39.02)	317831 (20.94)	105 (0.18)	3554 (2.91)	75 (0.5)	2087 (3.46)	7268 (1.33)	623742(97.45) (13.73)	-	16358 (2.55)	640100 (100)

2008-09	35579 **(3.24)**	130859 **(19.47)**	124602 **(27.48)**	317697 **(20.97)**	84 **(0.13)**	3610 **(2.81)**	57 **(0.34)**	1770 (3.15)	7484 **(1.38)**	621742(97.13) **(13.68)**	(0.32)	18358 (2.87)	640100 (100)
2009-10	37583 **(3.41)**	130859 **(19.47)**	124634 **(27.2)**	317549 **(21.16)**	101 **(0.15)**	3488 **(2.74)**	63 **(0.45)**	2005 **(3.32)**	7477 **(1.38)**	623759(97.45) **(13.72)**	0.32	16341 (2.55)	640100 (100)
2010-11	37583 **·(3.41)**	131126 **(19.93)**	124837 **(26.37)**	317595 **(21.23)**	88 **(0.13)**	3488 **(2.53)**	115 **(0.86)**	1876 **(2.99)**	7602 **(1.41)**	624310(97.54) **(13.74)**	0.09	15790 (2.46)	640100 (100)
2011-12	37583 **(3.41)**	133335 **(20.33)**	124840 **(26.37)**	317535 **(21.29)**	116 **(0.18)**	3444 **(2.52)**	134 **(0.92)**	1974 **(3.11)**	7553 **(1.4)**	624305(97.54) **(13.740)**	(0.00)	15795 (2.46)	640100 (100)
2012-13	37530 **(3.4)**	133335 **(20.33)**	117743 **(25.21)**	322281 **(21.49)**	116 **(0.17)**	3488 **(2.56)**	102 **(0.58)**	7136 **(11.86)**	7884 **(1.45)**	629615(98.37) **(13.84)**	0.85	10485 (1.63)	640100 (100)
2013-14	37612 **(3.4)**	133335 **(20.38)**	117794 **(25.17)**	322344 **(21.44)**	98 **(0.14)**	3289 **(2.43)**	56 **(0.28)**	1821 **(3.07)**	7866 **(1.45)**	624215(97.52) **(13.72)**	(0.85)	15885 (2.48)	640100 (100)
2014-15	38563 **(3.48)**	132430 **(16.90)**	117877 **(33.80)**	322170 **(21.42)**	107 **(0.15)**	3322 **(2.59)**	87 **(0.39)**	1624 **(2.70)**	8034 **(1.49)**	624214(97.52) **(13.69)**	(0.00)	15886 (2.48)	640100 (100)
	38590 **(3.42)**	132444 **(17.01)**	117878 **(33.42)**	322043 **(21.36)**	101 **(0.15)**	3254 **(2.62)**	83 **(0.38)**	1513 **(2.63)**	8310 **(1.52)**	624216(97.52) **(13.64)**	0.00	15884 (2.48)	640100 (100)
C.G											**6.42**		
MEAN	**36145.11**	**110416.16**	**91893.44**	**280591.16**	**168.55**	**4259.22**	**138.39**	**2027**	**7648.61**	**533164.38**			
SD	**3725.12**	**46730.30**	**45224.93**	**65698.84**	**229.18**	**1322.23**	**87.14**	**1285.93**	**245.74**	**155328.75**			
CV	**10.3**	**42.32**	**49.21**	**23.41**	**135.97**	**31.04**	**62.96**	**63.44**	**3.21**	**29.13**			

Source: Annual Season Crop Report, Directorate of Land Records, Kasumpti, Shimla-9,1998-99 to 2015-16.

Land-Use – Wise Geographical Area of Lahaul & Spiti

(in hectares)

LAHAUL & SPITI													
Year	Forest	B.U.L	L.P.N.A	P.P& GL	L.U Mis	C.W.	OFL	CF	NAS	TUA	Growth	Land not utilized	TGA
1998-99	110055 (10.55)	4414 (2.99)	1555 (0.77)	95500 (7.97)	108 (0.23)	654 (0.55)	22 (0.1)	190 (0.38)	3128 (0.55)	215626(15.59) (6.34)		1167874 (84.41)	1383500 (100)
1999-2000	110056 (10.49)	4416 (2.96)	1599 (0.8)	95453 (8)	96 (0.2)	682 (0.58)	2 (0.01)	185 (0.33)	3147 (0.55)	215636(15.59) (6.34)	0.00	1,167,888 (84.41)	1383500 (100)
2000-2001	110056 (10.42)	1523 (1.1)	4408 (2.29)	95505 (7.94)	87 (0.19)	679 (0.55)	6 (0.02)	156 (0.3)	3192 (0.57)	215612(15.59) (6.35)	(0.01)	1,167,888 (84.41)	1383500 (100)
2001-02	135514 (12.49)	543371 (75.93)	4626 (2.04)	210260 (16.29)	102 (0.1)	663 (0.62)	0 (0)	175 (0.34)	3218 (0.58)	897929(64.91) (21.58)	316.46	485571 (35.09)	1383500 (100)
2002-03	135382 (12.46)	535594 (69.03)	4800 (2.14)	230888 (17.23)	378 (0.39)	638 (0.61)	21 (0.09)	141 (0.25)	3238 (0.58)	911080(65.86) (21.35)	1.48	472,420 (34.14)	1383500 (100)
2003-04	135382 (12.39)	535694 (59.14)	4901 (2.1)	231117 (15.5)	112 (0.17)	587 (0.55)	9 (0.03)	115 (0.2)	3219 (0.59)	911136(65.85) (20.11)	0.01	472,364 (34.13)	1383500 (100)
2004-05	135382 (12.37)	546695 (63.8)	4947 (1.64)	220045 (14.95)	87 (0.14)	497 (0.42)	9 (0.06)	106 (0.19)	3386 (0.61)	911140(65.859) (20.11)	0.00	12,92,386 (34.13)	1383500 (100)
2005-06	135369 (12.38)	546695 (67.73)	4640 (1.48)	220138 (14.4)	113 (0.2)	587 (0.47)	21 (0.16)	100 (0.18)	3487 (0.63)	911163(65.86) (20.04)	0.00	472,337 (34.14)	1383500 (100)
2006-07	135369 (12.32)	546695 (67.78)	4865 (1.53)	220112 (14.49)	114 (0.19)	588 (0.48)	18 (0.14)	106 (0.19)	3292 (0.6)	911159(65.86) (20.06)	0.00	472,341 (34.14)	1383500 (100)

2007-08	135369 (12.31)	546695 (67.81)	4865 (1.52)	220110 (14.5)	124 (0.21)	588 (0.48)	3 (0.02)	85 (0.14)	3326 (0.61)	911165(65.86) (20.06)	0.00	472,335 (34.14)	1383500 (100)
2008-09	135369 (12.32)	415831 (61.83)	135730 (29.93)	220098 (14.53)	127 (0.2)	597 (0.46)	5 (0.03)	365 (0.65)	3043 (0.56)	911165(68.86) (20.05)		472,335 (34.14)	1383500 (100)
2009-10	135369 (12.29)	415831 (61.88)	135730 (29.62)	220999 (14.73)	127 (0.18)	599 (0.47)	0 (0)	118 (0.2)	3292 (0.61)	912065(65.93) (20.07)	0.10	471,435 (34.07)	1383500 (100) .
2010-11	135369 (12.3)	415831 (63.38)	135730 (28.68)	220999 (14.77)	127 (0.19)	599 (0.43)	0 (0)	119 (0.19)	3291 (0.61)	912065(65.93) (20.07)		471,435 (34.07)	1383500 (100)
2011-12	135369 (12.29)	415831 (63.2)	135780 (28.68)	220097 (14.76)	127 (0.19)	597 (0.44)	0 (0)	131 (0.21)	3283 (0.61)	911215(65.87) (20.05)	(0.09)	472,285 (34.13)	1383500 (100)
2012-13	135369 (12.27)	415831 (63.41)	135780 (29.08)	220097 (14.67)	127 (0.19)	597 (0.44)	0 (0)	131 (0.22)	3283 (0.61)	911215(65.13) (20.03)		472,285 (34.13)	1383500 (100)
2013-14	135369 (12.27)	415831 (63.58)	135760 (29.01)	220058 (14.63)	126 (0.18)	589 (0.43)	1 (0)	102 (0.17)	3359 (0.62)	911195(65.87) (20.02)		472,305 (34.13)	1383500 (100)
2014-15	137376 (12.42)	541314 (69.09)	16857 (4.83)	211474 (14.06)	108 (0.15)	563 (0.43)	2 (0)	103 (0.17)	3398 (0.63)	911195(65.87) (19.98)		472,305 (34.13)	1383500 (100)
2015-16	137376 (12.20)	541314 (69.53)	16857 (4.77)	211474 (14.02)	111 (0.17)	568 (0.45)	2 (0)	108 (0.18)	3396 (0.62)	911206(65.87) (19.91)		472,294 (34.13)	1383500 (100)
C.G											318.05		
MEAN	131383.33	410522.55	49412.77	199134.67	127.83	604	6.72	140.89	3276.55	749052.27			
SD	9835.20	196235.21	62954.88	47994.58	63.87	45.23	8.12	63.76	109.56	311631.37			
CV	7.48	47.8	127.4	24.1	49.96	7.48	120.83	45.25	3.34	41.6			

Source: Annual Season Crop Report, Directorate of Land Records, Kasumpti, Shimla-9,1998-99 to 2015-16.

The data evinces that total utilised land area of Himachal Pradesh on village papers, has increased almost every year since 1998-99 to 2015-16, recording a compound growth of 1.88 percent. In 2015-16, the Land use wise geographical area was recorded 45,75,638 hectares (82.18%) against total geographical area of 55,67,300 hectares as per professional survey. Whereas, in 1998-99, it was 33,99,887 hectares (61.07%). The average area under forest in the State is 1,09,0971.61 hectares with S.D of 21,080.69 hectares and C.V. 1.93 percent, followed by 7,46,959.33 hectares average area under barren and uncultivated land with S.D of 83,000.93 hectare and C.V. 11.11 percent. The average land put to non agricultural uses is 3,34,663.83 hectares with S.D. = 1,04,408.35 hectare and C.V. 31.19 percent, average permanent pasture and grazing land is 1,43,1780.88 hectares with the S.D. of 1,23,948.20 hectares and 8.65 percent C.V. and average land use under miscellaneous category which is not included in area sown, is 65,184.72 hectares with S.D. = 13,941.95 hectares and 21.38 percent C.V. The cultivated waste area is 1,23,405.05 hectare with S.D. = 10,159.01 hectares and 8.23 percent C.V. The average of other fellow landwas18,691.55 hectare with S.D. = 4,444.69 hectares and C.V. 23.77 percent, average current fellow land 54,374.27 hectare with S.D. = 12,777.86 hectare and 23.49 percent C.V. The average net area sown is 55,008.77 hectare with S.D. = 10935.62 hectares and C.V. 1.98 percent. The average total gross area is 43,18,625.11 hectares with S.D. = 4,36,568.53 hectares and C.V. 10.1 percent.Data recording highest C.V. (31.19%) for land put to non agricultural uses indicates that land is occupied by buildings, roads and railways.

In the beginning i.e. 1998-99, area under Land Put to Non Agricultural Uses was recorded 2,01,744 hectares, which increased to 3,52,667 hectares in the year 2015-16. Moreover, the area under NAS (Net Area Sown) was recorded 5,71,744 hectares in the year 1998, which decreased to 5,43,365 hectares in 2015-16. It leads to the conclusion that as the population increased (1991 to 2011), total area under LPNA increased, but area under NAS decreased. Further, the growth rate was recorded 0.07 percent in the year 1999-2000, which immediately decreased to -0.18 percent in 2000-01. The highest growth rate of 22.53 percent was recorded in the year 2001-02. Moreover, 0.36 percent growth rate is recorded in the year 2015-16.

3.2 Status of Cropped Area in Tribal Regions of Himachal Pradesh

Table-3.2 : Status of Cropped Area in Tribal Regions of Himachal Pradesh

(in hectares)

Year	HP			Kinnaur			Lahaul-Spiti		
	Used Area	Cropped Area	Irrigated Area	Used Area	Cropped Area	Irrigated Area	Used Area	Cropped Area	Irrigated Area
1998-99	3399887 (100)	975231 (28.68)	99646 (2.93) *10.21*	247098 (100)	9553 (3.86)	4307 (1.74) *45.08*	215626 (100)	3280. (1.52)	3146 (1.45) *95.91*
1999-2000	3402429 (100)	967990 (28.44)	100454 (2.95) *10.37*	247098 (100)	9285 (3.75)	4517 (1.82) *48.64*	215636 (100)	3285 (1.52)	3147 (1.45) *95.79*
2000-01	3396203 (100)	968217 (28.50)	104790 (3.08) *10.82*	249332 (100)	9480 (3.80)	4405 (1.76) *46.46*	215612 (100)	3361 (1.55)	3147 (1.45) *93.63*
2001-02	4161263 (100)	949888 (22.82)	104792 (2.51) *11.03*	322904 (100)	9787 (3.03)	4337 (1.34) *44.31*	897929 (100)	3309 (0.36)	3208 (0.35) *96.94*
2002-03	4267196 (100)	986338 (23.11)	102617 (2.40) *10.40*	415441 (100)	9970 (2.39)	4335 (1.04) *43.48*	911080 (100)	3318 (0.36)	3318 (0.36) *100*
2003-04	4530672 (100)	970136 (21.41)	10110 (0.22) *1.04*	623742 (100)	9334 (1.49)	4293 (0.68) *45.99*	911136 (100)	3358 (0.36)	3219 (0.35) *95.86*
2004-05	4531828 (100)	956767 (21.11)	101907 (2.24) *10.65*	623742 (100)	9059 (1.45)	4690 (0.75) *51.77*	911140 (100)	3486 (0.38)	3386 (0.37) *97.13*
2005-06	4547280 (100)	947142 (20.82)	125506 (2.76) *13.25*	623742 (100)	9328 (1.49)	4552 (0.72) *48.79*	911163 (100)	3595 (0.39)	3487 (0.38) *96.99*
2006-07	4542759 (100)	955740 (21.03)	102106 (2.24) *10.68*	623742 (100)	9088 (1.45)	4530 (0.72) *49.84*	911159 (100)	3377 (0.37)	3296 (0.36) *97.60*
2007-08	4543146 (100)	945205 (20.80)	102263 (2.25) *10.81*	623742 (100)	8592 (1.37)	4418 (0.70) *51.41*	911165 (100)	3413 (0.37)	3326 (0.35) *97.45*
2008-09	4544156 (100)	955614 (21.02)	105081 (2.31) *10.99*	621742 (100)	8745 (1.40)	4487 (0.72) *51.30*	911165 (100)	3174 (0.34)	3043 (0.33) *95.87*
2009-10	4544839 (100)	952517 (20.95)	104452 (2.29) *10.96*	623759 (100)	9058 (1.45)	4482 (0.71) *49.48*	912065 (100)	3489 (0.38)	3292 (0.07) *94.35*
2010-11	4544829 (100)	943469 (20.75)	103640 (2.28) *10.98*	624310 (100)	9017 (1.44)	4768 (0.76) *52.87*	912065 (100)	3464 (0.37)	3291 (0.36) *95*

Contd. ...

2011-12	4544957 (100)	943784 (20.76)	104320 (2.29) *11.05*	624305 (100)	8969 (1.43)	4676 (0.74) *52.13*	911215 (100)	3460 (0.37)	3283 (0.36) *94.88*
2012-13	4549549 (100)	954824 (20.98)	108328 (2.38) *11.34*	629615 (100)	9629 (1.52)	4860 (0.77) *50.47*	911215 (100)	3441 (0.37)	3283 (0.36) *95.40*
2013-14	4549611 (100)	946134 (20.79)	107852 (2.37) *11.39*	624215 (100)	9619 (1.54)	4913 (0.78) *51.07*	911195 (100)	3547 (0.38)	3359 (0.36) *94.69*
2014-15	4559010 (100)	940597 (20.63)	106599 (2.34) *11.33*	624214 (100)	9545 (1.52)	4995 (0.80) *52.33*	911195 (100)	3591 (0.39)	3398 (0.37) *94.62*
2015-2016	4575638 (100)	938625 (20.51)	109940 (2.40) *11.71*	624216 (100)	10646 (1.70)	5434 (0.87) *51.04*	911206 (100)	3517 (0.38)	3389 (0.37) *96.36*
MEAN	4318625.11	955457.25	93966.83	533164.38	9282.06	4611.05	749052.27	3397.31	3278.78
SD	436568.53	13210.19	30192.92	155328.75	378.59	295.90	311631.37	110.12	110.78
CV	10.1	1.38	32.13	29.13	4.07	6.41	41.6	3.24	3.37

Source: Annual Season Crop Report, Directorate of Land Records, Kasumpti, Shimla, 1998-99 to 2015-16.

Further, the area under 'land not utilised' was recorded 38.99 percent in the year 2000-01. Whereas, it was minimum i.e. 17.81 percent in the year 2015-16. It indicates that out of the total geographical area, total utilised land increased year by year, during the study period. It is analyzed from the table that Net Area Sown in Himachal Pradesh has declined despite of the fact that there is increase in total land area used. Hence, it indicates that there is diversion of use of land from area sown or used for agricultural purposes to the other purposes, like construction. The total geographical area under land utilisation of district Kinnaur on village papers was recorded 6,24,216 hectares (97.51%) in 2015-16 against total geographical area of the district as per professional survey i.e. 6,40,100 hectare. In 1998-99, it was 2,47,098 hectare i.e. 38.60 percent of the total geographical area. Further, the total utilised land area of district Lahaul & Spiti on village papers was 9,11,206 hectare (65.86%) in 2015-16, against 13,83,500 hectare out of the total geographical area of the district. In 1998-99, it was 2,15,626 hectare i.e. 15.58 percent of the total geographical area of the district recording 6.42 percent compound growth. It is pertinent to mention that at the beginning of the study period, i.e. 1998-99, total utilised area in Kinnaur was 38.31 percent, which increased to 50.55 percent in the year 2001-02 and it suddenly increased to 97.45 percent in the year 2002-03. Whereas, in Lahaul & Spiti, only 15.59

percent area was utilised land, as compared to that of Kinnaur. Further, it increased to 64.91 percent in the year 2001-02.

Further, the highest growth (50.14%) was recorded under total utilised area in Kinnaur in the year 2003-04, against -0.85 percent in 2013-14. In Lahaul & Spiti, highest growth was 316.46 percent in 2001-02 and lowest -0.09 percent in 2011-12. In Kinnaur, the highest area was utilised under permanent pastures and other grazing lands, out of total utilised area on village papers (28591.16 hectare i.e. 52.62%) with S.D. = 65698.84 hectare and C.V. = 23.41 percent. Followed by, area under barren and uncultivated land, i.e. 1,10,146.16 hectare (25.31%), with S.D. = 46,730.30 hectare and C.V. = 42.32 percent. The average cultivated land is recorded 4,259.22 hectare with S.D. = 1,322.23 hectare and C.V. = 31.04 percent. Whereas, in Lahaul & Spiti, maximum area was under barren and uncultivated lands 4,10,522.5 hectare with S.D. = 1,96,235.21 and C.V. = 47.8 percent, followed by permanent pastures and other grazing lands i.e. 1,99,134.67 hectare with S.D. = 47,994.57 hectare and C.V. = 24.1 percent and average cultivated waste which was 604 hectare with S.D. = 45.23 hectare and C.V. = 7.48 percent. Moreover, in Kinnaur, the area under NAS (Net Area Sown) was recorded 7,513 hectares in the year 1998, which increased to 8,310 hectares in 2015-16 and in Lahaul & Spiti, it was 3,128 hectares in 1998-99, which increased to 3,396 hectares in 2015-16. It leads to the conclusion that the NAS increased in both the districts, whereas the NAS of the State decreased to 5,71,744 hectares in 1998 from 5,43,365 hectares in 2015-16.

Out of the average Used Area of Himachal Pradesh 22.12 percent is Cropped Area, and only 9.83 percent is Irrigated Area. At the beginning of the study period i.e. 1998-99, 28.68 percent of the used area was Cropped Area and only 10.21 percent was Irrigated Area. It is noticeable from the table that the Cropped Area has decreased till 2008-09, except slight increases in the years 2002-03, 2006-07 and 2008-09. The Cropped Area remained constant at 20 percent for the remaining period until 2015-16. It is worth mentioning that the Cropped Area has shown an overall decrease of 8 percent over the eighteen years. The Irrigated Area in the year 1998-99 was 99,646 hectares which is 10.21 percent of the Cropped Area. The Irrigated Area remained constant between 10 and 11 percent with a slight upward trend to 13 percent in the year 2005-06. The trend of cropped area and irrigated area in the two tribal districts has been found different.

Out of the average Used Area in Kinnaur only 1.74 percent area is Cropped Area and meager 49.67 percent is Irrigated Area. The Cropped Area remained constant at around 3 percent until 2001-02 and then declined, from the year 2002-03. Further, the Irrigated Area for crops remained between 45 to 52 percent during the research period ranging between 5.78 percent in the year 2004-05 to 0.11 percent in the year 2008-09. The coefficient of variance was calculated 4.07 percent in respect of Cropped Area showing high level of consistency.

On the contrary, out of the average Used Area in Lahaul & Spiti an average of 0.45 percent i.e. 3,397.31 hectares area is Cropped Area and above 95 percent (3,278.78 hectares) of the Cropped Area is Irrigated Area. The Cropped Area remained constant at around 1.51 percent until 2001-02 and then declined, from the year 2002-03.

Since, the Irrigated Area for crops is above 95 percent, it indicates that maximum Cropped Area is irrigated in Lahaul & Spiti with high standard deviation and C.V. of Used Area which shows that there is high level of inconsistency in Used Area.

3.3 Total Cropped Area

The share of Kinnaur and Lahaul & Spiti as regards total cropped area has recorded a kaleidoscopic growth over the period under study. The following table shows growth in Net Area Sown, Area Sown More than Once, and Total Cropped Area in Himachal Pradesh, as well as in Kinnaur and Lahaul & Spiti.

Average total cropped area is recorded 9,55,457.25 hectares with 1.38 percent variance and standard deviation of 13,210.19 hectares, showing a very slight variation in total cropped area in Himachal Pradesh during the past 18 years. The average Net Area Sown is recorded 57.69 percent of the average total cropped area, with a negative compound growth of -0.38 percent showing a decline of NAS. However, the C.V. is 2 percent, which recognises a little variation. On the contrary, the variation in 'Area Sown More Than Once' is quite high (2.21%) as compared to that of NAS, with S.D. of 8,989.76 hectares. It shows that NAS is more consistent as compared to Area Sown More Than Once. Further, Total Cropped Area has been recorded 9,75,231 hectares in the year 1998-99. This has decreased to 9,38,625 hectares in the year 2015-16. A negative compound growth of 0.19 percent was recorded in the last 18 years, under Total Cropped Area in Himachal Pradesh.

Table-3.3 : Total Cropped Area in Kinnaur and Lahaul & Spiti

(in hectares)

Year	Himachal Pradesh						Kinnaur						Lahaul & Spiti					
	Net area sown	Growth	Area sown more than once	Growth	Total cropped area	Growth	Net area sown	Growth	Area sown more than once	Growth	Total cropped area	Growth	Net area sown	Growth	Area sown more than once	Growth	Total cropped area	Growth
1998-99	571744.00 (100)		403487.00 (100)		975231.00 (100)		7513.00 (1.31)		2040.00 (0.51)		9553.00 (0.98)		3128.00 (0.55)		152.00 (0.04)		3280.00 (0.34)	
1999-2000	568338.00 (100)	-0.60	399652.00 (100)	-0.95	967990.00 (100)	-0.74	7607.00 (1.34)	1.25	1678.00 (0.42)	-17.75	9285.00 (0.96)	-2.81	3147.00 (0.55)	0.61	138.00 (0.03)	-9.21	3285.00 (0.34)	0.15
2000-01	567534.00 (100)	-0.14	400683.00 (100)	0.26	968217.00 (100)	0.02	7537.00 (1.33)	-0.92	1943.00 (0.48)	15.79	9480.00 (0.98)	2.10	3218.00 (0.57)	2.26	143.00 (0.04)	3.62	3361.00 (0.35)	2.31
2001-02	557742.00 (100)	-1.73	392146.00 (100)	-2.13	949888.00 (100)	-1.89	7449.00 (1.34)	-1.17	2338.00 (0.60)	20.33	9787.00 (1.03)	3.24	3192.00 (0.57)	-0.81	117.00 (0.03)	-18.18	3309.00 (0.35)	-1.55
2002-03	560154.00 (100)	0.43	426184.00 (100)	8.68	986338.00 (100)	3.84	7602.00 (1.36)	2.05	2338.00 (0.56)	1.28	9970.00 (1.01)	1.87	3238.00 (0.58)	1.44	80.00 (0.02)	-31.62	3318.00 (0.34)	0.27
2003-04	549419.00 (100)	-1.92	420717.00 (100)	-1.28	970136.00 (100)	-1.64	7517.00 (1.37)	-1.12	1817.00 (0.43)	-23.27	9334.00 (0.96)	-6.38	3219.00 (0.59)	-0.59	139.00 (0.03)	73.75	3358.00 (0.35)	1.21
2004-05	551457.00 (100)	0.37	405310.00 (100)	-3.66	956767.00 (100)	-1.38	7806.00 (1.42)	3.84	1253.00 (0.31)	-31.04	9059.00 (0.95)	-2.95	3386.00 (0.61)	5.19	100.00 (0.02)	-28.06	3486.00 (0.36)	3.81
2005-06	554592.00 (100)	0.57	392550.00 (100)	-3.15	947142.00 (100)	-1.01	7586.00 (1.37)	-2.82	1742.00 (0.44)	39.03	9328.00 (0.98)	2.97	3487.00 (0.63)	2.98	108.00 (0.03)	8.00	3595.00 (0.38)	3.13
2006-07	549643.00 (100)	-0.89	406097.00 (100)	3.45	955740.00 (100)	0.91	7580.00 (1.38)	-0.08	1508.00 (0.37)	-13.43	9088.00 (0.95)	-2.57	3292.00 (0.60)	-5.59	81.00 (0.02)	-25.00	3377.00 (0.35)	-6.06

2007-08	544575.00 (100)	-0.92	400630.00 (100)	-1.35	945205.00 (100)	-1.10	7268.00 (1.33)	-4.12	1324.00 (0.33)	-12.20	8592.00 (0.91)	-5.46	3326.00 (0.61)	1.03	87.00 (0.02)	7.41	3413.00 (0.36)	1.07
2008-09	540518.00 (100)	-0.74	415096.00 (100)	3.61	955614.00 (100)	1.10	7484.00 (1.38)	2.97	1261.00 (0.30)	-4.76	8745.00 (0.92)	1.78	3043.00 (0.56)	-8.51	131.00 (0.03)	50.57	3174.00 (0.33)	-7.00
2009-10	542550.00 (100)	0.38	409967.00 (100)	-1.24	952517.00 (100)	-0.32	7477.00 (1.38)	-0.09	1581.00 (0.39)	25.38	9058.00 (0.95)	3.58	3292.00 (0.61)	8.18	197.00 (0.05)	50.38	3489.00 (0.37)	9.92
2010-11	539020.00 (100)	-0.65	404449.00 (100)	-1.35	943469.00 (100)	-0.95	7602.00 (1.41)	1.67	1415.00 (0.35)	-10.50	9017.00 (0.96)	-0.45	3291.00 (0.61)	-0.03	173.00 (0.04)	-12.18	3464.00 (0.37)	-0.72
2011-12	540820.00 (100)	0.33	402964.00 (100)	-0.37	943784.00 (100)	0.03	7553.00 (1.40)	-0.64	1416.00 (0.35)	0.07	8969.00 (0.95)	-0.53	3283.00 (0.61)	-0.24	177.00 (0.04)	2.31	3460.00 (0.37)	-0.12
2012-13	542500.00 (100)	0.25	412324.00 (100)	2.32	954824.00 (100)	1.14	7884.00 (1.45)	4.38	1745.00 (0.42)	23.23	9629.00 (1.01)	7.36	3283.00 (0.61)	0.00	158.00 (0.04)	-10.73	3441.00 (0.36)	-0.55
2013-14	539462.00 (100)	-0.56	406672.00 (100)	-1.37	946134.00 (100)	-0.91	7866 (1.45)	-0.22	1753 (0.43)	0.45	9619 (1.01)	-0.10	3359 (0.62)	2.31	188 (0.04)	18.98	3547 (0.37)	3.08
2014-15	538412 (100)	-.19	402202 (100)	-1.10	940597 (100)	-.58	8034 (1.49)	2.13	1511 (0.37)	-13.80	9545 (1.01)	-0.76	3398 (0.63)	1.16	193 (0.04)	2.65	3591 (0.38)	1.24
2015-16	543365 (100)	.91	395260 (100)	-1.72	938625 (100)	-0.20	8310 (1.52)	3.43	2336 (0.59)	54.59	10646 (1.13)	11.53	3396 (0.62)	-0.05	121 (0.03)	-37.30	3517 (0.37)	-2.06
Compound Growth		**-0.38**		**0.09**		**-0.19**		**0.33**		**0.84**		**0.11**		**0.54**		**5.34**		**0.59**
Mean	**551254.25**		**405355**		**955457.25**		**7583.19**		**1697**		**9282.06**		**3261.5**		**135.56**		**3397.31**	
S.D	**11030.39**		**8989.76**		**13210.19**		**157.52**		**342.17**		**378.59**		**106.90**		**37.68**		**110.12**	
C.V	2		2.21		1.38		2.077		20.16		4.07		3.27		27.79		3.24	

Source: Annual Crop Report, Directorate of Land Records, Kasumpti, Shimla, 1998-99 to 2015-16.

Moreover, Net Area Sown and Area Sown more than once have been recorded 5,71,744 hectares and 4,03,487 hectares respectively in the year 1998-99. Both NAS and Area Sown more than once have recorded a decreasing trend. Net Area Sown decreased by 28,379 hectares between 1998-99 and 2015-16, and Area Sown More than once has decreased by 8,227 hectares in the same years. It is analysed from the data that Total Cropped Area has decreased by 36,606 hectares.

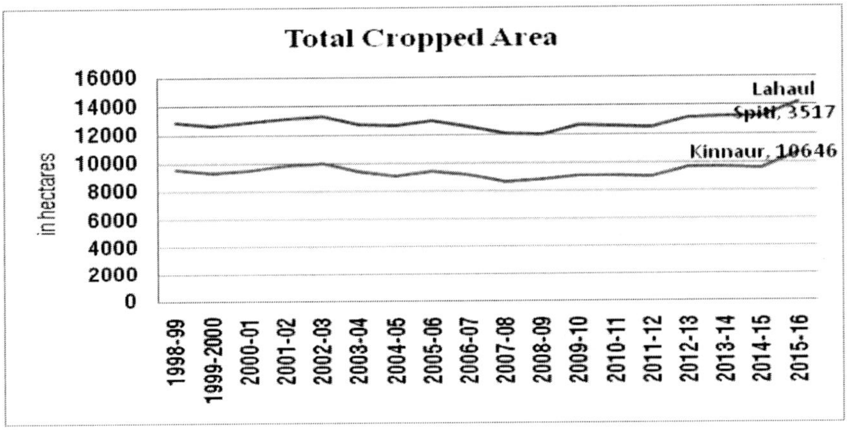

Figure-3.1 : Total Cropped Area in Kinnaur and Lahaul & Spiti

On an average, 9,282.06 hectares area is recorded in total cropped area in Kinnaur, with C.V. of 4.07 percent which is higher than that of the State (1.38%). Out of total cropped area, 81.69 percent (7,583.19 hectares) is covered by NAS with C.V. of 2.07 percent with S.D. 157.52, indicating a consistency of NAS in the district during the study period. The coefficient of variance of area sown more than once is recorded 20.16 percent with mean calculated as 1,697 hectares with S.D. 342.17 hectares. Further, 9,553 hectares area has been registered under Total Cropped Area in the year 1998-99. It is 0.98 percent of Total Cropped Area of Himachal Pradesh. This has increased to 10,646 hectares in the year 2015-16. Moreover, a positive compound growth of 0.11 percent in Total Cropped Area has been calculated in the district.

In Lahaul & Spiti, average total cropped area is 3,397.31 hectares. It is 0.34 percent of Total Cropped Area of Himachal Pradesh. About 96 percent area is under NAS in Lahaul & Spiti with C.V. of 3.27 percent indicating that maximum area in the district is under NAS. Rest of the area with high C.V. 27.29 percent is area sown more than once which is very meagre (4%). Total Cropped Area in the year 1998-99 was 3,280 hectares, which increased to 3,517 hectares in the year 2015-16. Thus, both the tribal districts have recorded increase in Total Cropped Area, Net Area Sown and Area Sown More Than Once.

3.4 Cropping Intensity in Kinnaur & Lahaul-Spiti

Cropping intensity of Kinnaur and Lahaul & Spiti districts of Himachal Pradesh envisages that the Net Area Sown in these regions has although registered growth, yet it is low in comparison to the State.

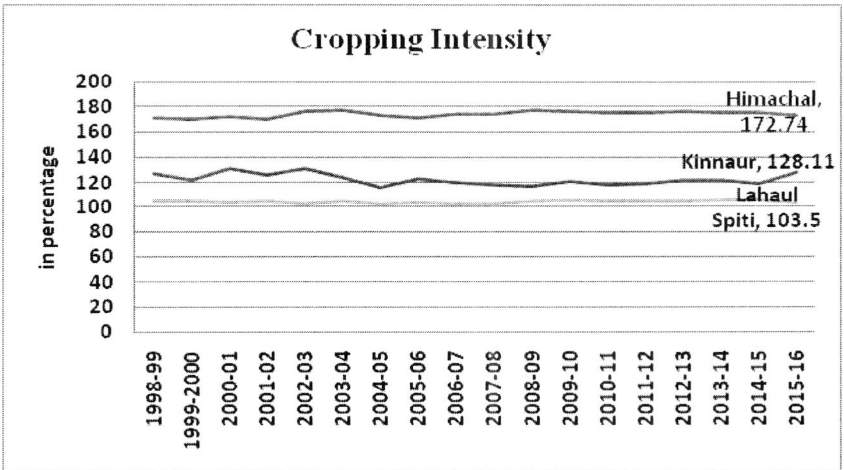

Figure-3.2 : Cropping Intensity in Kinnaur and Lahaul & Spiti

The average cropping intensity of Himachal Pradesh during the last 18 years has been recorded 173.84 percent. The lowest cropping intensity has been recorded 170.30 percent in the year 1999-2000. As shown in the table, cropping intensity has been recorded 171.1 percent in the year 1998-99, which increased to 172.74 percent in the year 2015-16. The coefficient of variance in cropping intensity is recorded least (1.23%) with S.D. of 2.15 percent. In Kinnaur, average cropping intensity during the last 18 years has been recorded 122.50 percent ranged between maximum cropping intensity of 131.20 percent in the year 2000-01 and minimum 116.10 percent in the year 2004-05. In Lahaul & Spiti, the average cropping intensity has been recorded 104.19 percent. The maximum was 106 percent in the year 2009-10, and minimum 102.4 percent in the year 2002-03. It is found that cropping intensity in Kinnaur is more consistent as compared to Lahaul & Spiti.

Table-3.4 : Cropping Intensity in Kinnaur and Lahaul & Spiti

(in hectares)

	Himachal Pradesh					Kinnaur					Lahaul & Spiti				
Year	NAS	Growth	TCA	Growth	Intensity %	NAS	Growth	TCA	Growth	Intensity %	NAS	Growth	TCA	Growth	Intensity %
1998-99	571744.00 (100)		975231.00 (100)		171.1	7513.00 (1.31)		9553.00 (0.98)		127.1	3128.00 (0.55)		3280.00 (0.34)		104.8
1999-2000	568338.00 (100)	-0.60	967990.00 (100)	-0.74	170.3	7607.00 (1.34)	1.25	9285.00 (0.96)	-2.81	122.1	3147.00 (0.55)	0.61	3285.00 (0.34)	0.15	104.4
2000-01	567534.00 (100)	-0.14	968217.00 (100)	0.02	171.8	7537.00 (1.33)	-0.92	9480.00 (0.98)	2.10	131.2	3218.00 (0.57)	2.26	3361.00 (0.35)	2.31	103.6
2001-02	557742.00 (100)	-1.73	949888.00 (100)	-1.89	170.6	7449.00 (1.34)	-1.17	9787.00 (1.03)	3.24	125.8	3192.00 (0.57)	-0.81	3309.00 (0.35)	-1.55	104.4
2002-03	560154.00 (100)	0.43	986338.00 (100)	3.84	176	7602.00 (1.36)	2.05	9970.00 (1.01)	1.87	131.1	3238.00 (0.58)	1.44	3318.00 (0.34)	0.27	102.4
2003-04	549419.00 (100)	-1.92	970136.00 (100)	-1.64	176.6	7517.00 (1.37)	-1.12	9334.00 (0.96)	-6.38	124.2	3219.00 (0.59)	-0.59	3358.00 (0.35)	1.21	104.3
2004-05	551457.00 (100)	0.37	956767.00 (100)	-1.38	173.5	7806.00 (1.42)	3.84	9059.00 (0.95)	-2.95	116.1	3386.00 (0.61)	5.19	3486.00 (0.36)	3.81	102.9
2005-06	554592.00 (100)	0.57	947142.00 (100)	-1.01	170.9	7586.00 (1.37)	-2.82	9328.00 (0.98)	2.97	123	3487.00 (0.63)	2.98	3595.00 (0.38)	3.13	103.1
2006-07	549643.00 (100)	-0.89	955740.00 (100)	0.91	173.8	7580.00 (1.38)	-0.08	9088.00 (0.95)	-2.57	119.9	3292.00 (0.60)	-5.59	3377.00 (0.35)	-6.06	102.5
2007-08	544575.00 (100)	-0.92	945205.00 (100)	-1.10	173.8	7268.00 (1.33)	-4.12	8592.00 (0.91)	-5.46	118.2	3326.00 (0.61)	1.03	3413.00 (0.36)	1.07	102.6
2008-09	540518.00 (100)	-0.74	955614.00 (100)	1.10	176.8	7484.00 (1.38)	2.97	8745.00 (0.92)	1.78	116.8	3043.00 (0.56)	-8.51	3174.00 (0.33)	-7.00	104.3
2009-10	542550.00 (100)	0.38	952517.00 (100)	-0.32	175.6	7477.00 (1.38)	-0.09	9058.00 (0.95)	3.58	121.1	3292.00 (0.61)	8.18	3489.00 (0.37)	9.92	106
2010-11	539020.00 (100)	-0.65	943469.00 (100)	-0.95	175.0	7602.00 (1.41)	1.67	9017.00 (0.96)	-0.45	118.6	3291.00 (0.61)	-0.03	3464.00 (0.37)	-0.72	105.2
2011-12	540820.00 (100)	0.33	943784.00 (100)	0.03	174.5	7553.00 (1.40)	-0.64	8969.00 (0.95)	-0.53	118.7	3283.00 (0.61)	-0.24	3460.00 (0.37)	-0.12	105.4
2012-13	542500.00 (100)	0.25	954824.00 (100)	1.14	176.0	7884.00 (1.45)	4.38	9629.00 (1.01)	7.36	122.1	3283.00 (0.61)	0.00	3441.00 (0.36)	-0.55	104.8
2013-14	539462.00 (100)	-0.56	946134.00 (100)	-0.91	175.38	7866 (1.45)	-0.22	9619 (1.01)	-0.10	122.2	3359 (0.62)	2.31	3547 (0.37)	3.08	105.6
2014-15	538412 (100)	-0.19	940614 (100)	-0.58	174.69	8034 (1.49)	2.13	9545 (1.01)	-0.76	118.80	3398 (0.63)	1.16	3591 (0.38)	1.24	105.6
2015-16	543365 (100)	0.91	938625 (100)	-0.20	172.74	8310 (1.52)	3.43	10646 (1.13)	11.53	128.11	3396 (0.62)	-0.05	3517 (0.37)	-2.06	103.5
Compound Growth		-0.26		-0.2			0.62		0.73			.54		.84	
Mean	550102.5		955456.56		173.84	7648.61		9372.45		122.50	3276.56		3414.72		104.19
S.D	10923.07		13211.32		2.15	245.75		480.96		4.60	109.56		115.89		1.159
C.V	1.98		1.38		1.23	3.21		5.13		3.76	3.34		3.39		1.11

Source: Annual Season Crop Report, Directorate of Land Records, Kasumpti, Shimla, 1998-99 to 2015-16.

Table-3.5 : Sources of Water for Irrigation

(in numbers)

Year	Himachal Pradesh								Kinnaur		Lahaul & Spiti	
	Canals	Tube – well	Wells	Reservoirs	Tanks	Oil Engines	Kulhs	Lift Irrigation Scheme	Kulhs	Lift Irrigation Scheme	Kuhls	Lift Irrigation Scheme
1998-99	0	1454	2109	-	18	39	-	489 (100)	0	0	0	3 **0.61**
1999-2000	0	2061	828	59	758	475	16887 **(100)**	45 **(100)**	670 **(3.97)**	0 **0.00**	552 (3.27)	0 **0.00**
2000-01	0	2061	828	59	758	475	16887 **(100)**	0 **(100)**	670 **(3.97)**	0	552 (3.27)	0
2001-02	6	2061	828	59	758	475	16887 **(100)**	0 **(100)**	670 **(3.97)**	0	552 (3.27)	0
2002 03	6	2061	828	59	758	475	16887 **(100)**	0 **(100)**	670 **(3.97)**	0	552 (3.27)	0
2003-04	6	2061	828	59	758	475	16887 (100)	0 **(100)**	670 **(3.97)**	0	552 (3.27)	0
2004-05	6	2061	828	59	758	475	16887 (100)	0 **(100)**	670 **(3.97)**	0	552 (3.27)	0
2005-06	6	2061	828	59	758	475	16887 **(100)**	0 **(100)**	670 **(3.97)**	0	552 (3.27)	0
2006-07	6	2061	828	59	758	475	16887 **(100)**	489 **(100)**	670 **(3.97)**	0	552 (3.27)	0 **0.00**
2007-08	6	2061	828	59	758	475	16887 **(100)**	489 **(100)**	670 **(3.97)**	0	119 (0.70)	0 **0.00**
2008-09	7	4316	1885	7	292	151	14340 **(100)**	550 **(100)**	670 **(4.67)**	0	552 (3.85)	3 **0.55**
2009-10	7	4722	1948	59	193	556	14373 **(100)**	685 **(100)**	670 **(4.66)**	0	513 (3.57)	1 **0.15**
2010-11	11	5408	1257	58	822	634	11339 **(100)**	341 **(100)**	657 **(5.79)**	0	518 (4.57)	0
2011-12	11	5342	1270	9	786	619	11545 **(100)**	372 **(100)**	657 (-)	0	518 (4.57)	0
2012-13	11	5438	1461	78	822	628	11831 **(100)**	349 **(100)**	657 (-)	0	518 (-)	0
2013-14	11	5455	1506	85	863	626	11301 **(100)**	402 **(100)**	657 (-)	0	518 (-)	0
2014-15	11	6322	1368	58	874	863	11523 (100)	397 (100)	630	0	518	0
Mean	**6.53**	**3353.29**	**1191.52**	**55.31**	**676**	**493.59**	**14889.69**	**271.06**	**625.18**	-	**481.76**	**0.41**
S.D	**3.79**	**1717.38**	**453.96**	**20.04**	**250.39**	**183.46**	**2501.14**	**242.09**	**161.44**	-	**156.36**	**1.0**
C.V	**58.12**	**51.21**	**38.1**	**36.23**	**37.03**	**37.17**	**16.79**	**89.31**	**25.82**	-	**32.46**	**243.9**

Source: Annual Season Crop Report, Directorate of Land Records, Kasumpti, Shimla.

3.5 Sources of Water for Irrigation

The major sources of irrigation in Himachal Pradesh are Canals, Tube well, Wells, Reservoirs, Tanks etc. However, kulhs and lift irrigation are the sources for irrigation in the tribal areas. The following table (3.5) shows the sources of water for irrigation.

As shown in the above table, canals have been used as one of the sources of irrigation in the State. Canals increased to 11 and Tube wells have registered a tremendous growth as one of the sources of irrigation. In the year 1998-99, the total number of tube wells was 1454 which has increased to 6322 in the year 2014-15. Similarly, the number of tanks and oil engines has increased rapidly. It is pertinent to state that out of all sources of irrigation, none is being used in the two districts of the present research. Only kulh and lift irrigation schemes are being used and their number is quite scanty. In both the districts only 4 percent of the total irrigation through kulh in Himachal Pradesh is being used as a source of irrigation. Moreover, in Lahaul & Spiti lift irrigation scheme is being used only in a very limited landscape (0.3%). Hence, it is concluded from the table that the most viable sources of irrigation are kulh and lift which are just 3 to 4 percent in Kinnaur and Lahaul & Spiti.

3.6 Irrigated Area under Different Sources of Water

The total area irrigated in Himachal Pradesh under different sources of irrigation in the year 1998-99 was 99,646 hectares. This has increased to 1,09,940 hectares in the year 2015-16. Data shows that maximum area irrigated was 1,25,506 hectares in 2005-06. The following table-3.6 shows the irrigated area under different sources of water in Himachal Pradesh as well as Kinnaur and Lahaul & Spiti.

As shown in the below table-3.6, in Himachal, total 3,631 hectares area was being irrigated through canals during 1999-2000, which has increased to 4,123 hectares in the year 2015-16. Further, in the year 1998-99, it was 2,119 through tube wells, which has increased to 20,023 hectares in the year 2015-16. Only 122 hectares was through tanks, which has decreased to 33,91,402 hectares irrigated under kulhs which increased to 1,05,898 hectares, following by a decreasing trend to 83,854 hectares. An area of 1,556 hectares came under lift irrigation schemes and wells. In 1998-99, the area irrigated through other sources of irrigation is 1,446 hectares, which has decreased to 90 hectares in the year 2015-16. It is analysed from the data that with the passage of

Table-3.6 : Irrigated Area under Different Sources of Water: Himachal Pradesh

(in hectares)

Year	Himachal Pradesh												
	Canals	Tubewell	Tanks	Kulhs	Lift irrigation Scheme	Wells	Others	Total	Growth	Area irrigated more than once	Growth	Gross area Irrigated	Growth
1998-99	0.00	2119.00	122.00	91402.00	1556.00	3001.00	1446.00	99646.00		71708.00		171354.00	
1999-2000	3631.00	7608.00	871.00	82012.00	1942.00	4390.00	0.00	100454.00	**0.81**	77384.00	**7.92**	177838.00	**3.78**
2000-01	3393.00	9744.00	397.00	85100.00	2813.00	3338.00	5.00	104790.00	**4.32**	72297.00	**-6.57**	177087.00	**-0.42**
2001-02	3574.00	8558.00	325.00	72209.00	3319.00	3272.00	13535.00	104792.00	**0.00**	74362.00	**2.86**	179154.00	**1.17**
2002-03	3398.00	8548.00	255.00	83968.00	3174.00	3272.00	2.00	102617.00	**-2.08**	77807.00	**4.63**	180424.00	**0.71**
2003-04	3173.00	8238.00	258.00	83873.00	2777.00	3186.00	5.00	10110.00	**-1.08**	81044.00	**4.16**	182554.00	**1.18**
2004-05	3337.00	9969.00	270.00	83499.00	1629.00	3200.00	3.00	101907.00	**0.39**	76789.00	**-5.25**	178696.00	**-2.11**
2005-06	3463.00	10210.00	263.00	105898.00	1522.00	4150.00	0.00	125506.00	**23.16**	5769.00	**-27.37**	181275.00	**1.44**
2006-07	3666.00	9713.00	257.00	80902.00	3782.00	3386.00	400.00	102106.00	**-18.64**	78860.00	**41.40**	180966.00	**-0.17**
2007-08	3510.00	10219.00	267.00	78335.00	2937.00	3595.00	3400.00	102263.00	**0.15**	84299.00	**6.90**	186562.00	**3.09**
2008-09	3520.00	10580.00	3.00	77991.00	6667.00	2959.00	3361.00	105081.00	**2.76**	76039.00	**-9.80**	181120.00	**-2.92**
2009-10	3379.00	12797.00	28.00	77844.00	6193.00	2720.00	1491.00	104452.00	**-0.60**	78522.00	**3.27**	182974.00	**1.02**
2010-11	4010.00	14374.00	654.00	77257.00	4924.00	1826.00	595.00	103640.00	**-0.78**	81907.00	**4.31**	185547.00	**1.41**
2011-12	4107.00	14375.00	701.00	83768.00	0.00	1369.00	0.00	104320.00	**0.66**	82360.00	**0.55**	186680.00	**0.61**
2012-13	3979.00	15754.00	526.00	85398.00	0.00	2671.00	0.00	108328.00	**3.84**	84408.00	**2.49**	192736.00	**3.24**
2013-14	4046	15555	283	74231	6126	1877	5734	107852	**-0.43**	83845	**-0.66**	191697	**-0.53**
2014-15	4104	17652	149	75924	6613	1705	456	106599	**-1.16**	79961	**-4.63**	186560	**-2.68**
2015-16	4123	20023	33	83854	0	1817	90	109940	**3.13**	83069	**3.88**	193009	**3.46**
Compound Growth									**0.85**		**1.65**		**0.72**
Mean	**3467.39**	**11446.44**	**314.55**	**82414.72**	**3109.67**	**2874.11**	**1695.72**	**93966.83**		**75023.89**		**183124.06**	
S.D	**919.15**	**4250.38**	**238.46**	**7504.43**	**2236.78**	**853.14**	**3362.56**	**30192.92**		**17719.98**		**5758.67**	
C.V	**26.51**	**37.13**	**75.8**	**9.1**	**71.92**	**29.68**	**198.29**	**32.13**		**23.62**		**3.14**	

Contd. ...

Irrigated Area under Different Sources of Water in Kinnaur and Lahaul & Spiti

(in hectares)

	Kinnaur								Lahaul & Spiti							
Year	Kulhs	Lift irrigation scheme	Total	Growth	Area irrigated more than once	Growth	Gross area irrigated	Growth	Kulhs	Lift irrigation scheme	Total	Growth	Area irrigated more than once	Growth	Gross area irrigated	Growth
1998-99	4307.00	0.00	4307.00		1107.00		5414.00		3146.00	0.00	3146.00		134.00		3280.00	
1999-2000	4517.00	0.00	4517.00	4.88	1105.00	-0.18	5622.00	3.84	3147.00	0.00	3147.00	0.03	138.00	2.99	3285.00	0.15
2000-01	4405.00	0.00	4405.00	-2.48	1118.00	1.18	5523.00	-1.76	3147.00	0.00	3147.00	0.00	160.00	15.94	3307.00	0.67
2001-02	4337.00	0.00	4337.00	-1.54	1391.00	24.42	5728.00	3.71	3208.00	0.00	3208.00	1.94	147.00	-8.13	3355.00	1.45
2002-03	4335.00	0.00	4335.00	-0.05	1534.00	10.28	5869.00	2.46	3318.00	0.00	3318.00	3.43	0.01	-100	3318.00	-1.10
2003-04	4293.00	0.00	4293.00	-0.97	1120.00	-26.99	5413.00	-7.77	3219.00	0.00	3219.00	-2.98	139.00	139	3358.00	1.21
2004-05	4690.00	0.00	4690.00	9.25	800.00	-28.57	5490.00	1.42	3386.00	0.00	3386.00	5.19	100.00	-28.06	3486.00	3.81
2005-06	4552.00	0.00	4552.00	-2.94	1275.00	59.38	5827.00	6.14	3474.00	13.00	3487.00	2.98	108.00	8.00	3595.00	3.13
2006-07	4530.00	0.00	4530.00	-0.48	948.00	-25.65	5478.00	-5.99	3283.00	13.00	3296.00	-5.48	81.00	-25.00	3377.00	-6.06
2007-08	4418.00	0.00	4418.00	-2.47	932.00	-1.69	5350.00	-2.34	3326.00	0.00	3326.00	0.91	87.00	7.41	3413.00	1.07
2008-09	4487.00	0.00	4487.00	1.56	863.00	-7.40	5350.00	0.00	3031.00	12.00	3043.00	-8.51	131.00	50.57	3174.00	-7.00
2009-10	4482.00	0.00	4482.00	-0.11	1145.00	32.68	5627.00	5.18	3292.00	0.00	3292.00	8.18	197.00	50.38	3489.00	9.92
2010-11	4768.00	0.00	4768.00	6.38	1001.00	-12.58	5769.00	2.52	3291.00	0.00	3291.00	-0.03	173.00	-12.18	3464.00	-0.72
2011-12	4676.00	0.00	4676.00	-1.93	977.00	-2.40	5653.00	-2.01	3270.00	13.00	3283.00	-0.24	177.00	2.31	3460.00	-0.12
2012-13	4860.00	0.00	4860.00	3.93	1155.00	18.22	6015.00	6.40	3270.00	13.00	3283.00	0.00	158.00	-10.73	3441.00	-0.55
2013-14	4913	0.00	4913	1.09	904	-21.73	5817	-3.29	3346	13.00	3359	2.31	188	18.98	3547	3.08
2014-15	4995	0.00	4995	1.66	1115	23.34	6110	5.03	3385	. 13	3398	1.15	193	2.66	3591	1.24
2015-16	5434	0.00	5434	8.79	2336	109.50	6847	12.06	3389	0.00	3389	-0.26	121	-37.30	3516	-2.09
C. G				1.45		8.43		1.50				0.51		4.52		0.48
Mean	4611.05	0.00	4611.05		1157		5716.78		3273.78	5	3278.78		135.11		3414.22	
SD	295.90	0.00	295.90		346.39		358.86		109.47	6.45	110.78		48.60		116.1	
CV	6.41	0.00	6.41		29.94		6.27		3.34	129	3.37		35.97		3.4	

Source: Annual Season Crop Report, Directorate of Land Records, Kasumpti, Shimla, 1998-99 to 2015-16.

time, dependence on tanks, wells and lift irrigation schemes has decreased, and shifted to the other sources of irrigation such as kulhs, tube wells and canals. It leads to the conclusion that in Himachal Pradesh, the maximum cultivable land area is irrigated through tube wells, canals and kulhs. The average irrigated area through kulhs in Kinnaur has been found 4611.05 hectares (5.59% of the State) with S.D. of 295.90 hectares and C.V. 6.41 percent. The area irrigated under kulh is not so large in the district. In Lahaul & Spiti, average irrigated area is 3,414.22 hectares (4.14% of the State), with S.D. calculated as 116.1 hectares and C.V. of 3.4 percent, indicating more consistency in irrigation through kulhs as compared to Kinnaur. Since 2005-06, only 13 hectares was irrigated through lift irrigation schemes till 2014-15. From the above analysis, it is found that in both the districts, land is irrigated only through kulhs.

3.7 Irrigation Intensity in Tribal Regions

The average Cropping Intensity of Himachal Pradesh was 173.84 percent ranged between 170.3 percent in the year 1999-2000 to 172.74 percent in the year 2015-16. The average Irrigation Intensity was recorded 174.13 percent during the 18 years under study. However, highest Irrigation Intensity was recorded 182.43 percent in the year 2007-08, and the minimum was 144.44 percent in 2005-06. It is pertinent to state that the gap between maximum and minimum Irrigation Intensity is high i.e. 37.99 percent (182.43-144.44). However, coefficient of variance is less in Cropping Intensity as compared to Irrigation Intensity. The Cropping Intensity and Irrigation Intensity were same in the year 1998-99, Irrigation Intensity was higher than Cropping Intensity in the year 1999-2000. It was less than Cropping Intensity in the year 2000-01. In the years 2003-04 & 2004-05 Irrigation Intensity was higher (179%, 175%) than Cropping Intensity (176.6%, 173.5%).

Surprisingly, in the year 2005-06 Irrigation Intensity declined by about 15 percent and Cropping Intensity declined by 3 percent (170.9%) in Himachal Pradesh. Further, the highest Irrigation Intensity was recorded 182.4 percent in the year 2007-08, but there was no change in Cropping Intensity. The coefficient of variance in Cropping Intensity is recorded least (1.23%) with S.D. of 2.15 percent, whereas the coefficient of variance in Irrigation Intensity is higher (4.65%) than Cropping Intensity showing inconsistency in Irrigation Intensity during the study period in Himachal Pradesh.

Table-3.7 : Irrigation Intensity in Tribal Regions

(in percentage)

Year	HP		Kinnaur		Lahaul-Spiti	
	Cropping Intensity	Irrigation Intensity	Cropping Intensity	Irrigation Intensity	Cropping Intensity	Irrigation Intensity
1998-99	171.1 (100)	171.9 (100)	127.1 (100)	125.7 (98.89)	104.8 (100)	104.2 (100)
1999-2000	170.3 (100)	177.0 (104.1)	122.1 (100)	124.4 (98.15)	104.4 (100)	104.3 (100)
2000-01	171.8 (100)	168.9 (98.31)	131.2 (100)	125.3 (95.50)	103.6 (100)	105.0 (101.35)
2001-02	170.6 (100)	170.9 (100)	125.8 (100)	132.0 (105)	104.4 (100)	145.36 (139)
2002-03	176 (100)	175.5 (99)	131.1 (100)	135.3 (103)	102.4 (100)	100 (98.03)
2003-04	176.6 (100)	179.8 (101)	124.2 (100)	126.0 (101)	104.3 (100)	104.32 (100)
2004-05	173.5 (100)	175.3 (101)	116.1 (100)	117.0 (100)	102.9 (100)	102.95 (100)
2005-06	170.9 (100)	144.4 (84.70)	123 (100)	128.6 (104)	103.1 (100)	103.1 (100)
2006-07	173.8 (100)	177.2 (102)	119.9 (100)	120.9 (100)	102.5 (100)	102.46 (100)
2007-08	173.8 (100)	182.4 (105)	118.2 (100)	121.1 (102)	102.6 (100)	102.62 (100)
2008-09	176.8 (100)	172.3 (97.72)	116.8 (100)	119.2 (102)	104.3 (100)	104.3 (100)
2009-10	175.6 (100)	175.1 (100)	121.1 (100)	125.5 (103)	106 (100)	102.86 (96.22)
2010-11	175.0 (100)	177.8 (101)	118.6 (100)	124.1 (105)	105.2 (100)	105.97 (100)
2011-12	174.5 (100)	178.9 (102)	118.7 (100)	120.8 (101)	105.4 (100)	105.39 (100)
2012-13	176.0 (100)	177.9 (100)	122.1 (100)	123.7 (100)	104.8 (100)	104.81 (100)
2013-14	175.3 (100)	177.7 (101)	122.2 (100)	118.4 (96.72)	105.6 (100)	105.60 (100)
2014-15	174.6 (100)	175.0 (100)	118.8 (100)	122.3 (103)	105.6 (100)	105.68 (100)
2015-2016	172.7 (100)	175.5 (101)	128.1 (100)	126.0 (98.43)	103.5 (100)	103.75 (100)
MEAN	**173.84**	**174.13**	**122.50**	**124.10**	**104.19**	**106.25**
SD	**2.15**	**8.11**	**4.60**	**4.56**	**1.159**	**9.59**
CV	**1.23**	**4.65**	**3.76**	**3.67**	**1.11**	**9.02**

Source: Annual Season Crop Report, Directorate of Land Records, Kasumpti, Shimla, 1998-99 to 2015-16.

In Kinnaur, average Cropping Intensity during the last 18 years has been recorded 122.50 percent which ranged between 131.20 percent in the year 2000-01 and 116.10 percent in the year 2004-05. Further, the Average Irrigation Intensity was 124.10 percent, with considerable fluctuation (maximum 135.39% and minimum 118.40%). The coefficient of variance was 3.67 percent which indicates slight variation in Irrigation Intensity. The irrigation intensity increased from 125.30 percent to 132 percent in the year 2000-01 to 2001-02 whereas, a decline in Cropping Intensity is found from 131.20 percent to 125.80 percent in the same years.

In Lahaul & Spiti, the average Cropping Intensity has been recorded 104.19 percent ranging between maximum 106 percent in the year 2009-10, and minimum 102.40 percent in the year 2002-03. The Irrigation Intensity has been recorded 105.88 percent in the year 1998-99. The highest Irrigation Intensity was 145.36 percent in 2001-02. Further, in the year 2009-10 a 2 percent decrease is recorded in Irrigation Intensity, while 4 percent increase is recorded in Cropping Intensity in the same year. However, Average Irrigation Intensity of the district was 106.25 percent, with S.D. = 9.59 percent and C.V. = 9.02 percent, showing less consistency.

3.8 Irrigation Intensity

The detail of Gross Area Irrigated, Net Area Irrigated and Irrigation Intensity in Himachal Pradesh, Kinnaur and Lahaul & Spiti districts is shown in table 3.8.

Data shown in table 3.8 followed by figure 3.3 reveals that the Average Net Irrigated Area and Gross Irrigated Area in Himachal Pradesh since 1998-99 to 2015-16 were accounted for 1,05,363.5 hectares with S.D. of 5,729.96 and C.V. = 5.44 percent and 1,83,110.72 hectares recording S.D. = 5,768.89 hectares and C.V. = 3.15 percent respectively. It indicates that the coefficient of variance is less i.e. 3.15 percent in Gross Irrigated Area as compared to 5.15 percent Net Irrigated Area in the State. It leads to the conclusion that out of total land area of the State, around 34.06 percent is irrigated having slight variation of 3 to 5 percent.

In 1998-99 the irrigation intensity was recorded 176.80 percent, which decreased to 175.56 percent (1%) in the year 2015-16. The average irrigation intensity was recorded 174.13 percent during the 18 years. However, highest irrigation intensity was recorded 182.43 percent in the year 2007-08, and the minimum was 144.44 percent in 2005-06. It

Table-3.8 : Irrigation Intensity in Kinnaur and Lahaul & Spiti

(in Percentage)

	Himachal Pradesh					Kinnaur					Lahaul & Spiti				
Year	NIA	Growth	GIA	Growth	Intensity (%)	NIA	Growth	GIA	Growth	Intensity (%)	NIA	Growth	GIA	Growth	Intensity (%)
1998-99	99646 (100)		171354 (100)		171.96	4307 (4.32)		5414 (3.16)		125.7	3146 (3.16)		3280 (1.91)		104.26
1999-2000	100454 (100)	0.81	177838 (100)	3.78	177.03	4517 (4.50)	4.88	5622 (3.16)	3.84	124.46	3147 (3.13)	0.03	3285 (1.85)	0.15	104.39
2000-2001	104790 (100)	4.32	177087 (100)	-0.42	168.99	4405 (4.20)	-2.48	5523 (3.12)	-1.76	125.38	3147 (3.00)	0	3307 (1.87)	0.67	105.08
2001-02	104792 (100)	0	179154 (100)	1.17	170.96	4337 (4.14)	-1.54	5728 (3.20)	3.71	132.07	2308 (2.20)	-26.66	3355 (1.87)	1.45	145.36
2002-03	102617 (100)	-2.08	180124 (100)	0.54	175.53	4335 (4.22)	-0.05	5869 (3.26)	2.46	135.39	3318 (3.23)	43.76	3318 (1.84)	-1.1	100
2003-04	101510 (100)	-1.08	182554 (100)	1.35	179.84	4293 (4.23)	-0.97	5413 (2.97)	-7.77	126.09	3219 (3.17)	-2.98	3358 (1.84)	1.21	104.32
2004-05-	101907 (100)	0.39	178696 (100)	-2.11	175.35	4690 (4.60)	9.25	5490 (3.07)	1.42	117.06	3386 (3.32)	5.19	3486 (1.95)	3.81	102.95
2005-06	125506 (100)	23.16	181275 (100)	1.44	144.44	4452 (3.55)	-5.07	5727 (3.16)	4.32	128.64	3487 (2.78)	2.98	3595 (1.98)	3.13	103.1
2006-07	102106 (100)	-18.64	180966 (100)	-0.17	177.23	4530 (4.44)	1.75	5478 (3.03)	-4.35	120.93	3296 (3.23)	-5.48	3377 (1.87)	-6.06	102.46
2007-08	102263 (100)	0.15	186562 (100)	3.09	182.43	4418 (4.32)	-2.47	5350 (2.87)	-2.34	121.1	3326 (3.25)	0.91	3413 (1.83)	1.07	102.62
2008-09	105081 (100)	2.76	181120 (100)	-2.92	172.36	4487 (4.27)	1.56	5350 (2.95)	0	119.23	3043 (2.90)	-8.51	3174 (1.75)	-7	104.3
2009-10	104452 (100)	-0.6	182974 (100)	1.02	175.18	4482 (4.29)	-0.11	5627 (3.08)	5.18	125.55	3392 (3.25)	11.47	3489 (1.91)	9.92	102.86
2010-11	104380 (100)	-0.07	185607 (100)	1.44	177.82	4518 (4.33)	0.8	5610 (3.02)	-0.3	124.17	3282 (3.14)	-3.24	3478 (1.87)	-0.32	105.97
2011-12	104320 (100)	-0.06	186680 (100)	0.58	178.95	4676 (4.48)	3.5	5653 (3.03)	0.77	120.89	3283 (3.15)	0.03	3460 (1.85)	-0.52	105.39
2012-13	108328 (100)	3.84	192736 (100)	3.24	177.92	4860 (4.49)	3.93	6015 (3.12)	6.4	123.77	3283 (3.03)	0	3441 (1.79)	-0.55	104.81
2013-14	107852 (100)	-0.43	191697 (100)	-0.53	177.74	4913 (4.55)	1.09	5817 (3.03)	-3.29	118.40	3359 (3.11)	2.31	3547 (1.85)	3.08	105.60
2014-15	106599 (100)	-1.16	186560 (100)	-2.68	175.01	4995 (4.68)	1.67	6110 (3.27)	5.04	122.32	3398 (3.19)	1.16	3591 (1.92)	1.24	105.68
2015-16	109940 (100)	3.13	193009 (100)	3.46	175.56	5434 (4.94)	8.79	6847 (3.55)	12.06	126.00	3389 (3.08)	-0.26	3516 (1.82)	-2.09	103.75
C.G.		0.85		0.57			1.43		1.70			1.15		0.36	
Mean	105363.5		183110.72		174.13	4574.05		5672.95		124.10	3229.21		3410.58		106.25
SD	5729.96		5768.89		8.11	297.48		371.08		4.56	250.49		114.86		9.59
CV	5.44		3.15		4.65	6.5		6.54		3.67	7.76		3.36		9.02

Source: Annual Season Crop Report, Directorate of Land Records, Kasumpti, Shimla, 1998-99 to 2015-16.

is pertinent to state that the gap between maximum and minimum irrigation intensity is high.

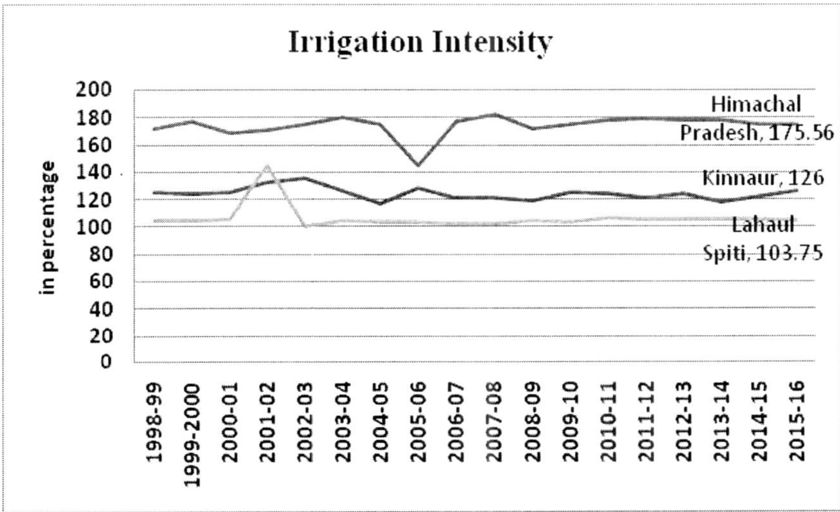

Figure-3.3 : Irrigation intensity in Kinnaur and Lahaul & Spiti

The average Gross Irrigated Area in Kinnaur, was 5,672.98 hectares with S.D 371.08 hectares and coefficient of variance 6.54 percent. The Average Net Area Irrigated was recorded 4,574.05 hectares with S.D. 297.48 hectares and C.V. 6.5 percent. It is analysed from the data that the variation is equal i.e. 6.5 percent for both, Net Area Irrigated and Gross Area Irrigated during the study period. Further, the Average Irrigation Intensity was recorded 124.10 percent, with considerable fluctuation (maximum 135.39% and minimum 118.40%). The 3.67 percent coefficient of variance indicates a very slight change in irrigation intensity.

In Lahaul & Spiti, the irrigation intensity has been recorded 105.88 percent in the year 1998-99. The highest irrigation intensity was 145.36 percent in 2001-02, which decreased in the year 2002-03. However, Average Irrigation Intensity of the district was 106.25 percent, with S.D. = 9.59 percent and with C.V. = 9.02 percent, showing less consistency as compared to Kinnaur as well as the State. From the above analyses, it is concluded that both the districts have less irrigation intensity as compared to the State. For the last 18 years Kinnaur has recorded an increase in irrigation intensity. On the contrary, Lahaul & Spiti district recorded slight decrease.

3.9 Crop- wise Irrigated Area in Tribal Regions

Table 3.9 shows that out of the average Area under cereal crops an average 19.15 percent Area was irrigated for Cereal Crops. From 1998-99 to 2006-07, only 18 percent Irrigated Area was covered by cereal crops. From 2007-08 to 2011-12 it increased to 19 percent and 2012-13 to 2015-16 it was between 19 to 20 percent. Data shows that there is a slight variation in Irrigated Area for Cereal crops in Himachal during the study period.

In Kinnaur, the Irrigated Area under cereals was between 41 to 55 percent and in Lahaul & Spiti to Area for cereal crops was under Irrigation. Out of area for production of pulses in the State, an average 14.92 percent area was irrigated. The coefficient of variance is 13.66 percent showing inconsistency in Irrigated Area for production of pulses in Himachal Pradesh.

Further, in Kinnaur 83.33 percent area is irrigated for production of pulses and in Lahaul & Spiti, the average irrigated area for production of pulses was 859.68 hectares with coefficient of variance as 80.16 percent. It indicates that Lahaul & Spiti has much confined area for production of pulses but is widely Irrigated Area as compared to Kinnaur as well as the State. Irrigated Area for Production of Vegetables in Himachal Pradesh is 29.23 percent. Whereas, in Kinnaur, area for production of vegetables is 50.35 percent with 83.71 percent coefficient of variance and in Lahaul & Spiti, which again analyses that in Lahaul - Spiti, Vegetables are being grown in very limited area but are being irrigated through traditional systems of constructing kulhs.

Fresh fruits are being grown in more land area in Himachal Pradesh during the past nearly two decades an average 60,546.33 hectares Area is used for Production of Fresh Fruits in the State. During the study period Irrigated Area for Production of Fresh Fruits varies between 6 to 9 percent and Average Irrigated Area was only 8.02 percent of the area under Fresh Fruits. The coefficient of variance is calculated 23.69 percent with standard deviation 1,150.88 hectares which shows considerable fluctuation in Irrigated area for fresh fruits.

In Kinnaur, an average 2,593.61 hectares Area was covered under Fresh Fruits which has increased from 1,536 hectares in 1998-99 to 4,696 hectares in 2015-16 and the Average Irrigated Area is calculated 72.34 percent. Further, Area for Production of Fresh Fruits is only 79.27 hectares in Lahaul & Spiti which is irrigated.

Table-3.9 : Crop- wise Irrigated Area in Tribal Regions

(in hectares)

Year	H.P. (Cereals)		Kinnaur (Cereals)		Lahaul-Spiti (Cereals)		H.P. (Pulses)		Kinnaur (Pulses)		Lahaul-Spiti (Pulses)		H.P. (Vegetables)		Kinnaur (Vegetables)	
	Area	Irrigated Area	Area	Irrigated Area	Area	Irrigated Area	Area	Irrigated Area	Area	Irrigated Area	Area	Irrigated Area	Area	Irrigated Area	Area	Irrigated Area
1998-99	815337 (100)	146939.00 (18.02)	5827 (100)	2834.00 (48.63)	1110 (100)	1110 (100)	39500 (100)	4882 (12.35)	1257 (100)	1244 (98.96)	1103 (100)	1103 (100)	27917 (100)	7033 (25.19)	350 (100)	151 (43.14)
1999-2000	811137 (100)	147315.00 (18.16)	5471 (100)	3015.00 (55.10)	1082 (100)	1082 (100)	36512 (100)	5117 (14.01)	2683 (10.26)	753 (28.06)	1116 (100)	1116 (100)	27824 (100)	8404 (30.20)	725 (100)	432 (59.58)
2000-01	795358 (100)	147287.00 (18.51)	5235 (100)	2708.00 (51.72)	953 (100)	953 (100)	36058 (100)	4776 (13.24)	1973 (100)	784 (39.73)	1198 (100)	1198 (100)	29958 (100)	7236 (24.15)	723 (100)	190 (26.27)
2001-02	803842 (100)	147581.00 (18.35)	5160 (100)	2630.00 (50.96)	1256 (100)	1256 (100)	36982 (100)	5604 (15.15)	1154 (100)	930 (80.58)	1215 (100)	1215 (100)	32590 (100)	8763 (26.88)	790 (100)	623 (78.86)
2002-03	819560 (100)	148200.00 (18.08)	5155 (100)	2537.00 (49.21)	912 (100)	912 (100)	35930 (100)	5268 (14.66)	1333 (100)	916 (68.71)	1267 (100)	1267 (100)	33745 (100)	8925 (26.44)	816 (100)	531 (65.07)
2003-04	806498 (100)	151585.00 (18.79)	4721 (100)	2324.00 (49.22)	1045 (100)	1045 (100)	33849 (100)	5125 (15.14)	1685 (100)	822 (48.78)	1239 (100)	1239 (100)	33240 (100)	8776 (26.40)	921 (100)	678 (73.61)
2004-05	791957 (100)	146657.00 (18.51)	4683 (100)	2480.00 (52.95)	923 (100)	923 (100)	32556 (100)	5532 (16.99)	1985 (100)	1340 (67.50)	1453 (100)	1453 (100)	36675 (100)	8869 (24.18)	844 (100)	116 (13.74)
2005-06	787375 (100)	149161.00 (18.94)	4536 (100)	2504.00 (55.20)	1,131 (100)	1,131 (100)	31093 (100)	5821 (18.72)	1443 (100)	1325 (91.82)	1669 (100)	1669 (100)	33915 (100)	8537 (25.17)	218 (100)	106 (48.62)
2006-07	783609 (100)	148916.00 (1.90)	4730 (100)	2345.00 (49.57)	945 (100)	945 (100)	29559 (100)	5126 (17.34)	1,495 (100)	1243 (83.14)	1539 (100)	1539 (100)	33984 (100)	9346 (27.50)	243 (100)	123 (50.61)
2007-08	779625 (100)	155201.00 (19.90)	4143 (100)	2108.00 (50.88)	791 (100)	791 (100)	30128 (100)	5244 (17.40)	1,539 (100)	1324 (86.02)	1620 (100)	1620 (100)	34289 (100)	8919 (26.01)	262 (100)	88 (33.58)
2008-09	782580 (100)	148930.00 (19.03)	3916 (100)	1911.00 (48.79)	712 (100)	712 (100)	28859 (100)	3766 (13.04)	1788 (100)	1471 (82.27)	26 (100)	26 (100)	39238 (100)	14409 (36.72)	200 (100)	97 (48.5)
2009-10	781542 (100)	150340.00 (19.23)	3710 (100)	1763.00 (47.52)	865 (100)	865 (100)	27955 (100)	3911 (13.99)	1990 (100)	1679 (84.37)	36 (100)	27 (75)	39830 (100)	10850 (27.24)	212 (100)	91 (42.92)
2010-11	771547 (100)	150770.00 (19.54)	3331 (100)	1657.00 (49.74)	838 (100)	838 (100)	33016 (100)	4416 (13.37)	1785 (100)	1614 (90.42)	36 (100)	33 (91.66)	34105 (100)	11290 (33.10)	192 (100)	85 (44.27)
2011-12	771277 (100)	152238.00 (19.73)	3432 (100)	1659.00 (48.33)	736 (100)	736 (100)	26149 (100)	4734 (18.10)	2683 (100)	1460 (54.41)	33 (100)	33 (100)	32707 (100)	10368 (31.69)	170 (100)	73 (42.94)
2012-13	779581 (100)	158156.00 (20.28)	3197 (100)	1539.00 (48.13)	737 (100)	737 (100)	31943 (100)	4229 (13.23)	1973 (100)	1235 (62.59)	31 (100)	31 (100)	35769 (100)	11569 (32.34)	317 (100)	317 (100)
2013-14	768293 (100)	156931 (20.42)	1417 (100)	1417 (100)	591 (100)	591 (100)	31158 (100)	4224 (13.55)	1154 (100)	1154 (100)	177 (100)	177 (100)	33013 (100)	11290 (34.19)	126 (100)	126 (100)
2014-15	757656 (100)	150699 (19.89)	1246 (100)	1246 (100)	576 (100)	576 (100)	29373 (100)	3888 (13.23)	1333 (100)	1095 (82.14)	46 (100)	46 (100)	35672 (100)	12302 (34.48)	418 (100)	285 (68.18)
2015-2016	762346 (100)	157345 (20.63)	2564 (100)	1059 (41.30)	587 (100)	587 (100)	34271 (100)	5852 (17.07)	1685 (100)	1334 (79.16)	1808 (100)	1808 (100)	30029 (100)	10510 (34.99)	1119 (100)	783 (69.97)
MEAN	787173	150791.72	4025.16	2096.44	877.22	877.22	32577.94	4861.94	1448.12	1206.83	859.68	867.94	33583.33	9816.82	480.33	241.88
SD	18276.8	3759.09	1316.31	582.55	199.81	199.81	3689.77	664.16	492.02	276.21	664.07	695.05	3290.02	1920.37	319.70	202.49
CV	2.32	2.49	32.7	27.78	22.77	22.77	11.32	13.66	33.97	22.88	77.24	27.85	9.79	19.56	66.55	83.71

Contd. ...

Year	Lahaul-Spiti (Vegetables)		H.P. (Fresh Fruits)		Kinnaur (Fresh Fruits)		Lahaul-Spiti (Fresh Fruits)		H.P. (Dry Fruits)		Kinnaur (Dry Fruits)		Lahaul-Spiti (Dry Fruits)	
	Area	Irrigated Area	Area	Irrigated Area	Area	Irrigated Area	Area	Irrigated Area	Area	Irrigated Area	Area	Irrigated Area	Area	Irrigated Area
1998-99	862 (100)	862 (100)	50450 (100)	3029 (6)	1536 (100)	1178 (76.69)	27 (100)	27 (100)	776 (100)	187 (24.09)	529 (100)	184 (34.78)	27 (100)	27 (100)
1999-2000	859 (100)	859 (100)	49930 (100)	3526 (7.06)	1566 (100)	1208 (77.13)	26 (100)	26 (100)	978 (100)	214 (21.88)	546 (100)	190 (34.79)	2 (100)	2 (100)
2000-01	895 (100)	895 (100)	45986 (100)	3657 (7.95)	2098 (100)	1567 (74.69)	31 (100)	31 (100)	1381 (100)	271 (19.62)	428 (100)	195 (45.56)	0	0 0.00
2001-02	868 (100)	868 (100)	51767 (100)	3489 (6.73)	1823 (100)	1333 (73.12)	39 (100)	39 (100)	1045 (100)	294 (28.13)	679 (100)	191 (29.42)	2 (100)	2 (100)
2002-03	935 (100)	935 (100)	54504 (100)	4407 (8.08)	2183 (100)	1641 (75.17)	52 (100)	52 (100)	1025 (100)	267 (26.04)	685 (100)	236 (34.45)	0	0
2003-04	900 (100)	900 (100)	55644 (100)	3946 (7.09)	1915 (100)	1342 (70.07)	59 (100)	59 (100)	1124 (100)	272 (24.19)	609 (100)	233 (38.25)	0	0
2004-05	951 (100)	951 (100)	56474 (100)	4303 (7.61)	1798 (100)	1286 (71.52)	58 (100)	58 (100)	1248 (100)	356 (28.52)	623 (100)	251 (40.28)	0	-
2005-06	838 (100)	838 (100)	58458 (100)	4650 (7.95)	2097 (100)	1617 (77.11)	56 (100)	56 (100)	1449 (100)	468 (32.29)	707 (100)	251 (35.50)	0	0
2006-07	832 (100)	829 (99.63)	61035 (100)	4389 (7.19)	2259 (100)	1638 (72.50)	67 (100)	67 (100)	1180 (100)	215 (18.22)	552 (100)	103 (18.65)	2 (100)	0
2007-08	826 (100)	826 (100)	60442 (100)	4459 (7.37)	2152 (100)	1708 (79.36)	62 (100)	62 (100)	1260 (100)	262 (20.79)	412 (100)	97 (23.54)	153 (100)	0
2008-09	2263 (100)	2263 (100)	62836 (100)	4698 (7.47)	2389 (100)	1753 (73.37)	51 (100)	51 (100)	1396 (100)	274 (19.62)	417 (100)	102 (24.46)	15 (100)	15 (100)
2009-10	2376 (100)	785 (33.03)	61857 (100)	4869 (7.87)	2707 (100)	1978 (73.06)	71 (100)	71 (100)	1162 (100)	247 (21.25)	416 (100)	103 (24.75)	15 (100)	15 (100)
2010-11	2331 (100)	2331 (100)	64367 (100)	6173 (9.59)	3015 (100)	2276 (75.48)	86 (100)	86 (100)	1119 (100)	212 (18.94)	421 (100)	107 (25.41)	3 (100)	3 (100)
2011-12	2447 (100)	2447 (100)	64691 (100)	5743 (8.87)	3080 (100)	2335 (75.81)	93 (100)	93 (100)	264 (100)	264 (100)	97 (100)	97 (100)	3 (100)	3 (100)
2012-13	2387 (100)	2387 (100)	66323 (100)	5977 (9.01)	3646 (100)	2679 (73.47)	118 (100)	118 (100)	174 (100)	174 (100)	96 (100)	80 (83.33)	3 (100)	3 (100)
2013-14	2391 (100)	2391 (100)	73208 (100)	6116 (8.35)	2978 (100)	2974 (99.86)	122 (100)	122 (100)	243 (100)	243 (100)	99 (100)	99 (100)	3 (100)	3 (100)
2014-15	2626 (100)	2626 (100)	77754 (100)	7023 (9.03)	4747 (100)	3385 (71.30)	207 (100)	207 (100)	1268 (100)	192 (15.14)	350 (100)	89 (25.42)	3 (100)	3 (100)
2015-2016	794 (100)	794 (100)	74106 (100)	6972 (9.40)	4696 (100)	3328 (70.86)	202 (100)	202 (100)	1238 (100)	1238 (100)	450 (100)	450 (100)	3 (100)	3 (100)
MEAN	**1463.83**	**1416.76**	**60546.33**	**4857**	**2593.61**	**1876.35**	**79.27**	**78.72**	**1018.33**	**313.88**	**485.28**	**169.88**	**11.39**	**4.70**
SD	**774.79**	**770.64**	**8737.75**	**1150.88**	**958.27**	**641.33**	**53.09**	**52.63**	**398.055**	**240.41**	**148.45**	**93.75**	**35.63**	**7.48**
CV	**52.92**	**54.39**	**14.43**	**23.69**	**36.94**	**34.17**	**66.97**	**61.64**	**39.08**	**7.67**	**30.58**	**55.18**	**312.89**	**159.14**

Source: Annual Season Crop Report, Directorate of Land Records, Kasumpti, Shimla, 1998-99 to 2015-16.

The average Area covered under dry fruits was 1,018.33 hectares in the State, with standard deviation of 398.05 hectares and C.V. = 39.08 percent and only 30.82 percent Area is Irrigated with S.D. 240.41 hectares and coefficient of variance 7.67 percent which is indicating uniformity in Irrigated Area for production of dry fruits in Himachal Pradesh.

In Kinnaur, the average Area for dry fruits was 485.28 hectares, which is 47.65 percent of the State's total Irrigated Area and 35 percent Area is Irrigated. The C.V. is 55.18 percent which indicates that there is more variation in Irrigated Area under dry fruits.

In Lahaul & Spiti, the average area for production of dry fruits is only 11.39 percent, which is only 1.11 percent of the State's total. Out of this, 41.26 percent area is irrigated, with C.V. 159.14 percent which shows huge variation.

3.10 Area for Production of Cereals

The main crops in the State under cereals include; wheat, rice, maize, barley and millets etc. An average of 32,577.94 hectares area is under cereal crops in Himachal Pradesh. The total area under cereal crops cultivation in Himachal Pradesh, Kinnaur and Lahaul & Spiti is shown in the table 3.10.

In Himachal Pradesh, maximum land area under cereal crops was covered by wheat (46.08%), followed by maize (37.39%) and rice (10.75%), out of the total land area of 8,15,337 hectares under cereals crops in the year 1998-99. A continuous decline in area under cultivation of rice, wheat and barley has been registered after 2009-10 till 2015-16 in Himachal Pradesh. The area under wheat cultivation has decreased between 1998-99 to 2015-16 from 3,75,751 hectares to 3,57,673 hectares. Rice covered 87,716 hectares land area in the year 1998-99, which decreased to 77,027 hectares in the year 2015-16. Barley covered only 3.38 percent (27,585 hectare) area followed by, millets 1.99 percent (16,289 hectares) and a meagre area was covered by other crops 0.36 percent (2,967 hectares), out of total area under cereal crops. A decrease is recorded in 2015-16 in trend of area under cereal crops (barley 2.94%), millets (0.90%) and area under other crops (0.19%). Despite, of decreasing trends in a number of years, there has been a positive compound growth rate of 10.39 percent in Himachal Pradesh.

Table 3.10 Area for Production of Cereals in Kinnaur

(in hectares)

	Himachal Pradesh								Kinnaur							
Year	**Rice**	**Maize**	**Wheat**	**Barley**	**Millets**	**Other**	**Total**	**Growth**	**Rice**	**Maize**	**Wheat**	**Barley**	**Millets**	**Other**	**Total**	**Growth**
1998-99	87716.00	304927	375751	27587	16289	2967	**815337 (100)**		26	470	678	1531	2957	165	**5827 (0.71)**	
1999-2000	82754.00	308476	374938	26352	15488	3249	**811137 (100)**	**(6.11)**	31	483	598	1561	2631	167	**5471 (0.67)**	**(0.52)**
2000-01	83021.00	309480	357715	26970	17852	320	**795358 (100)**	**(4.31)**	27	470	495	1510	2733	0	**5235 (0.66)**	**(1.95)**
2001-02	81740.00	307291	372992	24587	12645	4587	**803842 (100)**	**(1.43)**	22	431	502	1441	2608	156	**5160 (0.64)**	**1.07**
2002-03	86178.00	311861	377343	27693	7900	8585	**819560 (100)**	**(0.10)**	23	420	527	1547	2483	155	**5155 (0.63)**	**1.96**
2003-04	82125.00	300976	379718	26752	11763	4564	**806498 (100)**	**(8.42)**	23	295	470	1456	2328	149	**4721 (0.59)**	**(1.59)**
2004-05	80221.00	29990	370587	25901	11201	4141	**791957 (100)**	**(0.80)**	30	404	371	1420	2327	131	**4683 (0.59)**	**(1.80)**
2005-06	81519.00	298052	362680	25017	9811	4107	**787375 (100)**	**(3.14)**	29	387	399	1394	2258	69	**4536 (0.58)**	**(0.58)**
2006-07	80580.00	301282	366518	25643	11060	4655	**783609 (100)**	**4.28**	23	383	479	1475	2268	102	**4730 (0.60)**	**(0.48)**
2007-08	83273.00	292801	359439	23596	10670	3346	**779625 (100)**	**(12.41)**	31	338	347	1188	2062	177	**4143 (0.53)**	**(0.51)**
2008-09	81345.00	298542	363369	24330	8121	6873	**782580 (100)**	**(5.48)**	27	428	349	1133	1917	62	**3916 (0.50)**	**0.38**
2009-10	79518.00	297773	367490	24206	8857	3698	**781542 (100)**	**(5.26)**	41	264	361	1187	1763	94	**3710 (0.47)**	**(0.13)**
2010-11	79366.00	294560	361640	23344	8402	4235	**771547 (100)**	**(10.22)**	22	321	323	1019	1551	95	**3331 (0.43)**	**(1.28)**
2011-12	79226.00	299050	358428	23695	8612	2266	**771277 (100)**	**303**	28	296	343	1048	1608	109	**3432 (0.44)**	**(0.03)**
2012-13	78571.00	300174	366557	23500	9289	1490	**779581 (100)**	**(6.85)**	13	273	248	1061	1599	3	**3197 (0.41)**	**1.06**
2013-14	76720	298806	360070	22633	7764	2300	**768293 (100)**	**(56.33)**	0	156	33	666	541	0	**1396 (0.18)**	**(1.46)**
2014-15	76825	296936	353723	20981	7150	2041	**757656 (100)**	**(10.74)**	17	102	32	650	445	0	**1246 (0.16)**	**(-1.38)**
2015-16	77027	296814	357673	22450	6875	1507	**762346 (100)**	**1.05**	15	163	181	935	1263	0	**2564 (0.33)**	**0.61**
C.G								10.39								-0.32
Mean	**80984.72**	**285988.39**	**365923.94**	**24735.94**	**10541.6**	**3607.27**	**787173**		**23.78**	**338**	**374.22**	**1234.56**	**1963.44**	**90.78**	**4025.16**	
SD	**2996.78**	**64108.44**	**7767.38**	**1890.96**	**3220.51**	**1964.69**	**18276.8**		**8.82**	**114.06**	**173.09**	**292.86**	**705.27**	**66.24**	**1316.31**	
CV	**3.7**	**22.41**	**2.12**	**7.64**	**30.55**	**54.46**	**2.32**		**37.08**	**33.74**	**46.26**	**23.72**	**35.92**	**72.96**	**32.7**	

Contd. ...

Area for Production of Cereals in Lahaul & Spiti

(in hectares)

	Himachal Pradesh								Lahaul & Spiti							
Year	Rice	Maize	Wheat	Barley	Millets	Other	Total	Growth	Rice	Maize	Wheat	Barley	Millets	Other	Total	Growth
1998-99	87716.00	304927	375751	27587	16289	2967	**815337 (100)**		0	41	205	694	170	0	**1110 (0.14)**	
1999-2000	82754.00	308476	374938	26352	15488	3249	**811137 (100)**	**(6.11)**	0	25	206	683	0	168	**1082 (0.13)**	**(2.52)**
2000-2001	83021.00	309480	357715	26970	17852	320	**795358 (100)**	**(4.31)**	0	30	181	590	152	0	**953 (0.12)**	**(11.92)**
2001-2002	81740.00	307291	372992	24587	12645	4587	**803842 (100)**	**(1.43)**	0	41	199	637	169	0	**1256 (0.16)**	**31.79**
2002-03	86178.00	311861	377343	27693	7900	8585	**819560 (100)**	**(0.10)**	0	34	173	550	0	0	**912 (0.11)**	**(27.39)**
2003-04	82125.00	300976	379718	26752	11763	4564	**806498 (100)**	**(8.42)**	0	35	185	647	178	0	**1045 (0.13)**	**14.58**
2004-2005	80221.00	29990	370587	25901	11201	4141	**791957 (100)**	**(0.80)**	0	34	175	553	161	0	**923 (0.12)**	**(11.67)**
2005-06	81519.00	298052	362680	25017	9811	4107	**787375 (100)**	**(3.14)**	0	42	121	576	65	7	**1,131 (0.14)**	**22.54**
2006-07	80580.00	301282	366518	25643	11060	4655	**783609 (100)**	**4.28**	0	38	142	616	149	0	**945 (0.12)**	**(16.45)**
2007-08	83273.00	292801	359439	23596	10670	3346	**779625 (100)**	**(12.41)**	0	49	118	573	51	0	**791 (0.10)**	**(16.30)**
2008-09	81345.00	298542	363369	24330	8121	6873	**782580 (100)**	**(5.48)**	0	47	107	473	0	85	**712 (0.09)**	**(9.99)**
2009-10	79518.00	297773	367490	24206	8857	3698	**781542 (100)**	**(5.26)**	0	85	81	592	107	0	**865 (0.11)**	**21.49**
2010-11	79366.00	294560	361640	23344	8402	4235	**771547 (100)**	**(10.22)**	0	46	75	608	0	109	**838 (0.11)**	**(3.12)**
2011-12	79226.00	299050	358428	23695	8612	2266	**771277 (100)**	**303**	0	34	64	545	0	93	**736 (0.10)**	**(12.17)**
2012-13	78571.00	300174	366557	23500	9289	1490	**779581 (100)**	**(6.85)**	0	34	63	554	0	86	**737 (0.09)**	**0.14**
2013-14	76720	298806	360070	22633	7764	2300	**768293 (100)**	**(56.33)**	0	23	57	511	0	0	**591 (0.07)**	**(19.81)**
2014-15	76825	296936	353723	20981	7150	2041	**757656 (100)**	**(10.74)**	0	19	46	403	103	0	**576 (0.07)**	**(2.53)**
2015-16	77027	296814	357673	22450	6875	1507	**762346 (100)**	**1.05**	0	20	46	429	0	92	**587 (0.07)**	**1.90**
C.G								10.39								-2.43
Mean	**80984.72**	**285988.39**	**365923.94**	**24735.94**	**10541.6**	**3607.27**	**787173**		**0**	**37.61**	**124.66**	**558.55**	**72.5**	**35.55**	**877.22**	
SD	**2996.78**	**64108.44**	**7767.38**	**1890.96**	**3220.51**	**1964.69**	**18276.8**		**0**	**14.79**	**59.29**	**4052.57**	**74.61**	**53.76**	**199.81**	
CV	**3.7**	**22.41**	**2.12**	**7.64**	**30.55**	**54.46**	**2.32**		**0**	**39.32**	**47.56**	**725.55**	**102.91**	**151.22**	**22.77**	

Source: Annual Season Crop Report, Directorate of Land Records, Kasumpti, Shimla, 1998-99 to 2015-16.

Further, 2.32 percent coefficient of variance shows a very low variation. Moreover, 2.12 percent coefficient of variance was found in area under wheat with S.D. of 7,767.38 hectares. It is concluded that wheat is the continuous growing crop of the State since 1998-99, whereas the area under millets was highly fluctuating which indicates a shifting of area from traditional crops (1.99% in 1998-99 to 0.90% in 2015-16) to other crops.

In Kinnaur, the total area under cereal crops was 5,827 hectares in the year 1998-99 with a tremendous decreasing trend (44%) in the succeeding years. Out of average 4,025.16 hectares area under cereal crops in Kinnaur, 48.77 percent is under millets, followed by barley (30.67%). These two crops covered about 78.78 percent of the total area under cereals and only 21.22 percent is under rice, maize, wheat and other cereals. Coefficient of variance during the period was 32.70 percent, indicating inconsistency of area under cereal crops in Kinnaur. A negative compound growth of 0.32 percent shows an overall decrease in the area cropped under cereals in the district. It indicates that area under cereal crops has shifted to other purposes in the district.

Similarly, in Lahaul & Spiti, the total area under cereal crops was 1,110 hectares in the year 1998-99. An average of 877.22 hectares land area is recorded under cereals with 199.81 hectares standard deviation and 22.77 percent coefficient of variance with negative growth recorded in most of the years resulting to -2.43 percent compound growth. It is indicating overall decrease in area under cereals in the district from 1998-99 to 2015-16. As per table, out of total area for cereals, area under barley was 63.67 percent, followed by wheat (14.21%), millets (8.26%), maize (4.28%) and 4.05 percent for other cereals. Moreover, Lahaul & Spiti has less area under cereals.

3.11 Area for Production of Pulses

The land area under different pulses in Himachal Pradesh with reference to the study area is shown in table 3.11.

Note*= In the year 2014-15and 2015-16 area under gram, peas, horse gram and masur and other pulses is included in total pulses as per government records. After the year 2003-04 area under peas (pulses) has been included in area under vegetables in Lahaul & Spiti as per government records.

Table-3.11 : Area for Production of Pulses

(in hectares)

Year	Himachal Pradesh								Kinnaur						Lahaul & Spiti						
	Gram	Black, Red and Green gram	Peas	Hourse gram (kuth)	Masur	Other pulses	Total	Growth	Black, Red and Green gram	Peas	Masur	Other pulses	Total	Growth	Black, Red and Green gram	Peas	Hourse gram (kuth)	Masur	Other pulses	Total	Growth
1998-99	3291	18108	5066	4605	1440	6990	39500 (100)		6	422	15	814	1257 (3.18)		34	1066	0	3	0	1103 (2.79)	
1999-2000	3072	17263	3771	4037	1525	6844	36512 (100)	(7.56)	13	0	6	898	917 (2.51)	(27.05)	0	1089	0	0	27	1116 (3.06)	1.18
2000-01	2138	17158	4220	3411	1381	7750	36058 (100)	(1.24)	27	0	3	913	943 (2.62)	2.84	27	1166	0	5	0	1198 (3.32)	7.35
2001-02	2470	17890	4104	3496	1340	7682	36982 (100)	2.56	16	0	5	1050	1071 (2.90)	13.57	27	1186	0	2	0	1215 (3.29)	1.42
2002-03	2379	17985	4589	3348	1474	6155	35930 (100)	(2.84)	9	0	2	1057	1068 (2.97)	(0.28)	35	1232	0	0	0	1267 (3.53)	4.28
2003-04	1908	15345	4845	3028	1168	7555	33849 (100)	(5.79)	13	0	4	1062	1079 (3.19)	1.03	0	1210	0	0	29	1239 (3.66)	(2.21)
2004-05	1691	15109	5046	3307	1061	6342	32556 (100)	(3.82)	7	0	0	978	985 (3.03)	(8.71)	0	1415	0	1	37	1453 (4.46)	17.27
2005-06	1403	14721	5510	2807	993	5659	31093 (100)	(4.49)	13	494	5	931	1443 (4.64)	46.50	0	1598	45	0	26	1669 (5.37)	14.87
2006-07	1144	14842	5294	2418	751	5110	29559 (100)	(4.93)	13	521	2	959	1,495 (5.06)	3.60	0	1,497	0	4	38	1539 (5.21)	(7.79)
2007-08	1351	13398	6285	2582	872	5640	30128 (100)	1.92	9	650	1	879	1,539 (5.11)	2.94	0	1,497	65	0	58	1620 (5.38)	5.26
2008-09	1338	14500	3974	2537	794	5716	28859 (100)	(4.21)	5	778	1	1004	1788 (6.20)	16.18	0	0	0	0	26	26 (0.09)	(98.40)
2009-10	1345	13482	4251	2435	742	5700	27955 (100)	(3.13)	8	1157	0	825	1990 (7.12)	11.30	0	0	0	0	36	36 (0.13)	38.46
2010-11	1339	12870	10439	2411	724	5233	33016 (100)	18.10	7	890	1	887	1785 (5.41)	(10.30)	0	0	0	0	33	33 (0.10)	(8.33)
2011-12	1312	14115	3261	2556	710	4195	26149 (100)	-20.79	7	890	1	1785	2683 (10.26)	50.30	0	0	0	0	33	33 (0.12)	0
2012-13	1172	15751	8754	2471	624	3171	31943 (100)	22.15	5	1090	3	875	1973 (6.18)	(26.46)	0	0	0	0	31	31 (0.8)	(6.06)
2013-14	760	12769	10582	2167	682	4198	31158 (100)	-2.45	4	0	0	1150	1154 (3.70)	(41.51)	0	140	0	0	37	177 (0.56)	470.96
2014-15*	-	-	-	-	-	-	29373 (100)	-5.72	-	--	-	1333	1333 (4.55)	15.51	-	-	-	-	-	46 (0.15)	-74.01
2015-16*	-	-	-	-	-	-	34271 (100)	16.67	-	-	-	1685	1685 (4.91)	26.40	-	-	-	-	-	1808 (5.27)	3830
C.G								-0.32						4.46							246.72
Sigma	28113*	245306*	89991*	47616*	16281*	93940*	584891*		162*	6892*	49*	19085*	26188*		123*	13096	110*	15*	411*	15609*	
Mean	1757.06	15331.62	5624.43	2976	1017.56	5871.25	32577.94		10.12	430.75	3.06	1004.18	1448.12		7.68	818.5	6.87	0.93	25.68	859.68	
SD	724.35	1846.73	2285.48	677.02	323.72	1321.19	3689.77		5.75	436.92	3.71	228.21	492.02		13.89	653.64	19.14	1.65	17.02	664.07	
CV	41.22	12.04	40.63	22.74	31.81	22.5	11.32		56.71	101.43	121.24	22.72	33.97		180.72	79.85	278.45	177.41	66.27	77.24	

Source: Annual Season Crop Report, Directorate of Land Records, Kasumpti, Shimla-9, 1998-99 to 2015-16.

Data reveals that the Average Area under Pulses in Himachal Pradesh is 32,577.94 hectares. About 50 percent of the area, is cultivated under black, red and green gram. Production of pulses is expected to be declined as the area under pulses which was 39,500 hectares in the year 1998-99 has decreased to 34,271 hectares in the year 2015-16. The average area covered under black, red and green gram is 47.06 percent, other Pulses is 18.02 percent, horse gram 9.13 percent, gram 5.39 percent, and masur 3.12 percent. Overall, the area under pulses has declined by 0.32 percent.

Further, in Kinnaur, total area under pulses has been recorded 26,188 hectares. A fluctuating trend has been recorded in area under pulses in the district. Out of the total area under pulses in Kinnaur, 69.34 percent is cultivated under other pulses, followed by peas 2.97 percent, masur 0.69 percent, and meagre area 0.21 percent under black and green gram. However, there is a positive compound growth of 4.46 percent in area under pulses in the district.

In Lahaul & Spiti, the area under pulses has been recorded 15,609 hectares, which is only 2.66 percent of the State's total area. Peas covered 95.20 percent area, followed by other pulses with 2.98 percent area, black and green gram with 0.89 percent area and 0.79 percent area is under kuth and horse gram. In Kinnaur maximum area (69.34%) is covered under other pulses, whereas in Lahaul & Spiti, peas is the most dominating crop. Further, both the regions have recorded positive compound growth, Lahaul & Spiti has recorded a huge growth rate of 246.72 percent as compared to 4.46 percent of Kinnaur. It leads to the conclusion, that there is extensive expansion of land used for production of pulses in Lahaul & Spiti.

3.12 Area for Production of Fresh Fruits

Table 3.12, shows that production of fresh fruits has taken place in more land area in Himachal Pradesh during the past nearly two decades whereas, area under cereals crops (table 3.10) shows a decrease which indicates that there is shifting of cropping pattern from cereal crops to fruits crops. Further, 75.81 percent area is dominated by apple. It concludes that in Himachal, apple is the major fruit crop consistently.

Note*= In the year 2014-15 and 2015-16 area under grapes, peaches, plum, lichi and pears has been included in other fresh fruits.

Table-3.12 : Area for Production of Fresh Fruits

(in hectares)

Year	Himachal Pradesh									Kinnaur						Lahaul & Spiti						
	Apple	Grapes	Peaches	Plum	Lichi	Pears	Others	Total	Growth	Apple	Grapes	Peaches	Others	Total	Growth	Apple	Grapes	Peaches	Plum	Others	Total	Growth
1998-99	39935	7	189	2403	28	34	7854	50450 (100)		1529	7	0	0	1536 (3.04)		4	0	0	0	23	27 (0.05)	
1999-2000	38650	11	309	2104	72	175	8699	49930 (100)	-1.03	1559	7	0	0	1566 (3.14)	1.95	19	0	4	3	0	26 (0.05)	-3.70
2000-01	38785	15	348	2587	116	63	4072	45986 (100)	-7.90	2088	10	0	0	2098 (4.56)	33.97	31	0	0	0	0	31 (0.07)	19.23
2001-02	39236	9	297	2132	98	120	9875	51767 (100)	12.57	1814	9	0	0	1823 (3.52)	-13.11	31	0	4	0	4	39 (0.08)	25.81
2002-03	37062	15	513	1793	142	58	14921	54504 (100)	5.29	2174	9	0	0	2183 (4.01)	19.75	52	0	0	0	0	52 (0.10)	33.33
2003-04	38681	6	356	1355	226	133	14817	55644 (100)	2.09	1909	6	0	0	1915 (3.44)	-12.28	59	0	0	0	0	59 (0.11)	13.46
2004-05	40662	9	578	787	44	87	14307	56474 (100)	1.49	1791	7	0	0	1798 (3.18)	-6.11	42	0	0	0	16	58 (0.10)	-1.69
2005-06	42251	9	647	1707	47	79	13618	58458 (100)	3.51	2090	7	0	0	2097 (3.59)	16.63	40	0	0	0	16	56 (0.10)	-3.45
2006-07	43871	9	638	949	133	106	15329	61035 (100)	4.41	2137	7	0	155	2259 (3.70)	7.73	48	0	19	0	0	67 (0.11)	19.64
2007-08	44281	5	782	712	76	159	14427	60442 (100)	-0.97	2120	4	0	28	2152 (3.56)	-4.74	47	1	0	0	14	62 (0.10)	-7.46
2008-09	45120	4	721	1430	97	282	15182	62836 (100)	3.96	2214	4	0	171	2389 (3.80)	11.01	51	0	0	0	0	51 (0.08)	-17.74
2009-10	45679	5	749	1560	135	241	13488	61857 (100)	-1.56	2524	4	0	179	2707 (4.38)	13.31	71	0	0	0	0	71 (0.11)	39.22
2010-11	46815	7	670	1433	223	260	14959	64367 (100)	4.06	2851	6	0	158	3015 (4.68)	11.38	71	0	0	0	15	86 (0.13)	21.13
2011-12	51582	15	813	2123	85	300	13094	64691 (100)	0.50	2947	6	-	127	3080 (4.76)	2.16	71	-	-	-	22	93 (0.14)	8.14
2012-13	52766	14	933	1570	162	291	13545	66323 (100)	2.52	3514	5	-	127	3646 (5.50)	18.38	96	-	-	-	22	118 (0.18)	26.88
2013-14	58576	12	1644	2203	63	194	11739	73208 (100)	10.38	2968	5	1	4	2978 (4.06)	(18.32)	100	0	0	0	22	122 (0.17)	3.38
2014-15	60418	-	-	-	-	-	17336	77754 (100)	6.21	4587	-	-	103	4747 (6.10)	59.40	195	-	-	-	12	207 (0.26)	69.67
2015-16	61891	-	-	-	-	-	5981	74106 (100)	-4.69	4742	-	-	5	4696 (6.33)	-1.07	190	-	-	-	12	202 (0.27)	-2.41
C.G									2.40						8.23							14.32
Sigma	826261*	152*	10187*	26848*	1747*	2582*	223243*	1089832*		45558*	103*	1*	1057*	46685*		1218*	1*	27*	3*	178*	1427*	
Mean	45903.39	9.5	636.68	1678	109.18	161.37	12354.11	60546.33		2531	6.43	0.07	58.72	2593.61		67.66	0.07	1.92	0.21	9.88	79.27	
SD	7929.75	3.79	344.44	561.96	58.83	90.32	3560.46	8737.75		935.84	1.82	0.26	73.52	958.27		51.45	0.26	5.12	0.80	9.26	53.09	
C.V	17.27	39.93	54.10	33.48	53.88	55.97	28.82	14.43		36.97	28.33	376.05	125.20	36.94		76.04	371.42	266.66	380.95	93.72	66.97	

Source: Annual Season Crop Report, Directorate of Land Records, Kasumpti, Shimla-9 1998-99 to 2015-16.

In Kinnaur, fresh fruits are produced in 46,685 hectares area. Needless to state that it has increased from 1,536 hectares in 1998-99 to 4,696 hectares in 2015-16. Further, 97.58 percent area is dominated by apple. Thus apple is the main fruit crop of the district.

Similarly, in Lahaul & Spiti, 85 percent area is under apple, followed by, others 12.47 percent, area where other fresh fruits are produced 1.89 percent area where peach is produced and rest of 0.64 percent area is under plum and grapes. It is analysed that apple is the major fresh fruit crop of Himachal Pradesh which is produced in the hilly regions of Shimla district and the tribal regions like Kinnaur and Lahaul & Spiti.

3.13 Area for Production of Dry Fruits

Table 3.13 shows that in 47 percent area (8,649 hectares) almond is produced while, other dry fruits covered 27.34 percent, chilgoza in 21.31 percent, and walnut in 3.99 percent, out of total 18,330 hectares area under dry fruits in Himachal Pradesh. The area under production of dry fruits during the study period ranged between 174 hectares in the year 2012-13 to 1,449 hectares in the year 2005-06. Further, the average area under almond in the State is 540.56 hectares with S.D. = 285.96 hectares and C.V. of 52.90 percent, chilgoza averaged 244.19 hectare with standard deviation of 147.73 hectare and C.V. = 60.49 percent. Thus, almond is the major dry fruit crop of the State.

Out of 8,735 hectares area under dry fruits in Kinnaur, chilgoza is being produced in 52.80 percent area, other dry fruits in 28.32 percent area, almond in 17.27 percent and walnut in 1.8 percent area. The study finds that there has been decline in the area covered under production of dry fruits in Kinnaur district.

In Lahaul & Spiti, only 205 hectare (1.11%) area produces dry fruits. Walnut is the most dominating (73.65%) dry fruit in the district against the remaining 26.33 percent area where almond and other dry fruits are produced. So, production of dry fruits is very limited in Lahaul & Spiti district.

Note*= in the year 2014-15 and 2015- 16 area under walnut, almond and chilgoza has been included in other dry fruits.

Table-3.13 : Area for Production of Dry Fruits

(in hectares)

	Himachal Pradesh						Kinnaur						Lahaul & Spiti					
Year	Walnut	Almond	Chilgoza	Other	Total	Growth	Walnut	Almond	Chilgoza	Other	Total	Growth	Walnut	Almond	Chilgoza	Other	Total	Growth
1998-99	22	324	0	430	776 (100)		15	84	0	430	529 (68.17)		0	0	0	0	0	
1999-2000	27	359	312	280	978 (100)	26.03	10	84	308	144	546 (55.83)	3.21	2	0	0	0	2 (0.20)	
2000-01	77	975	322	7	1381 (100)	41.21	7	99	322	0	428 (30.99)	-21.61	0	0	0	0	0	-100
2001-02	18	174	381	452	1045 (100)	-24.33	17	112	381	187	679 (64.98)	58.64	0	0	0	0	0	-
2002-03	26	470	312	217	1025 (100)	-1.91	17	148	312	208	685 (66.83)	0.88	0	0	0	0	0	-
2003-04	37	600	314	173	1124 (100)	9.66	9	113	314	173	609 (54.18)	-11.09	0	0	0	0	0	-
2004-05	59	684	321	184	1248 (100)	11.03	11	110	318	184	623 (49.92)	2.30	0	0	0	0	0	-
2005-06	40	833	393	183	1449 (100)	16.11	17	114	393	183	707 (48.79)	13.48	0	0	0	0	0	-
2006-07	38	337	309	516	1180 (100)	-18.56	12	82	309	149	552 (46.78)	-21.92	0	1	0	1	2 (0.17)	-
2007-08	71	869	313	7	1260 (100)	6.78	6	93	313	0	412 (32.70)	-25.36	3	150	0	0	153 (12.14)	7550.00
2008-09	174	888	312	22	1396 (100)	10.79	8	98	311	0	417 (29.87)	1.21	3	0	0	12	15 (1.07)	-90.20
2009-10	82	761	307	12	1162 (100)	-16.76	10	99	307	0	416 (35.80)	-0.24	3	0	0	12	15 (1.29)	0.00
2010-11	35	762	311	11	1119 (100)	4.65	9	101	311	0	421 (34.62)	1.20	3	0	0	0	3 (0.25)	-80.00
2011-12	10	229	0	25	264 (100)	-76.40	5	94	298	0	397 (30.24)	-5.70	3	0	0	0	3 (0.23)	0.00
2012-13	8	166	0	0	174 (100)	-34.09	0	0	415	0	415 (34.35)	4.53	3	0	0	0	3 (0.25)	0.00
2013-14	9	218	0	16	243 (100)	-39.65	5	78	0	16	99 (40.74)	-76.14	3	0	0	0	3 (1.23)	0.00
2014-15	-	-	-	1238	1268 (100)	421.81	-	-	-	350	350 (27.60)	253.53	3	0	0	0	3 (0.23)	0.00
2015-16	-	-	-	1238	1238 (100)	-2.36	-	-	-	450	450 (36.34)	28.57	3	0	0	0	3 (0.24)	0.00
Sum	733*	8649*	3907*	5011*	18330* (100)		158*	1509*	4612*	2474*	8735* (47.65)		29*	151*	0	25*	205* (1.11)	
CG						18.57						12.09						727.98
Mean	45.81	540.56	244.19	278.39	1018.33		9.88	94.31	288.25	137.44	485.28		1.61	8.39	0	1.39	11.39	
SD	41.61	285.96	147.73	387.32	398.055		4.89	30.34	117.76	151.18	148.45		1.50	0	0	3.87	35.63	
CV	90.81	52.90	60.49	139.12	39.08		49.44	32.16	40.84	109.99	30.58		93.10	0	0	278.60	312.89	

Source: Annual Season Crop Report, Directorate of Land Records, Kasumpti, Shimla-9, 1998-99 to 2015-16.

3.14 Area for Production of Vegetables

The area wise vegetables grown in Kinnaur and Lahaul & Spiti is shown in the table 3.14. The table 3.14 clearly indicates that land area used for production of vegetables has increased rapidly averaging 33,583.33, hectares recording growth of 0.61 percent with a slight variation of 9.79 percent indicating consistency in use of land for Vegetables in the State. Out of all vegetables, area under production of potato is recorded 15,052.5 hectares which is 44.82 percent of the area under all vegetables, whereas, area for peas is 5,845 hectares (17.40%), tomato 4,509.25 hectares (13.42%), cabbage and cauliflower 2,561.94 hectares (7.62%), other vegetables 5,241.56 hectares (15.60%), onion 845.31 hectares (2.51%) and lady finger 241.69 hectares (0.71%). The data indicates that in most of the area of the State under vegetables potato and cauliflower are being produced. However, coefficient of variance for these vegetables is high.

In Kinnaur, an average 480.33 percent area is under vegetables, out of which 40 percent is used for production of potato and peas. Where, potato is produced in 189.89 hectares with S.D. = 65.63 hectares and C.V. = 34.56% and peas are produced in 195.37 hectare with S.D. = 242.28 hectares and C.V. = 124%. The compound growth is 26.83%, ranging between -74.17% in 2005-06 to 231.74 in 2014-15.

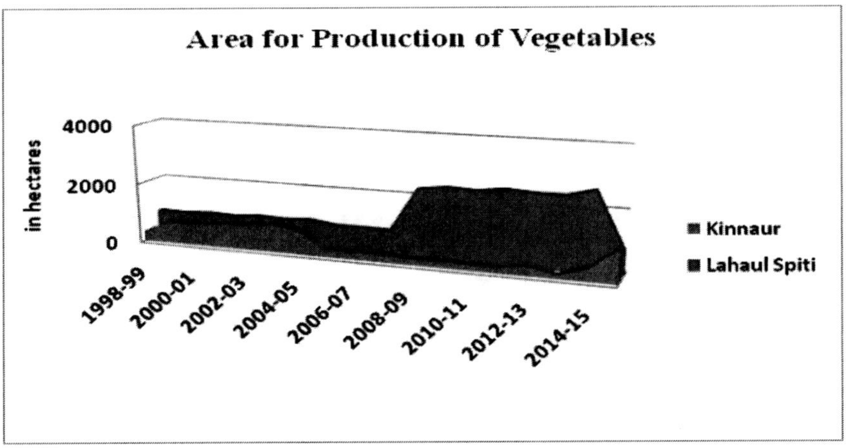

Figure-3.4 : Area for Production of Vegetables in Kinnaur and Lahaul & Spiti

Table-3.14 : Area for Production of Vegetables in Kinnaur

(in hectares)

Year	Himachal Pradesh									Kinnaur								
	Potato	Peas	Onion	Tomato	Lady finger	Cabbage	Others	Total	Growth	Potato	Peas	Onion	Tomato	Lady finger	Cabbage	Others	Total	Growth
1998-99	14420	0	759	2274	98	1197	9196	27917 (100)		274	0	0	0	0	20	36	350 (1.25)	
1999-2000	25414	5796	802	2548	304	1517	3333	27824 (100)	-0.33	271	390	0	2	0	26	36	725 (2.61)	107.14
2000-01	14422	6895	810	2856	269	1544	3162	29958 (100)	7.67	238	428	0	0	0	23	34	723 (2.41)	-0.28
2001-02	13199	8944	790	3714	147	1891	3905	32590 (100)	8.79	255	486	0	0	0	21	28	790 (2.42)	9.27
2002-03	14923	8063	760	3556	121	2658	3664	33745 (100)	3.54	240	524	0	1	0	16	35	816 (2.42)	3.29
2003-04	14144	7334	778	4133	202	2830	3819	33240 (100)	-1.50	244	539	0	1	0	121	16	921 (2.77)	12.87
2004-05	12548	7410	848	4267	181	2975	4486	36675 (100)	10.33	244	562	0	2	0	23	13	844 (2.30)	-8.36
2005-06	14022	6669	766	4451	182	2885	4940	33915 (100)	-7.53	192	0	0	0	0	22	4	218 (0.64)	-74.17
2006-07	13869	7788	1112	5201	116	2,979	4919	33984 (100)	0.20	199	0	0	0	0	36	9	243 (0.72)	11.47
2007-08	14661	6928	807	4981	132	2621	4159	34289 (100)	0.90	239	0	0	0	0	23	0	262 (0.76)	7.82
2008-09	22362	2576	999	5271	182	2917	4931	39238 (100)	14.43	169	0	0	0	0	31	0	200 (0.51)	-23.66
2009-10	14807	10849	702	5432	267	3068	4705	39830 (100)	1.51	183	0	0	0	0	29	0	212 (0.53)	6.00
2010-11	13986	3211	854	5623	166	3446	6819	34105 (100)	-14.37	134	0	0	0	0	58	0	192 (0.56)	-9.43
2011-12	12786	3327	865	5620	668	2478	6963	32707 (100)	-4.10	143	0	0	0	0	27	0	170 (0.36)	-11.46
2012-13	13368	3838	1070	5546	462	2692	8793	35769 (100)	6.31	57	197	0	0	0	11	52	317 (1.28)	86.47
2013--14	11909	3892	803	6675	370	3293	6071	33013 (100)	-7.70	109	0	0	0	0	1	16	126 (0.38)	-60.25
2014-15*	-	-	-	-	-	-	-	35672 (100)	8.05	129	-	-	-	-	-	289	418 (1.17)	231.74
2015-16*	-	-	-	-	-	-	-	30029 (100)	-15.81	98	-	-	-	-	-	1021	1119 (3.72)	167.70
Sum	**240840***	**93520***	**13525***	**72148***	**3867***	**40991***	**83865***	**604500* (100)**		**3418***	**3126***	**0**	**6***	**0**	**488***	**1589***	**8646* (1.43)**	
CG									**0.61**									**26.83**
Mean	**15052.5**	**5845**	**845.31**	**4509.25**	**241.69**	**2561.94**	**5241.56**	**33583.33**		**189.89**	**195.375**	**0**	**0.37**	**0**	**30.5**	**88.28**	**480.33**	
SD	**3594.50**	**2792.04**	**115.82**	**1256.79**	**151.03**	**668.18**	**1843.51**	**3290.02**		**65.63**	**242.28**	**0**	**0.72**	**0**	**26.97**	**241.91**	**319.70**	
CV	**23.87**	**47.76**	**13.7**	**27.87**	**62.48**	**26.08**	**35.17**	**9.79**		**34.56**	**124**	**0**	**191.46**	**0**	**88.42**	**274.05**	**66.55**	

Contd. ...

Area for Production of Vegetables in Lahaul S iti

(in hectares)

	Himachal Pradesh									Lahaul S iti								
Year	**Potato**	**Peas**	**Onion**	**Tomato**	**Lady finger**	**Cabbage**	**Others**	**Total**	**Growth**	**Potato**	**Peas**	**Onion**	**Tomato**	**Lady finger**	**Cabbage**	**Others**	**Total**	**Growth**
1998-99	14420	0	759	2274	98	1197	9196	27917 (100)		849	0	0	0	0	0	13	862 (3.09)	
1999-2000	25414	5796	802	2548	304	1517	3333	27824 (100)	-0.33	813	0	0	0	0	2	16	831 (2.99)	-3.60
2000-01	14422	6895	810	2856	269	1544	3162	29958 (100)	7.67	885	0	0	0	0	2	8	895 (2.99)	7.70
2001-02	13199	8944	790	3714	147	1891	3905	32590 (100)	8.79	850	0	0	0	0	6	12	868 (2.66)	-3.02
2002-03	14923	8063	760	3556	121	2658	3664	33745 (100)	3.54	925	10	0	0	0	0	0	935 (2.77)	7.72
2003-04	14144	7334	778	4133	202	2830	3819	33240 (100)	-1.50	874	0	0	0	0	17	9	900 (2.71)	-3.74
2004-05	12548	7410	848	4267	181	2975	4486	36675 (100)	10.33	928	0	0	0	0	16	7	951 (2.59)	5.67
2005-06	14022	6669	766	4451	182	2885	4940	33915 (100)	-7.53	807	0	4	0	0	21	6	838 (2.47)	-11.88
2006-07	13869	7788	1112	5201	116	2,979	4919	33984 (100)	0.20	813	0	0	0	0	0	19	832 (2.45)	-0.72
2007-08	14661	6928	807	4981	132	2621	4159	34289 (100)	0.90	813	0	0	0	0	4	5	822 (2.40)	-1.20
2008-09	22362	2576	999	5271	182	2917	4931	39238 (100)	14.43	2242	0	0	0	0	12	1	2263 (5.77)	175.30
2009-10	14807	10849	702	5432	267	3068	4705	39830 (100)	1.51	759	1591	0	0	0	8	18	2376 (5.97)	4.99
2010-11	13986	3211	854	5623	166	3446	6819	34105 (100)	-14.37	755	1560	0	0	0	0	16	2331 (6.83)	-1.89
2011-12	12786	3327	865	5620	668	2478	6963	32707 (100)	-4.10	819	1612	0	0	0	0	16	2447 (7.48)	4.98
2012-13	13368	3838	1070	5546	462	2692	8793	35769 (100)	6.31	824	1535	0	0	0	0	28	2387 (6.67)	-2.45
2013-14	11909	3892	803	6675	370	3293	6071	33013 (100)	-7.70	788	1574	0	1	0	17	11	2391 (7.24)	0.16
2014-15*	-	-	-	-	-	-	-	35672 (100)	8.05	737	-	-	-	-	-	1889	2626 (7.36)	9.82
2015-16*	-	-	-	-	-	-	-	30029 (100)	-15.81	748	-	-	-	-	-	40	794 (2.64)	-69.76
CG									**0.61**									**6.95**
Sum	**240840***	**93520***	**13525***	**72148***	**3867***	**40991***	**83865***	**604500* (100)**		**16229***	**7882***	**4***	**1***	**0**	**105***	**2114***	**26349* (4.35)**	
Mean	**15052.5**	**5845**	**845.31**	**4509.25**	**241.69**	**2561.94**	**5241.56**	**33583.33**		**901.61**	**492.62**	**0.25**	**0.06**	**0**	**6.56**	**117.44**	**1463.83**	
SD	**3594.50**	**2792.04**	**115.82**	**1256.79**	**151.02**	**668.18**	**1843.51**	**3290.02**		**339.12**	**753.40**	**1**	**0.25**	**0**	**7.55**	**442.23**	**774.79**	
CV	**23.87**	**47.76**	**13.7**	**27.87**	**62.48**	**26.08**	**35.17**	**9.79**		**37.61**	**152.93**	**400**	**403.22**	**0**	**114.93**	**376.54**	**52.92**	

Source: , , , , 1998-99 2015-16.

ote* 2014-15, 2015-16 , , ,

.

In Lahaul & Spiti also, coefficient of variance in respect of area for production of potato is calculated 37.61 percent in comparison to peas; 152.93 percent, cabbage & cauliflower; 114.93 percent and onion; 400 percent. The average area under production of all vegetables in the district is 1463.83 hectares (S.D. = 774.79 hectares and C.V. = 52.92%) spread as 901.61 hectares under potato and 492.62 hectares for peas. The compound growth is 6.95 percent. It is analysed that in comparison to Lahaul & Spiti (26.83%), Kinnaur (0.61%) has less area for production of all vegetables.

3.15 Irrigated Area for Production of Cereals

The average irrigated area for production of cereals in Himachal Pradesh (table 3.15) is 1,50,791.72 hectares accounting for 3,759.09 hectares standard deviation and 2.40 percent coefficient of variance. It was 1,46,939 hectares in the year 1998-99, which increased to 1,57,345 hectares in 2015-16. It has not grown much as the compound growth is calculated only 0.43 percent. Further, 46.57 percent (70,235.61 hectares) land area has been irrigated for wheat, 33.20 percent (50,077.88 hectares) for rice, and 16.78 percent (25,306.72 hectares) land for maize. These three crops covered about 95 percent area out of the total area irrigated for cereals. Coefficient of variance for production of rice is 1.42 percent, wheat 4.12 percent maize 6.71 percent, other cereals is 89.72 percent and millets 45.92 percent.

In Kinnaur and Lahual & Spiti, the irrigated area for cereals has decreased consistently resulting in to negative compound which is -5.54 percent in Kinnaur and -4.17 percent in Lahaul & Spiti. Average irrigated land area for cereals in district Kinnaur is 2,096.44 hectare spread as 879.33 hectares (41.94%) under barley with 33.89 percent coefficient of variance and 848.83 hectares (40.48%) under millets with 30.69 percent coefficient of variance. These two crops have covered about 82 percent of the total irrigated area for cereals and rest have only 18 percent including maize, wheat, rice, and others in the district.

Table-3.15 : rrigated Area for Production of Cereals in Kinnaur

(in hectares)

	Himachal Pradesh								Kinnaur							
	ice	Mai e	heat	arley	Millets	Other	Total	Growth	ice	Mai e	heat	arley	Millets	Other	Total	Growth
1998-99	50221.00 (100)	23608.00 (100)	67295.00 (100)	4141.00 (100)	1651.00 (100)	23.00 (100)	146939.00 (100)		0	328.00 (1.39)	201.00 (0.30)	1135.00 (27.41)	1170.00 (70.87)	0	2834.00 (1.93)	
1999-2000	50433.00 (100)	23221.00 (100)	67304.00 (100)	4141.00 (100)	2216.00 (100)	0.00 (100)	147315.00 (100)	0.26	2.00 (0.00)	338.00 (1.46)	160.00 (0.24)	1215.00 (29.34)	1300.00 (58.66)	0	3015.00 (2.05)	6.39
2000-01	50156.00 (100)	24047.00 (100)	67634.00 (100)	3421.00 (100)	1958.00 (100)	71.00 (100)	147287.00 (100)	-0.02	3.00 (0.01)	309.00 (1.28)	129.00 (0.19)	1150.00 (33.62)	1117.00 (57.05)	0	2708.00 (1.84)	-10.18
2001-02	49536.00 (100)	23570.00 (100)	68316.00 (100)	4211.00 (100)	1674.00 (100)	274.00 (100)	147581.00 (100)	0.20	1.00 (0.00)	292.00 (1.24)	136.00 (0.20)	1105.00 (26.24)	1074.00 (64.16)	22.00 (8.03)	2630.00 (1.78)	-2.88
2002-03	50690.00 (100)	23952.00 (100)	67606.00 (100)	4112.00 (100)	1021.00 (100)	819.00 (100)	148200.00 (100)	0.42	0	275.00 (1.15)	106.00 (0.16)	1192.00 (28.99)	938.00 (91.87)	26.00 (3.17)	2537.00 (1.71)	-3.54
2003-04	50492.00 (100)	24778.00 (100)	70293.00 (100)	4183.00 (100)	1579.00 (100)	260.00 (100)	151585.00 (100)	2.28	0	164.00 (0.66)	111.00 (0.16)	1072.00 (25.63)	955.00 (60.48)	22.00 (8.46)	2324.00 (1.53)	-8.40
2004-05	49508.00 (100)	23582.00 (100)	68010.00 (100)	3721.00 (100)	1654.00 (100)	182.00 (100)	146657.00 (100)	-3.25	0	245.00 (1.04)	92.00 (0.14)	1049.00 (28.19)	1079.00 (65.24)	15.00 (8.24)	2480.00 (1.69)	6.71
2005-06	51529.00 (100)	24706.00 (100)	66954.00 (100)	3944.00 (100)	1642.00 (100)	386.00 (100)	149161.00 (100)	1.71	0	240.00 (0.97)	125.00 (0.19)	1168.00 (29.61)	971.00 (59.14)	0	2504.00 (1.68)	0.97
2006-07	50330.00 (100)	25639.00 (100)	67688.00 (100)	3625.00 (100)	1500.00 (100)	134.00 (100)	148916.00 (100)	-0.16	0	253.00 (0.99)	107.00 (0.16)	1027 (28.33)	953.00 (63.53)	5.00 (3.73)	2345.00 (1.57)	-6.35
2007-08	50296.00 (100)	27627.00 (100)	73097.00 (100)	2730.00 (100)	1409.00 (100)	42.00 (100)	155201.00 (100)	4.22	0	256.00 (0.93)	840.00 (1.15)	83.00 (3.04)	917.00 (65.08)	12.00 (28.57)	2108.00 (1.36)	-10.11
2008-09	49603.00 (100)	23888.00 (100)	70682.00 (100)	3352.00 (100)	1186.00 (100)	219.00 (100)	148930.00 (100)	-4.04	0	252.00 (1.05)	55.00 (0.08)	783.00 (23.36)	816.00 (68.80)	5.00 (2.28)	1911.00 (1.28)	-9.35
2009-10	49461.00 (100)	25058.00 (100)	70969.00 (100)	3459.00 (100)	1079.00 (100)	314.00 (100)	150340.00 (100)	0.95	19.00 (0.04)	148 (0.59)	80.00 (0.11)	785.00 (22.69)	689.00 (63.86)	42.00 (13.38)	1763.00 (1.17)	-7.74
2010-11	48231.00 (100)	26685.00 (100)	70857.00 (100)	3289.00 (100)	1179.00 (100)	529.00 (100)	150770.00 (100)	0.29	0	183.00 (0.69)	51.00 (0.07)	717.00 (21.80)	690.00 (58.52)	16.00 (3.02)	1657.00 (1.10)	-6.01
2011-12	50309.00 (100)	26418.00 (100)	71019.00 (100)	3422.00 (100)	824.00 (100)	246.00 (100)	152238.00 (100)	0.97	0	181.00 (0.69)	49.00 (0.07)	752.00 (21.98)	639.00 (77.55)	38.00 (15.45)	1659.00 (1.09)	0.12
2012-13	50866.00 (100)	28822.00 (100)	73872.00 (100)	3297.00 (100)	1047.00 (100)	252.00 (100)	158156.00 (100)	3.89	0	162.00 (0.56)	51.00 (0.07)	765.00 (23.20)	558.00 (53.30)	3.00 (1.19)	1539.00 (0.97)	-7.23
2013-14	50355 (100)	28014 (100)	74003 (100)	3249 (100)	1143 (100)	167 (100)	156931 (100)	(0.77)	0	156 (0.55)	33 (0.04)	666 (20.49)	562 (49.16)	0	1417 (0.90)	-7.92
2014-15	49467 (100)	25414 (100)	71563 (100)	3192 (100)	904 (100)	0	150699 (100)	(3.97)	17 (0.03)	102 (0.40)	32 (0.04)	650 (20.36)	445 (49.22)	0	1246 (0.82)	-13.72
2015-16	49919 (100)	26492 (100)	77079 (100)	2826 (100)	862 (100)	0	157345 (100)	4.41	15 (0.03)	101 (0.38)	23 (0.02)	514 (18.18)	406 (47.09)	0	1059 (0.67)	-15.00
CG								0.43								-5.54
Mean	50077.88	25306.72	70235.61	3573.05	1264.55	315.77	150791.72		3.16	221.38	132.27	879.33	848.83	11.44	2096.44	
SD	715.416	1699.40	2897.87	464.03	580.77	283.31	3759.09		6.45	73.91	183.19	298.08	260.52	13.67	582.55	
CV	1.42	6.71	4.12	12.98	45.92	89.72	2.49		204.11	33.38	138.49	33.89	30.69	119.49	27.78	

Contd. ...

rrigated Area for Production of Cereals in Lahaul S iti

	Himachal Pradesh								Lahaul S iti							
Year	ice	Mai e	heat	arley	Millets	Other	Total	Growth	ice	Mai e	heat	arley	Millets	others	Total	Growth
1998-99	50221.00 (100)	23608.00 (100)	67295.00 (100)	4141.00 (100)	1651.00 (100)	23.00 (100)	146939.00 (100)		0	41 (0.17)	205 (0.30)	694 (16.75)	170 (10.29)	0 (0)	1110 (0.75)	
1999-2000	50433.00 (100)	23221.00 (100)	67304.00 (100)	4141.00 (100)	2216.00 (100)	0.00 (100)	147315.00 (100)	0.26	0	25 (0.10)	206 (0.30)	683 (16.49)	168 (7.93)	0	1082 (0.73)	-2.52
2000-01	50156.00 (100)	24047.00 (100)	67634.00 (100)	3421.00 (100)	1958.00 (100)	71.00 (100)	147287.00 (100)	-0.02	0	30 (0.12)	181 (0.26)	590 (17.24)	152 (7.76)	0	953 (0.65)	-11.92
2001-02	49536.00 (100)	23570.00 (100)	68316.00 (100)	4211.00 (100)	1674.00 (100)	274.00 (100)	147581.00 (100)	0.20	0	41 (0.17)	199 (0.29)	637 (15.12)	160 (10.09)	0	1037 (0.70)	-8.81
2002-03	50690.00 (100)	23952.00 (100)	67606.00 (100)	4112.00 (100)	1021.00 (100)	819.00 (100)	148200.00 (100)	0.42	0	34 (0.14)	173 (0.25)	550 (13.37)	155 (0)	0	912 (0.62)	-12.05
2003-04	50492.00 (100)	24778.00 (100)	70293.00 (100)	4183.00 (100)	1579.00 (100)	260.00 (100)	151585.00 (100)	2.28	0	35 (0.14)	185 (0.26)	647 (15.46)	178 (11.27)	0	1045 (0.69)	14.58
2004-05	49508.00 (100)	23582.00 (100)	68010.00 (100)	3721.00 (100)	1654.00 (100)	182.00 (100)	146657.00 (100)	-3.25	0	34 (0.14)	175 (0.25)	553 (14.86)	161 (9.73)	0	923 (0.63)	-11.67
2005-06	51529.00 (100)	24706.00 (100)	66954.00 (100)	3944.00 (100)	1642.00 (100)	386.00 (100)	149161.00 (100)	1.71	0	42 (0.16)	121 (0.18)	576 (14.60)	149 (3.95)	0	945 (0.63)	2.38
2006-07	50330.00 (100)	25639.00 (100)	67688.00 (100)	3625.00 (100)	1500.00 (100)	134.00 (100)	148916.00 (100)	-0.16	0	38 (0.14)	142 (0.20)	616 (16.99)	65 (9.93)	0	811 (0.54)	-14.18
2007-08	50296.00 (100)	27627.00 (100)	73097.00 (100)	2730.00 (100)	1409.00 (100)	42.00 (100)	155201.00 (100)	4.22	0	49 (0.17)	118 (0.16)	573 (20.98)	51 (3.61)	0	791 (0.51)	-2.47
2008-09	49603.00 (100)	23888.00 (100)	70682.00 (100)	3352.00 (100)	1186.00 (100)	219.00 (100)	148930.00 (100)	-4.04	0	47 (0.19)	107 (0.15)	473 (14.11)	85 (7.17)	0	712	-9.99
2009-10	49461.00 (100)	25058.00 (100)	70969.00 (100)	3459.00 (100)	1079.00 (100)	314.00 (100)	150340.00 (100)	0.95	0	85 (0.34)	81 (0.11)	592 (17.11)	107 (9.91)	0	865	21.49
2010-11	48231.00 (100)	26685.00 (100)	70857.00 (100)	3289.00 (100)	1179.00 (100)	529.00 (100)	150770.00 (100)	0.29	0	46 (0.17)	75 (0.11)	608 (18.49)	109 (9.25)	0	838	-3.12
2011-12	50309.00 (100)	26418.00 (100)	71019.00 (100)	3422.00 (100)	824.00 (100)	246.00 (100)	152238.00 (100)	0.97	0	34 (0.13)	64 (0.09)	545 (15.93)	93 (11.29)	0	736	-12.17
2012-13	50866.00 (100)	28822.00 (100)	73872.00 (100)	3297.00 (100)	1047.00 (100)	252.00 (100)	158156.00 (100)	3.89	0	22 (0.08)	63 (0.08)	554 (16.80)	86 (8.21)	0	725	-1.49
2013-14	50355 (100)	28014 (100)	74003 (100)	3249 (100)	1143 (100)	167 (100)	156931 (100)	(0.77)	0	23 (0.08)	57 (0.07)	511 (15.72)	0	0	591	-18.48
2014-15	49467 (100)	25414 (100)	71563 (100)	3192 (100)	904 (100)	0	150699 (100)	(3.97)	0	19 (0.07)	46 (0.06)	403 (12.62)	103 (11.39)	0	576	-2.53
2015-16	49919 (100)	26492 (100)	77079 (100)	2826 (100)	862 (100)	0	157345 (100)	4.41	0	20 (0.07)	46 (0.05)	429 (15.18)	92 (10.67)	0	587	1.9
CG								0.43								-4.17
Mean	50077.88	25306.72	70235.611	3573.05	1264.55	315.78	150791.72		0	37.61	124.66	558.55	72.5	0	846.61	
SD	715.416	1699.40	2897.87	464.03	580.77	283.31	3759.09		0	14.79	59.28	78.68	49.03	0	169.32	
CV	1.42	6.71	4.12	12.98	45.92	89.72	2.49		0	39.32	47.55	14.08	67.62	0	19.99	

Source: , , , , 1998-99 2015-16.

Further, in Lahaul & Spiti it is 846.61 hectares out of which, 558.55 hectares (65.97%) for barley with 14.08 percent coefficient of variance, 124.66 hectares (14.72%) for wheat with coefficient of variance 47.55 percent. Both crops covered 80 percent irrigated area and rest of the 20 percent area is covered under maize and millets. It is analysed from the data that majority of the area of both the districts is dominated by Barley, but it is quite meagre as compared to that of the State, calculated only 1.39 percent area in Kinnaur and 0.56 percent in Lahaul & Spiti.

3.16 Irrigated Area for Production of Pulses

The following table 3.16 depicts that, 56 percent is irrigated area for peas (2,747.14 hectare), 30 percent for other crops, 15.94 percent red, black and green gram, and 2.61 percent gram. The coefficient of variation is 19.11 percent in production of gram (red, black and green), and 20.47 percent peas.

The average irrigated area for pulses is 1,206.83 hectares in Kinnaur, with S.D. = 276.21 hectares and 22.88 percent C.V. About 70 percent area is covered under other pulses followed by, 29.61 percent under peas and a very small (0.39 %) under masur and gram (black, red, green). The irrigated area for production of pulses has grown by 2.37 percent in Kinnaur and 219.43 percent in Lahaul & Spiti.

In district Lahaul & Spiti, 83.82 percent (727.55 hectares) irrigated area is under peas with 56.84 percent coefficient of variance, followed by, other pulses (13.81%) percent with 351.77 percent coefficient of variance. Only peas has covered about 83 percent of the total irrigated area for pulses. Thus in Kinnaur district, irrigated area in majority, is under other pulses, whereas, peas has covered maximum area in Lahaul & Spiti.

ote* 2014-15 2015-16, , ,

Table-3.16 : rrigated Area for Production of Pulses

(in hectares)

	Himachal Pradesh								Kinnaur						Lahaul S iti					
	Gram	Gram (lac ed Green)	Peas	Horse Gram (Kuth)	Masur	Other Pulses	Total	Growth	Gram (lac ed Green)	Peas	Masur	Other Pulses	Total	Growth	Gram (lac ed Green)	Peas	Masur	Other Pulses	Total	Growth
1998-99	214	979	2581	66	176	866	4882 (100)		11	551	4	678	**1244 (25.48)**		34	1066	3	0	**1103 (22.59)**	
1999-2000	327	1020	2346	192	168	1064	5117 (100)	**4.81**	11	0	5	737	**753 (14.72)**	**(39.47)**	0	1089	0	27	**1116 (21.81)**	**1.18**
2000-01	216	615	2609	91	201	1044	4776 (100)	**-6.66**	15	0	2	767	**784 (16.42)**	**4.12**	27	1166	5	0	**1198 (25.08)**	**7.35**
2001-02	233	818	2899	76	203	1375	5604 (100)	**17.34**	11	0	4	915	**930 (16.60)**	**18.62**	27	1186	2	0	**1215 (21.68)**	**1.42**
2002-03	189	878	2763	105	183	1150	5268 (100)	**-6.00**	3	0	1	912	**916 (17.39)**	**(1.51)**	35	1232	0	0	**1267 (24.05)**	**4.28**
2003-04	161	762	2837	128	214	1023	5125 (100)	**-2.71**	9	0	3	810	**822 (16.04)**	**(10.26)**	0	1210	0	29	**1239 (24.18)**	**(2.21)**
2004-05	42	756	3577	60	145	952	5532 (100)	**7.94**	5	558	1	776	**1340 (24.22)**	**63.02**	37	1415	1	0	**1453 (26.27)**	**17.27**
2005-06	108	887	3597	133	137	959	5821 (100)	**5.22**	8	481	1	835	**1325 (22.76)**	**(1.12)**	0	1598	0	26	**1669 (28.67)**	**14.87**
2006-07	107	631	3309	64	91	924	5126 (100)	**-11.94**	8	454	2	779	**1243 (24.25)**	**(6.19)**	58	1497	0	0	**1559 (30.41)**	**(6.59)**
2007-08	97	622	3375	136	134	880	5244 (100)	**2.30**	7	567	1	749	**1324 (25.25)**	**6.52**	0	1497	0	58	**1620 (30.89)**	**3.91**
2008-09	90	619	1946	30	139	942	3766 (100)	**-28.18**	4	667	1	799	**1471 (39.06)**	**11.10**	26	-	0	0	**26 (0.69)**	**(98.40)**
2009-10	75	553	2250	80	140	813	3911 (100)	**3.85**	4	984	2	689	**1679 (42.93)**	**14.14**	0	-	0	27	**27 (0.69)**	**3.85**
2010-11	107	831	2526	67	122	763	4416 (100)	**12.91**	7	1007	0	600	**1614 (36.55)**	**(3.87)**	0	-	0	36	**36 (0.82)**	**33.33**
2011-12	94	-	-	-	-	4640	4734 (100)	**7.20**	7	806	1	646	**1460 (30.84)**	**(9.54)**	0	-	0	33	**33 (0.70)**	**(8.33)**
2012-13	124	-		-	-	4105	4229 (100)	**-10.67**	-	-	-	1235	**1235 (29.20)**	**(15.41)**	0	-	0	31	**31 (0.73)**	**(6.06)**
2013-14	0	884	1845	79	110	1231	4224 (100)	**-0.11**	4	0	0	1150	**1154 (27.32)**	**-6.55**	0	140	0	37	**177 (4.19)**	**4.70**
2014-15	55	-	-	-	-	3833	3888 (100)	**-7.95**	0	0	0	1095	**1095 (30.27)**	**-5.11**	0	0	0	46	**46 (1.27)**	**-74.01**
2015-16	54	-	-	-	-	5798	5852 (100)	**50.51**	0	0	0	1334	**1334 (22.79)**	**21.82**	0	0	0	1808	**1808 (30.89)**	**3830.43**
Sum	2293	10855	38460	1307	2163	23617	87515 (100)		114	6075	28	14271	21723 (24.82)		244	13096	11	2158	15623 (17.85)	
CG								**2.23**						**2.37**						**219.23**
Mean	**127.38**	**775.35**	**2747.14**	**93.35**	**154.5**	**1459.18**	**4861.94**		**6.70**	**357.35**	**1.647**	**839.47**	**1206.83**		**13.56**	**727.55**	**0.611**	**119.88**	**867.94**	
SD	**81.46**	**148.20**	**562.38**	**41.67**	**37.05**	**1331.05**	**664.16**		**4.02**	**377.47**	**1.538**	**192.82**	**276.21**		**18.69**	**572.64**	**1.37**	**421.71**	**695.05**	
CV	**63.95**	**19.11**	**20.47**	**44.63**	**23.98**	**91.21**	**13.66**		**60.29**	**105.63**	**93.29**	**22.96**	**22.88**		**137.93**	**56.84**	**224.59**	**351.77**	**27.85**	

Source: , , , , 1998-99 2015-16.

3.17 Irrigated Area for Production of Fresh Fruits

Although Himachal Pradesh has favourable climatic conditions for production of different varieties of fruits, but the production highly depends on irrigation. The irrigated area under different fresh fruits is shown in table 3.17.

Data reveals that irrigated area under apple is 2,275.06 hectares (48.07%), whereas, 45.14 percent is covered by other fresh fruits and 7 percent by grapes, peaches, plum, lichi, and pears. The total irrigated area under apple and other crops in the year 1998-99 was 3,029 hectares which increased to 4,074 hectares in the year 2014-15. Moreover, irrigated area for fresh fruits has grown by 5.28 percent.

In Kinnaur, average 1,876.35 hectares irrigated area is covered by fresh fruits with S.D. = 635.72 hectares and C.V. = 34.80 percent, out of which 97 percent (1,826.64 hectares) area is irrigated for apple. Only 3 percent is under other fruits like, grapes etc. As shown in the table, peaches, plum, lichi and pears are not being covered under irrigation for commercial purpose in Kinnaur, whereas an average of 0.32 percent area (6.12 hectares) is irrigated for grapes and 2.30 percent (43.29 hectares) for other fruits. The coefficient of variance is calculated 34.80 percent for apples and compound growth in respect of fresh fruits is calculated 7.62 percent.

In Lahaul & Spiti, an average 71.47 hectare irrigated area covers fresh fruits, out of which 85.43 percent (61.06 hectares) is for apple. A compound growth of 15.74 percent is calculated and the coefficient of variance is 70.28 percent under apple.

Table-3.17 : rrigated Area for Production of resh ruits

(in hectares)

	Himachal Pradesh									Kinnaur							Lahaul S iti				
Year	A les	Gra es	Peaches	Plum	Lichi	Pears	Others	Total	Growth	A les	Gra es	Peaches	Plum	others	Total	growth	A les	Gra es	Others	Total	Growth
1998-99	1547	7	26	188	1	1	1259	3029 (100)		1171	7	0	0	0	1178 (38.89)		4	0	23	27 (0.89)	
1999-2000	1479	11	4	223	69	11	1729	3526 (100)	16.41	1201	7	0	0	0	1208 (34.25)	2.56	19	0 .	0	26 (0.74)	-4
2000-01	1981	15	78	134	51	5	1393	3657 (100)	3.72	1557	10	0	0	0	1567 (42.84)	29.72	31	0	0	31 (0.85)	19
2001-02	1706	9	4	249	75	7	1439	3489 (100)	-4.59	1324	9	0	0	0	1333 (38.20)	-14.93	31	0	4	39 (1.12)	26
2002-03	1988	9	67	122	110	11	2100	4407 (100)	26.31	1632	9	0	0	0	1641 (37.25)	23.11	52	0	0	52 (1.18)	33
2003-04	1772	6	31	94	116	6	1921	3946 (100)	-10.46	1336	6	0	0	0	1342 (34.01)	-18.22	59	0	0	59 (1.50)	13
2004-05	1727	8	64	82	1	23	2398	4303 (100)	9.05	1279	7	0	0	0	1286 (29.88)	-4.17	42	0	16	58 (1.35)	-2
2005-06	1884	8	77	136	34	6	2505	4650 (100)	8.06	1610	7	0	0	0	1617 (34.77)	25.74	40	0	16	56 (1.20)	-3
2006-07	1883	7	96	20	88	2	2293	4389 (100)	-5.61	1515	7	0	0	116	1638 (37.32)	1.3	48	0	0	67 (1.53)	20
2007-08	1994	5	62	131	65	2	2200	4459 (100)	1.59	1594	4	0	0	110	1708 (38.30)	4.27	47	1	14	62 (1.39)	-7
2008-09	2034	4	110	66	73	77	2334	4698 (100)	5.36	1637	4	0	0	112	1753 (37.31)	2.63	51	0	0	51 (1.09)	-18
2009-10	2234	4	143	158	111	1	2218	4869 (100)	3.64	1842	4	0	0	132	1978 (40.62)	12.84	71	0	0	71 (1.46)	39
2010-11	2608	6	78	91	24	82	3284	6173 (100)	26.78	2170	6	0	0	100	2276 (36.87)	15.07	71	0	15	86 (1.39)	21
2011-12	2689	8	99	171	65	20	2691	5743 (100)	-7.48	2233	6	0	0	96	2335 (40.65)	2.59	81	0	12	93 (1.61)	8.13
2012-13	3403	4	90	230	87	80	2083	5977 (100)	4.07	2672	0	1	0	4	2679 (44.82)	14.73	96	0	22	118 (1.97)	27
2013-14	3673	7	130	241	64	19	1982	6116 (100)	2.32	2968	5	1	0	0	2974 (48.62)	11.01	100	0	12	112 (1.83)	-5.08
2014-15	4074	9	111	202	119	18	2490	7023 (100)		3312	6	0	1	66	3385 (48.19)	13.81	195	0	12	207 (2.94)	84.82
CG									5.28							7.62					15.74
Mean	2275.06	7.47	74.70	149.29	67.82	21.82	2136.41	4732.59		1826.64	6.12	0.12	0.06	43.29	1876.35		61.06	0.06	8.59	71.47	
SD	766.49	2.78	40.47	66.73	36.86	28.47	504.81	1117.88		635.72	2.34	0.33	0.24	54.34	646.52		42.91	0.24	8.44	44.07	
CV	33.69	37.21	54.17	44.69	54.35	130.48	23.62	23.62		34.80	38.23	275	400	125.52	34.45		70.28	480	98.37	61.64	

Source: , , , .

3.18 Irrigated Area for Production of Dry Fruits

Kinnaur is known for production of Walnut, Almond, and Chilgoza. The irrigated area for dry fruits is sparse comprising of average 313.88 hectares in the State, out of which, 169.88 hectares is in Kinnaur and 4.70 hectares in Lahaul & Spiti. The following table shows irrigated area under dry fruits.

In the year 1998-99, irrigated area for dry fruits in the State was 184 hectares, which increased to 1,238 hectares in the year 2015-16. Similarly, in the tribal districts, total area under dry fruits increased from 184 hectares in 1998-99 to 450 hectares in 2015-16 in district Kinnaur. Whereas, in Lahaul & Spiti, it decreased to 3 hectares in 2015-16 from 27 hectares in 1998-99. Almond is the only fruit which covered about 60 percent of the irrigated area of the State with S.D. = 63.71 hectares and 34.26 percent C.V., followed by other dry fruits (103.01 hectares with S.D. = 61.84 hectares and C.V. 60.03%). Further, irrigated area under Chilgoza has accounted for highest C.V. (325%). It shows that area under Chilgoza is not consistent.

In Kinnaur, average 169.88 hectares irrigated area is covered for dry fruits, out of which 54.32 percent (92.29 hectares with S.D. = 29.09 hectares and C.V. = 31.52%) irrigated area is covered for almond and 32.19 percent is under other dry fruits (54.70 hectares with S.D. 57.51 hectares and 105.13% C.V.). Further, these two crops covered about 85 percent of the total irrigated area and the remaining 15 percent area is irrigated for chilgoza and walnut. The C.V. is 55.18 percent which indicates variation specially highest (377.04%) in chilgoza. There is 23.21 percent compound growth during the research period. Although, district Kinnaur is known for production of Chilgoza, yet it is in less irrigated area.

On the other hand, in Lahaul & Spiti, only an average 2.94 hectares (62.55%) area is irrigated for walnut, followed by 28.29 percent for other fruits and rest of the 10 percent area is irrigated under almond and chilgoza. Surprisingly, there has been a decline in Lahaul & Spiti in respect of the irrigated area for dry fruits by 25.57 percent being highly inconsistent (159.14%) during the period of the present study.

ote* 2015-16 , ,

Table-3.18 : rrigated Area for Production of Dry ruits

(in hectares)

Year	Himachal Pradesh						Kinnaur						Lahaul S iti					
	alnut	Almond	Chilgo a	Others	Total	Growth	alnut	Almond	Chilgo a	Others	Total	Growth	alnut	Almond	Chilgo a	Others	Total	Growth
1998-99	10	85	0	92	187 (100)		8	84	0	92	184 (98.40)		27	0	0	0	27 (14.44)	
1999-2000	6	97	7	104	214 (100)	14.44	4	84	7	95	190 (88.79)	3.26	2	0	0	0	2 (0.93)	-93
2000-01	12	129	0	140	271 (100)	26.64	12	112	0	134	195 (71.96)	2.63	0	0	0	0	0 0.00	(-100)
2001-02	5	96	0	193	294 (100)	8.49	5	82	0	104	191 (64.97)	(2.05)	0	2	0	0	2 (0.68)	-
2002-03	7	171	0	99	267 (100)	(9.18)	7	140	0	99	236 (88.39)	23.56	0	0	0	0	0	(-100)
2003-04	6	149	0	117	272 (100)	1.87	4	112	0	117	233 (85.39)	(1.27)	0	0	0	0	0	-
2004-05	8	213	0	135	356 (100)	30.88	6	110	0	135	251 (70.51)	7.73	0	0	0	0	-	-
2005-06	14	330	0	124	468 (100)	31.46	13	114	0	124	251 (53.63)	-	0	0	0	0	0	-
2006-07	4	208	0	3	215 (100)	(54.06)	4	99	0	0	103 (47.91)	(58.96)	0	0	0	0	0	-
2007-08	6	256	0	0	262 (100)	21.86	4	93	0	0	97 (37.02)	(5.83)	0	0	0	0	0	-
2008-09	22	228	1	23	274 (100)	4.58	4	98	0	0	102 (37.23)	5.15	3	0	1	12	16 (5.84)	-
2009-10	7	236	0	14	247 (100)	(9.85)	4	99	0	0	103 (41.70)	0.98	3	0	0	12	15 (6.07)	-
2010-11	9	192	0	11	212 (100)	(0.14)	6	101	0	0	107 (50.47)	3.88	3	0	0	0	3 (1.41)	-6
2011-12	10	218	0	27	264 (100)	24.52	3	94	0	0	97 (36.74)	(9.35)	3	0	0	0	3 (1.13)	-80
2012-13	8	166	1	6	174 (100)	-34.09	4	0	76	0	80 (45.97)	(17.52)	3	0	0	0	3 (1.72)	0
2013-14	9	218	0	22	243 (100)	39.66	5	78	0	16	99 (40.74)	23.75	3	0	0	0	3 (1.23)	0
2014-15	9	169	0	14	192 (100)	-20.99	6	69	0	14	89 (46.35)	-10.10	3	0	0	0	3 (1.56)	0
2015-16	-	-	-	-	1238 (100)	544.79	-	-	-	-	450 (36.34)	405.61	3	0	0	0	3 (0.24)	0
Sum	152	3161	9	1124	5650* (100)		99	1569	83	930	3058* (54.12)		53	2	1	24	80* (1.41)	
CG						36.52						23.21						-25.57
Mean	8.94	185.94	0.52	103.01	313.88		5.82	92.29	4.88	54.70	169.88		2.94	0.11	0.05	1.33	4.70	
S.D.	4.20	63.71	1.69	61.84	240.41		2.83	29.09	18.40	57.51	93.75		6.18	0.47	0.23	3.88	7.48	
C.V.	46.97	34.26	325	60.03	7.67		48.63	31.52	377.04	105.13	55.18		209.86	427.27	460	292.48	159.14	

Source: , , , -9, 1998-99 2015-16.

3.19 Irrigated area for Production of Vegetables

The irrigated area for vegetables in Himachal Pradesh in the year 1998-99 was 7,033 hectares, which increased to 12,302 hectares in the year 2015-16 with considerable fluctuation, ranging between 14,409 hectares in 2008-09 to 7,033 hectares in the year 1998-99.

Further, average irrigated area for vegetables is calculated 9,816.82 hectares, out of which 38.19 percent (3,749.35 hectares) area is under potato, 21.25 percent under tomato (2,086.17 hectares), 23.70 percent under other vegetables (2,326.70 hectares), 5.67 percent under onion (557.12 hectares), 5.31 percent under cauliflower (521.94 hectares) and 0.91 percent under lady finger (89.88 hectares). The coefficient of variance in respect of irrigated area for potato is 8.8 percent which indicate that potato is the crop which is grown consistently. Moreover, a compound growth of 4.99 percent is calculated in total irrigated area for vegetables in the State.

In Kinnaur, an average 241.48 hectares area is irrigated for vegetables and 43 percent irrigated area is under other vegetables, 31.61 percent under potato, and rest 25 percent under tomato and cauliflower. It is analysed that irrigated area for production of vegetables is quite scanty in the district due to which production of vegetables is meager except small amount of production of potato. Similar to Kinnaur, Lahaul & Spiti has not much irrigated land area for production of vegetables. The average area irrigated for vegetables is 1,416.76 hectares in Lahaul & Spiti, where potato is cropped in about 58 percent area (824.05 hectares).

Table-3.19 : rrigated Area for Production of Vegetables

(in hectares)

	Himachal Pradesh								Kinnaur						Lahaul S iti					
Year	Potato	Onion	Tomato	Lady finger	Cauliflower	Other	Total	Growth	Potato	Tomato	Cauliflower	Other	Total	Growth	Potato	Tomato	Cauliflower	Other	Total	Growth
1998-99	3035	486	1138	19	315	2040	7033 (100)		105	0	18	28	151 (2.15)		849	0	0	13	862 (12.26)	
1999-2000	4061	538	1321	137	339	1526	8404 (100)	19.49	97	0	26	0	432 (5.14)	186.09	813	. 0	30	16	859 (10.22)	-0.35
2000-01	3252	596	1444	161	321	1462	7236 (100)	-13.90	9	0	23	72	190 (2.63)	-56.02	885	0	2	8	895 (12.37)	4.19
2001-02	3468	583	1,771	80	783	2078	8763 (100)	21.10	124	0	21	478	623 (7.11)	227.89	850	0	6	6	862 (9.84)	-3.69
2002-03	3748	569	1781	68	436	2323	8925 (100)	1.85	80	0	11	440	531 (5.95)	-14.77	925	0	0	10	935 (10.48)	8.47
2003-04	3636	529	1854	78	585	2094	8776 (100)	-1.67	91	1	117	469	678 (7.73)	27.68	874	1	17	9	900 (10.26)	-3.74
2004-05	4259	544	1974	102	485	1505	8869 (100)	1.06	82	2	19	13	116 (1.31)	-82.89	928	2	16	7	951 (10.72)	5.67
2005-06	3876	510	2128	92	581	1350	8537 (100)	-3.74	86	0	19	1	106 (1.24)	-8.62	807	0	21	6	838 (9.82)	-11.88
2006-07	3758	933	2209	64	472	1,910	9346 (100)	9.48	81	0	33	9	123 (1.32)	16.04	813	0	7	6	829 (8.87)	-1.07
2007-08	4269	539	2133	89	397	1462	8919 (100)	-4.57	71	0	17	0	88 (0.99)	-28.46	813	0	4	9	826 (9.26)	-0.36
2008-09	3727	579	2294	52	458	1596	14409 (100)	61.55	73	0	24	0	97 0(0.67)	10.23	770	0	12	1472	2263 (15.71)	173.97
2009-10	3916	456	2359	73	537	1468	10850 (100)	-24.70	73	0	18	0	91 (0.84)	-6.19	759	0	8	18	785 (7.24)	-65.31
2010-11	4064	537	2370	65	639	3615	11290 (100)	4.06	50	0	35	0	85 (0.75)	-6.59	755	0	16	1560	2366 (20.96)	201.40
2011-12	3606	537	2326	76	547	3276	10368 (100)	-8.17	55	0	18	0	73 (0.70)	-14.12	819	0	26	1612	2473 (23.85)	4.52
2012-13	3933	509	2554	116	559	3898	11569 (100)	11.58	57	0	11	52	317 (2.74)	334.24	824	5	23	1535	2424 (20.95)	-2.18
2013-14	3654	516	2845	51	653	3571	11290 (100)	-2.41	109	0	1	16	126 (1.11)	-60.25	788	1	17	1585	2391 (21.17)	-1.36
2014-15	3477	510	2964	205	766	4380	12302 (100)	8.96	57	0	9	219	285 (2.31)	126.19	737	7	58	1824	2626 (21.34)	9.82
C.G.								4.99						40.65						19.88
Mean	3749.35	557.12	2086.17	89.88	521.94	2326.70	9816.82		76.47	0.17	24.70	105.70	241.88		824.05	0.94	15.47	570.35	1416.76	
SD	331.43	103.16	499.74	44.59	140.51	1006.32	1920.37		26.74	0.52	25.19	178.40	202.49		55.89	2.01	14.23	785.23	770.64	
CV	8.83	18.51	23.95	49.61	26.92	43.25	19.56		34.96	311.76	101.98	168.77	83.71		6.78	213.82	91.98	137.67	54.39	

Source: , , , .

Table-3.20 : Cro -wise Standard Yield

(in gs. hectare)

	Standard Yield of Cereals			Standard Yield of Pulses			Standard Yield of Vegetables			Standard Yield for on ood Cro s		
Year	HP	K	L S	HP	K	L S	HP	K	L S	HP	K	L S
1998-99	6278	6337	4692	1057	1007	795	12280	9892	23353	705	151	1533
1999-2000	7505.32	6696.3	4943.271	1912.53	1427	0	11773	5129	19280	1478	343	380
2000-01	6508.171	6994.029	4752.255	2740.79	2368	5533	10928	11040	20370	1444	314	1483
2001-02	6997.376	6829.154	5492.264	3392	2981	6889	12280	6698	28221	2487	3098	3118
2002-03	7441.028	7207.89	5593.401	3137	3011	5533	8458	6068	20976	2496	1463	2006
2003-04	6905.59	10205.467	5246.193	3169	3011	5533	11772	4509	23024	2300	0	1483
2004-05	7563.19	8440.01	5774.787	3000	1530	5533	13271	5906	24858	2170	0	1355
2005-06	6157.771	8262.505	4561.691	2398	3687	5533	13686	15246	22920	1731	2048	1483
2006-07	8333.564	9253.637	6307.391	2754	3535	5744	7802	5025	14438	2268	0	1483
2007-08	6065.11	7511.613	4980.537	2272	3135	5422	9975	6608	13697	2123	1413	44
2008-09	7191.818	8625.325	5379.791	2304	3631	2767	18771	7856	15793	2189	0	742
2009-10	7327.206	7792.227	5927.285	2112	4159	0	25567.87	41268	43994	2455	0	1489
2010-11	7217.88	6372.625	5041.957	1475	1495	5500	24490	31559	42410	2100	0	1355
2011-12	9188.322	7470.099	6396.288	4021.71	3647.36	5553.28	12838.03	8706.29	29201	2637	0	1489
2012-13	7396	8777	6012	2458	4159	5553	11335	26817	41494	2441	0	1489
2013-14	8823	7045	4884	2868	3092	1660	12141	22188	44847	2291	0	1489
2014-15	5838	6817	5095	2724	2926	2021	31247	28026	45871	3211	0	39
Mean	**7219.84376**	**7684.52235**	**5357.65359**	**2566.93938**	**2867.21**	**4221.7675**	**14624.40**	**14267.13**	**27926.29**	**2131.38889**	**490.55556**	**1249.38889**
S.D.	**931.72343**	**1089.69249**	**567.015751**	**736.293785**	**1009.2532**	**2319.71111**	**6522.05186**	**11339.5691**	**11328.2756**	**549.835712**	**902.16**	**768.324927**
C.V.	**12.9**	**14.18**	**10.58**	**28.68**	**35.19**	**54.94**	**44.59**	**79.48**	**40.56**	**25.79**	**183.9**	**61.49**

Source: , , .

3.20 Crop-wise Standard Yield

The two districts taken for the present research, have a very limited irrigated area for production of different crops and the volume of production is not much in these regions. Table depicts standard yield of cereals of these areas.

The average standard yield/production per hectare of cereals in Himachal Pradesh was 7,219.84 kg/hectares, with S.D. of 93.72 kg/hectare and coefficient of variance is 12.9 percent. The standard yield for cereal crops in Kinnaur is higher than that of the State, it was 7,684.52 kg/hectare. the coefficient of variance is slightly higher in Kinnaur from the State which shows more variation in standard yield of cereal crops in Kinnaur district. On the other hand, in Lahaul & Spiti, the average standard yield for cereals is 5,357.65 kg/hectares with S.D. 567.01 kg/hectare and coefficient of variance of 10.58 percent which is lower than that of Kinnaur. It indicates that the standard yield for cereals is lower in Lahaul & Spiti. Further, average standard yield of pulses in Himachal Pradesh was 2,566.93 kg/hectare. The maximum standard yield was 4,021.71 kg/hectare in the year 2011-12, and minimum was 1,057 kg/hectare in 1998-99. The average standard yield of pulses in Kinnaur was 2,867.21 kg/hectare, higher than the standard yield of the State. Further, Lahaul & Spiti had highest standard yield that of Kinnaur and the State, (4,221.76 kg/hectare). Moreover, the coefficient of variance has been calculated as; Himachal Pradesh 28.68 percent, Kinnaur 35.19 percent and Lahaul & Spiti 54.94 percent which shows that standard yield of pulses in Himachal Pradesh is more consistent in comparison to that in Kinnaur and Lahaul & Spiti.

Average standard yield of vegetables was highest (27,926.29 kg/hectare) in Lahaul & Spiti, followed by standard yield in the State (14,624.40 kg/hectare) and Kinnaur (14,267.13 kg/hectare). The coefficient of variance is calculated 40.56 percent in Lahaul-Spiti being more consistent in production of pulses.

The average standard yield for non-food crops in Himachal Pradesh was 2,131.38 kg/hectares with standard deviation of 549.83 kg/hectare and coefficient of variance calculated as 25.79 percent. In Kinnuar, standard yield registered higher coefficient of variation (183.9%), indicating more inconsistently in standard yield of non food crops. Whereas, in Lahaul & Spiti, standard deviation was 768.32 kg/hectare and coefficient of variance was 61.49 percent.

3.21 Standard Yield of Cereal

The two districts taken for the present research have a very limited irrigated area for production of different crops. Despite of that, these regions are characterised as fertile regions of production. However, in terms of volume of production, not much production is being contributed by these regions. In fact, the production is considered better in quality of cereals, pulses, vegetables and other crops. The following table 3.21 depicts standard yield of cereals of these areas.

The average standard yield/production per hectare of rice in the State is 1,419.38 kg, whereas in Kinnaur, it is 1,419.38 kg and rice is not produced in Lahaul & Spiti. The highest standard yield of rice was recorded 1,707.38 kg per hectare in the State and 1,707.38 kg per hectare in Kinnaur in 2006-07. Similarly, average standard yield for maize was recorded 212.14 kgs per hectare in Kinnaur and 2,102.76 kg per hectare in Lahaul & Spiti. It is analysed that rice is not produced in Lahaul & Spiti but its production of maize per hectare is almost equal to that of the State (2,134.94 kg/hectare of HP).

The coefficient of variance for rice, and maize was between 10 to 15 percent which shows that there is consistency in the production of these two crops. The average standard yield for wheat in the State was 1,388.25 kg per hectare with S.D. = 304.94 hectare and C.V. = 21.96 percent, it was 1,633.69 kg per hectare with S.D. = 235.75 and C.V. = 11.1 percent in Kinnaur and in Lahaul & Spiti; 1,389.65 kg per hectare. Thus, in Kinnaur, there is high yield with less variation. Further, average standard yield for barley in the State was 1,227.11 kg per hectare, whereas in Kinnaur, it was 1,619.88 kg/hectare and in Lahaul & Spiti, it was recorded 1,236.29 kg per hectare which is more than that of the State.

Millet is also grown in the two districts. The average standard yield for millets in the State was 498.80 kg per hectare, whereas in Kinnaur, it was 448.411 kg per hectare and in Lahaul & Spiti, it was 544.76 kg per hectare. For other cereals, average standard yield was calculated 551.34 kg per hectare within the State, whereas in Kinnaur, it was 441 kg per hectare and in Lahaul & Spiti, 84.17 kg per hectare. In the State, the standard deviation and coefficient of variance is found least for rice i.e. S.D. = 150.07 hectares and C.V. = 10.57 percent in comparison to other cereals indicating more uniformity in standard yield of rice. In Lahaul & Spiti, least variance is recoded for maize which is 12.94 percent, while in Kinnaur it was 11.1 percent.

Table-3.21 : Standard Yield er Hectare for the Princi al Cro s (Cereals)

(in gs hectare)

	Himachal Pradesh							Kinnaur							Lahaul S iti						
Year	ice	Mai e	heat	arley	Millets	Others	Total	ice	Mai e	heat	arley	Millets	Others	Total	ice	Mai e	heat	arley	Millets	Others	Total
1998-99	1238	2129	1103	1202	342	264	6278	1238	2129	1123	1127	595	125	6337	0	2129	1103	1202	258	0	4692
1999-2000	1351.185	2051.7	1564.346	1330.487	807.6	400	7505.318	1351.18	2039.05	1880.893	1035.176	390	0	6696.299	0	2039.056	1582.093	1322.122	0	0	4943.271
2000-01	1346.153	2143.715	1403.354	1268.669	346.28	0	6508.171	1346.153	2145.921	1653.145	1437.81	411	0	6994.029	0	2145.921	1411.441	1194.893	0	0	4752.255
2001-02	1328.9	1918.175	1505.55	1343.751	444	457	6997.376	1328.9	1918.175	1505.706	1665.373	411	0	6829.154	0	1918.175	1505.553	1657.536	411	0	5492.264
2002-03	1397.627	1990.257	1699.529	1492.615	458	403	7441.028	1397.627	1990.257	1795.686	1613.32	411	0	7207.89	0	1990.257	1699.529	1492.615	411	0	5593.401
2003-04	1422.789	2201.221	1267.04	1037.54	480	497	6905.59	1422.789	2201.221	2119.37	2166.087	411	1885	10205.467	0	2201.221	1267.43	1037.542	411	329	5246.193
2004-05	1500.42	2272.12	1573.99	1254.66	458	504	7563.19	1500.427	2272.126	1608.075	1308.382	411	1340	8440.01	0	2272.126	1573.993	1254.668	411	263	5774.787
2005-06	1532.08	2293.706	692.95	835.035	349	455	6157.771	1532.081	2093.706	1381.182	1363.536	411	1481	8262.505	0	2293.706	692.951	835.034	411	329	4561.691
2006-07	1707.38	2549.557	1738.16	1386.467	472	480	8333.564	1707.384	2549.77	1765.525	1338.958	411	1481	9253.637	0	2549.757	1738.167	1386.467	403	230	6307.391
2007-08	1028.58	1613.374	1378.69	1297.466	346	401	6065.11	1028.583	1613.374	1688.537	1585.119	411	1185	7511.613	0	1613.374	1378.697	1297.466	411	280	4980.537
2008-09	1483.03	2444.393	1367.6	1156.795	213	527	7191.818	1483.035	2444.393	1802.497	2484.4	411	0	8625.325	0	2444.393	1367.603	1156.795	411	0	5379.791
2009-10	1372.36	2136.843	1870.66	1392.75	75.78	478.813	7327.206	1372.369	2129.458	1743.25	2061.15	486	0	7792.227	0	1600	1869.246	1439.039	1019	0	5927.285
2010-11	1412.93	1838.7	1020.73	1163.52	480	1302	7217.88	1412.935	1838.7	1632.29	1077.7	411	0	6372.625	0	1838.7	1020.735	1163.522	1019	0	5041.957
2011-12	1559.05	2325.382	1646.65	1405.24	679	1573	9188.322	1559.057	2325.382	1487.63	1612.03	486	0	7470.099	0	2325.382	1646.657	1405.249	1019	0	6396.288
2012-13	1546	2274	1533	1309	734	0	7396	1546	2274	1857	2614	486	0	8777	0	2274	1532	1187	1019	0	6012
2013-14	1522	2273	1059	905	1433	1631	8823	1522	2273	1288	1476	486	0	7045	0	2273	1059	905	647	0	4884
2014-15	1381	1839	1176	1080	362	0	5838	1381	1839	1441	1572	584	0	6817	0	1839	1176	1080	1000	0	5095
Mean	**1419.38**	**2134.94**	**1388.25**	**1227.11**	**498.8**	**551.34**	**7219.84376**	**1419.38**	**2122.14**	**1633.69**	**1619.88**	**448.41**	**441**	**7684.52235**	**0**	**2102.76**	**1389.65**	**1236.29**	**544.76**	**84.17**	**5357.65359**
S.D.	**150.077**	**238.88**	**304.94**	**179.95**	**299.64**	**491.76**	**931.72343**	**150.07**	**235.75**	**244.17**	**461.56**	**62.71**	**700.41**	**1089.69249**	**0**	**272.04**	**305.46**	**208.92**	**348.06**	**136.12**	**567.015751**
C.V.	**10.57**	**11.18**	**21.96**	**14.66**	**60.07**	**89.19**	**12.9**	**10.57**	**11.1**	**14.94**	**28.49**	**13.98**	**158.82**	**14.18**	**0**	**12.94**	**21.98**	**16.89**	**63.89**	**161.72**	**10.58**

Source: , , , .

3.22 Standard Yield of Pulses

The standard yield of all the pulses is depicted in the table 3.22. Table 3.22 shows that average standard yield of pulses in Himachal Pradesh is 1,386.12 kg per hectare, followed by masur 432.88 kg per hectare, mash 425.56 kg per hectares, red gram 243.29 kg per hectare and other pulses is 79.07 kg per hectare. Further, the standard yield of peas has been 387 kg per hectare in the year 1998-99, which increased to 1,660 in the year 2013-14.

The maximum standard yield of peas was 2,063 kg per hectare in the year 2012-13. Moreover, the coefficient of variance has been calculated as; mash 22.46 percent, red gram 24.47 percent, masur 27.38 percent, peas 39.67 percent and other pulses 226.59 percent during the study period. It shows that yield of mash is more consistent in comparison to the yield of all other pulses in the State.

Standard yield of black gram in Kinnaur averaged 1,326.56 kg per hectare which is higher in comparison to all other pulses being produced in this district. Yield of this crop is 46.26 percent alone which indicates that it is the most dominating crop in terms of production in the district. Further, its production is consistent. Needless to state that in spite of adverse climatic conditions in majority of the period throughout the year, all major pulses crops are being produced in Kinnaur through production of other pulses has been calculated very limited confining below 30 percent.

On the contrary, in Lahaul & Spiti, Mash is not produced. Except peas which is the most dominating pulse crop of the district, other pulses are just 2.99 percent. Thus, in production of pulses, Lahaul & Spiti is much ahead particularly for production of peas which is a commercial crop of the district. However, black gram in Kinnaur is being largely produced and has emerged as the commercial crop of this district.

Table-3.22 : Standard Yield of Pulses

(in gs hectares)

	Himachal Pradesh						Kinnaur						Lahaul S iti					
Year	Mash (lac gram)	ed gram	Masur	Peas	Other Pulses	Total	Mash (lac gram)	ed gram	Masur	Peas	Other Pulses	Total	Mash (lac gram)	ed gram	Masur	Peas	Other Pulses	Total
1998-99	291	180	199	387	0	1057	312	0	200	495	0	1007	0	235	0	560	0	795
1999-2000	347.57	288.19	356.06	920.71	0	1912.53	307	0	500	620	0	1427	0	0	0	0	0	0
2000-01	275.1	232.55	362.05	1871.09	0	2740.79	1518	0	230	620	0	2368	0	0	0	5533	0	5533
2001-02	508	278	553	2053	0	3392	1530	0	1451	0	0	2981	0	0	1467	5422	0	6889
2002-03	490	274	479	1894	0	3137	1530	0	1481	0	0	3011	0	0	0	5533	0	5533
2003-04	512	236	541	1880	0	3169	1530	0	1481	0	0	3011	0	0	0	5533	0	5533
2004-05	490	242	451	1817	0	3000	1530	0	0	0	0	1530	0	0	0	5533	0	5533
2005-06	410	154	445	1389	0	2398	1530	152	1481	524	0	3687	0	0	0	5533	0	5533
2006-07	466	215	504	1569	0	2754	1530	0	1481	524	0	3535	0	0	322	5422	0	5744
2007-08	327	212	456	1277	0	2272	1331	0	1333	471	0	3135	0	0	0	5422	0	5422
2008-09	490	198	482	1134	0	2304	1530	0	1481	620	0	3631	0	0	0	2767	0	2767
2009-10	338	282	462	1030	0	2112	1543	468	636	1512	0	4159	0	0	0	0	0	0
2010-.11	347	317	185	626	0	1475	875	0	0	620	0	1495	0	0	0	5500	0	5500
2011-12	472.37	340	546.07	2063.15	600.12	4021.71	1543	468	1000	636.36	0	3647.36	0	0	0	5553.28	0	5553.28
2012-13	615	311	580	607	345	2458	1543	468	1512	636	0	4159	0	0	0	5553	0	5553
2013-14	430	133	325	1660	320	2868	1543	468	0	636	445	3092	0	0	0	1660	0	1660
Mean	**425.56**	**243.29**	**432.88**	**1386.12**	**79.07**	**2566.93938**	**1326.56**	**126.5**	**891.68**	**494.65**	**27.81**	**2867.21**	**0**	**14.6875**	**111.8125**	**4095.26**	**0**	**4221.7675**
SD	**95.59**	**59.54**	**118.53**	**549.92**	**179.17**	**736.293785**	**431**	**207.069**	**640.88**	**377.61**	**111.25**	**1009.2532**	**0**	**58.75**	**370.2018**	**2244.63**	**0**	**2319.71111**
CV	**22.46**	**24.47**	**27.38**	**39.67**	**226.59**	**28.68**	**32.49**	**163.68**	**71.87**	**76.34**	**400**	**35.19**	**0**	**400**	**331.09**	**54.81**	**0**	**54.94**

Source: , , , .

3.23 Standard Yield of Vegetables

Potato is the vegetable crop of Himachal Pradesh which is also being produced in the tribal regions of this research. The average standard yield of potato in the State was 10,533.58 kg/hectare being 72 percent of the average standard yield of all vegetables. The standard yield per hectare of potato was 12,280 kg per hectare in the year 1998-99, which decreased to 10,689 kg per hectare in 2014-15.

Further in Kinnaur, standard yield per kg of potato was 9,892 kg per hectare in the year 1998-99. However, cabbage and cauliflower had 19,023 kg per hectare followed by, other vegetables (5,736 kg per hectare) and peas (5,553 kg per hectare) in 2009-10. A considerable decrease in production of these vegetables was in the year 2014-15, (peas 572 kg per hectare, cabbage and cauliflower 14,268 kg per hectares and other vegetables 4,817 kg per hectare).

The average standard yield for potato is 8,008.54 kg per hectare followed by, cabbage and cauliflower as 4,598.82 kg per hectare and peas as 435.12 kg per hectares in the district. The coefficient of variance was 33.75 percent in respect of standard yield of potato with Standard Deviation calculated as 2,703.30 kg per hectare which is comparatively more consistent in comparison to the standard yield of all other vegetables in the district.

In Lahaul & Spiti, standard yield for potato was 23,353 kg per hectare in the year 1998-99, which decreased to 22,155 kg per hectare in the year 2014-15. Further, average standard yield of potato is 20,557.48 kg per hectares, cabbage & cauliflower is 4,714 kg per hectare and other vegetables is 1,766.05 kg per hectare. The coefficient of variance in respect of potato is least i.e. 22.24 percent.

Therefore, it can be concluded that the yield of potato is uniform despite of the fact that yield of potato has slightly declined in the district over the period under research.

Table-3.23 : Standard Yield per Hectare of Vegetables

(in kgs/hectare)

	Himachal Pradesh					Kinnaur					Lahaul & Spiti				
Year	Potato	Peas	Cabbage and Cauliflower	Other veg	Total	Potato	Peas	Cabbage and Cauliflower	Other Veg.	Total	Potato	Peas	Cabbage and Cauliflower	Other Veg.	Total
1998-99	12280	0	0	0	12280	9892	0	0	0	9892	23353	0	0	0	23353
1999-2000	10876	0	0	897	11773	5129	0	0	0	5129	19280	0	0	0	19280
2000-01	8531	0	0	2397	10928	11040	0	0	0	11040	20370	0	0	0	20370
2001-02	12280	0	0	0	12280	6698	0	0	0	6698	28221	0	0	0	28221
2002-03	8458	0	0	0	8458	6068	0	0	0	6068	20976	0	0	0	20976
2003-04	11772	0	0	0	11772	4509	0	0	0	4509	23024	0	0	0	23024
2004-05	13271	0	0	0	13271	5906	0	0	0	5906	24858	0	0	0	24858
2005-06	13686	0	0	0	13686	15246	0	0	0	15246	22920	0	0	0	22920
2006-07	7802	0	0	0	7802	5025	0	0	0	5025	14438	0	0	0	14438
2007-08	9975	0	0	0	9975	6608	0	0	0	6608	13697	0	0	0	13697
2008-09	11529	1362	0	5880	18771	7856	0	0	0	7856	15793	2765	0	4100	15793
2009-10	9967	1892	9838	3870.87	25567.87	10956	5553	19023	5736	41268	13682	5553	19023	5736	43994
2010-11	8140	1571	11263	3516	24490	8039	0	18071	5449	31559	17890	5497	19023	5736	42410
2011-12	10774.88	2063.15	0	0	12838.03	8706.29	0	0	0	8706.29	29201.32	0	0	0	29201
2012-13	9117	2218	0	0	11335	8814	636	12550	4817	26817	18487	4630	13560	4817	41494
2013-14	9923	2218	0	0	12141	7284	636	14268	4817	22188	21132	4630	14268	4817	44847
2014-15	10689	1473	14268	4817	31247	8369	572	14268	4817	28026	22155	4631	14268	4817	45871
Mean	**10533.58**	**752.77**	**2080.52**	**1257.52**	**14624.40**	**8008.54**	**435.12**	**4598.82**	**1508**	**14267.13**	**20557.48**	**1629.76**	**4714.234**	**1766.05**	**27926.29**
SD	**1781.45**	**953.11**	**4701.26**	**2012.31**	**6522.05186**	**2703.3**	**1340.55**	**7473.09**	**2417.96**	**11339.5691**	**4623.53**	**2343.39**	**7652.47**	**2489.99**	**11328.2756**
CV	**16.91**	**126.61**	**225.96**	**160.02**	**44.59**	**33.75**	**308.09**	**162.5**	**160.34**	**79.48**	**22.49**	**143.78**	**162.32**	**140.99**	**40.56**

Source: Annual Season Crop Report, Directorate of Land Records, Kasumpti, Shimla.

3.24 Standard Yield Per Hectare of Non Food Crops

Non food crops include sesamum, mustard and soyabeen etc. Standard yield per hectare of these non food crops is shown in the table 3.24. As per the table, average standard yield is recorded highest of soyabean amongst all non food crops in the State, which is 1,123.83 kg per hectare. It is 90.83 kg per hectare in both Kinnaur and Lahaul & Spiti districts which is 8.08 percent of the State. It indicates that both the tribal districts are far behind in production of soyabeen.

Further, the average standard yield of mustard is 657.55 kg per hectares followed by, sesamum (350 kg per hectares) in Himachal Pradesh. The coefficient of variance in respect of sesamum, mustard and soyabeen, has been calculated as 24.08 percent, 78.83 percent and 40.24 percent respectively. Thus, it signifies that sesamum is most consistent among the three crops. Further, high inconsistency has been found in the yield of mustard with high coefficient of variance i.e. 78.83 percent.

In Kinnaur, average standard yield of mustard, soyabeen and sesamum is 367.22 kg, 90.83 kg and 32.50 kg per hectare respectively. The standard yield of mustard was 151 kg per hectare at the beginning of the study period i.e. 1998-99. It indicates that mustard is the major non food crop in district Kinnaur.

In Lahaul & Spiti, an average standard yield of 1,129.5 kg/hectare was recorded of mustard, followed by, soyabeen (90.83 kg per hectare) and sesamum (29.05 kg per hectare). Standard yield of mustard was 1,533 kg per hectare in the year 1998-99, which decreased to 29 kg per hectare in the year 2015-16. Moreover, yield of sesamum was 523 kg per hectare in the year 2002-03 and soyabeen was 1,635 kg per hectare in the year 2001-02. It indicates that yield of mustard per hectare is more and much consistent.

Table-3.24 : Standard Yield per Hectare of Non Food Crops

(in kgs/hectare)

Year	Himachal Pradesh				Kinnaur				Lahaul & Spiti			
	Sesamum	Mustered	Soyabeen	Total	Sesamum	Mustered	Soyabeen	Total	Sesamum	Mustered	Soyabeen	Total
1998-99	237 (100)	138 (100)	330 (100)	705	0 (0.00)	151 (109.42)	0 (0.00)	151	0 (0.00)	1533 (1110.87)	0 (0.00)	1533
1999-2000	257 (100)	461 (100)	760 (100)	1478	0 (0.00)	343 (74.40)	0 (0.00)	343	0 (0.00)	380 (82.43)	0 (0.00)	380
2000-01	253 (100)	431 (100)	760 (100)	1444	0 (0.00)	314 (72.85)	0 (0.00)	314	0 (0.00)	1483 (344.08)	0 (0.00)	1483
2001-02	434 (100)	709 (100)	1344 (100)	2487	0 (0.00)	1463 (203.19)	1635 (121.65)	3098	0 (0.00)	1483 (209.17)	1635 (121.65)	3118
2002-03	435 (100)	720 (100)	1341 (100)	2496	0 (0.00)	1463 (204.04)	0 (0.00)	1463	523 (120.51)	1483 (205.97)	0 (0.00)	2006
2003-04	396 (100)	717 (100)	1187 (100)	2300	0 (0.00)	0 (0.00)	0 (0.00)	0	0 (0.00)	1483 (206.83)	0 (0.00)	1483
2004-05	423 (100)	641 (100)	1106 (100)	2170	0 (0.00)	0 (0.00)	0 (0.00)	0	0 (0.00)	1355 (211.39)	0 (0.00)	1355
2005-06	303 (100)	508 (100)	920 (100)	1731	585 138.30	1463 (212.95)	0 (0.00)	2048	0 (0.00)	1483 (291.93)	0 (0.00)	1483
2006-07	354 (100)	687 (100)	1227 (100)	2268	0 (0.00)	0 (0.00)	0 (0.00)	0	0 (0.00)	1483 (215.87)	0 (0.00)	1483
2007-08	272 (100)	453 (100)	1398 (100)	2123	0 (0.00)	1413 (274.90)	0 (0.00)	1413	0 (0.00)	44 (9.71)	0 (0.00)	44
2008-09	392 (100)	514 (100)	1283 (100)	2189	0 (0.00)	0 (0.00)	0 (0.00)	0	0 (0.00)	742 (144.36)	0 (0.00)	742
2009-10	500 (100)	537 (100)	1418 (100)	2455	0 (0.00)	0 (0.00)	0 (0.00)	0	0 (0.00)	1489 (277.28)	0 (0.00)	1489
2010-11	402 (100)	285 (100)	1413 (100)	2100	0 (0.00)	0 (0.00)	0 (0.00)	0	0 (0.00)	1355 (475.43)	0 (0.00)	1355
2011-12	449 (100)	507 (100)	1681 (100)	2637	0 (0.00)	0 (0.00)	0 (0.00)	0	0 (0.00)	1489 (293.69)	0 (0.00)	1489
2012-13	353 (100)	408 (100)	1680 (100)	2441	0 (0.00)	0 (0.00)	0 (0.00)	0	0 (0.00)	1489 (364.95)	0 (0.00)	1489
2013-14	351 (100)	267 (100)	1673 (100)	2291	0 (0.00)	0 (0.00)	0 (0.00)	0	0 (0.00)	1489 (557.68)	0 (0.00)	1489
2014-15	266 (100)	2427 (100)	518 (100)	3211	0 (0.00)	0 (0.00)	0 (0.00)	0	0 (0.00)	39 (7.52)	0 (0.00)	39
2015-16	223 (100)	1426 (100)	190 (100)	1839	0 (0.00)	0 (0.00)	0 (0.00)	0	0 (0.00)	29 (2.03)	0 (0.00)	29
Mean	350	657.55	1123.83	2131.38889	32.5	367.22	90.83	490.55556	29.055	1129.5	90.83	1249.38889
SD	84.30	518.37	452.32	549.835712	137.88	605.33	385.37	902.16	123.27	585.19	385.37	768.324927
CV	24.08	78.83	40.24	25.79	424.24	164.84	424.27	183.9	424.33	51.8	424.27	61.49

Source: Annual Season Crop Report, Directorate of Land Records, Kasumpti, Shimla-9, 1998-99 to 2015-16.

3.25 Outturn of Crops

The average outturn of cereals in Himachal was 13,53,617.39 metric tons ranged between 15,85,480 metric tons in 2005-06 and 10,38,710 in the year 2013-14 and the coefficient of variance was 12.14 percent.

On the contrary, in Kinnaur, average turnover of cereals during the study period was 4,456.38 metric tons (only 0.32% of average outturn of State) and in Lahaul & Spiti 1,030.27 metric tons (only 0.07% of average outturn of State). The coefficient of variance is calculated 22.22 percent in Kinnaur and 23.2 percent in Lahaul & Spiti which is indicating a meager difference between both the districts. However, the average Outturn of Cereal Crops is more in Kinnaur as compared to Lahaul & Spiti.

As per table 3.25 Average Outturn of Pulses of the State was 18,338.41 metric tons. Which ranged between 33,663 metric tons in the year 2002-03 and minimum 5,426 metric tons in the year 2014-15. The coefficient of variance was 35.66 percent with Standard Deviation of 6,541.67 metric tons.

In Kinnaur, the Average Outturn of Pulses was 1,020.33 metric tons (5.56% of the State) whereas, outturn of pulses was 1,556 metric tons in Lahaul & Spiti in the year 1998-99, which decreased to 15 metric tons in the year 2015-16. However, average outturn was 3,665.41 metric tons. It is analysed from the data that Lahaul & Spiti is much ahead as compared to Kinnaur in production of pulses.

The average outturn of vegetables in Himachal Pradesh is calculated 1,92,289.65 metric tons with S.D. = 62,885.55 metric tons and C.V. = 32.7 percent. It was 1,30,795 metric tons in the year 1998-99, which increased to 1,60,855 metric tons in 2015-16. In Kinnaur, average outturn of Vegetables is calculated 1,657.53 metric tons which is 0.86 percent of the State. In Lahaul & Spiti, it was 20,010.29 metric tons which is 10.40 percent of the State. It is concluded that the production of vegetables is more in Lahaul & Spiti as compared to Kinnaur.

Table-3.25 : Outturn of Crops

	Outturn of Cereals			Outturn of Pulses			Outturn of Vegetables		
Year	H.P	K	L&S	H.P	K	L&S	H.P	K	L&S
1998-1999	1377603 **(100)**	4419 **(0.32)**	1595 **(0.01)**	15335 **(100)**	961 **(6.27)**	1556 **(10.15)**	130795 **(100)**	1390 **(1.06)**	15675 **(11.98)**
1999-2000	1317679 **(100)**	5255 **(0.40)**	1123 **(0.01)**	18611 **(100)**	778 **(4.18)**	6468 **(34.75)**	124718 **(100)**	2892 **(2.32)**	18027 **(14.45)**
2000-01	1303459 **(100)**	5148 **(0.39)**	1172 **(0.09)**	22888 **(100)**	341 **(1.49)**	6446 **(28.16)**	149416 **(100)**	1708 **(1.14)**	23988 **(16.05)**
2001-02	1434071 **(100)**	5394 **(0.38)**	1255 **(0.01)**	25717 **(100)**	1634 **(6.35)**	6835 **(26.58)**	122653 **.(100)**	1450 **(1.18)**	19403 **(15.82)**
2002-03	1298460 **(100)**	5850 **(0.45)**	1055 **(0.01)**	33663 **(100)**	1452 **(4.31)**	6694 **(19.89)**	153303 **(100)**	1100 **(0.72)**	20123 **(13.13)**
2003-04	1427477 **(100)**	4428 **(0.31)**	1112 **(0.01)**	24316 **(100)**	1322 **(5.44)**	7829 **(32.20)**	182543 **(100)**	1441 **(0.79)**	23068 **(12.64)**
2004-05	1362166 **(100)**	5112 **(0.38)**	760 **(0.01)**	20322 **(100)**	1665 **(8.19)**	8862 **(43.61)**	191453 **(100)**	2927 **(1.53)**	18496 **(9.66)**
2005-06	1585480 **(100)**	4563 **(0.29)**	1145 **(0.01)**	22542 **(100)**	1716 **(7.61)**	8130 **(36.07)**	108207 **(100)**	1000 **(0.92)**	11738 **(10.85)**
2006-07	1100979 **(100)**	4028 **(0.37)**	1006 **(0.01)**	19206 **(100)**	1361 **(7.09)**	8149 **(42.43)**	143054 **(100)**	1779 **(1.24)**	11136 **(7.78)**
2007-08	1385706 **(100)**	6708 **(0.48)**	859 **(0.01)**	13884 **(100)**	2024 **(14.58)**	20 **(0.14)**	229421 **(100)**	1328 **(0.58)**	16848 **(7.34)**
2008-09	1476702 **(100)**	4522 **(0.31)**	1248 **(0.01)**	13335 **(100)**	1106 **(8.29)**	13 **(0.10)**	264750 **(100)**	2452 **(0.92)**	19475 **(7.28)**
2009-10	1058785 **(100)**	2975 **(0.28)**	979 **(0.01)**	14464 **(100)**	949 **(6.56)**	17 **(0.12)**	215550 **(100)**	1849 **(0.86)**	22413 **(10.40)**
2010-11	1450517 **(100)**	3823 **(0.26)**	1044 **(0.07)**	12164 **(100)**	981 **(8.06)**	15 **(0.12)**	264804 **(100)**	1673 **(0.63)**	33159 **(12.52)**
2011-12	1404658 **(100)**	4656 **(0.33)**	804 **(0.05)**	20147 **(100)**	0 **(0)**	451 **(2.23)**	307384 **(100)**	1815 **(0.59)**	22712 **(7.38)**
2012-13	1214531 **(100)**	3495 **(0.28)**	735 **(0.06)**	17642 **(100)**	867 **(4.91)**	790 **(4.47)**	243704 **(100)**	1002 **(0.41)**	24192 **(9.92)**
2013-14	1038710 **(100)**	2514 **(0.24)**	587 **(0.05)**	12091 **(100)**	570 **(4.71)**	20 **(0.16)**	279524 **(100)**	1427 **(0.51)**	25408 **(9.08)**
2014-15	1553630 **(100)**	3700 **(0.23)**	1087 **(0.07)**	5426 **(100)**	352 **(6.5)**	17 **(0.31)**	157645 **(100)**	945 **(0.60)**	14314 **(9.08)**
2015-16	1574500 **(100)**	3625 **(0.24)**	979 **(0.06)**	5955 **(100)**	287 **(4.81)**	15 **(.25)**	160855 **(100)**	1286 **(.8)**	15924 **(9.90)**
Mean	**1353617.39**	**4456.38**	**1030.27**	**18338.41**	**1020.33**	**3665.41**	**192289.65**	**1657.53**	**20010.29**
S.D	**164391.71**	**1035.66**	**231.67**	**6541.67**	**567.05**	**3725.71**	**62885.547**	**604.64**	**5437.57**
C.V	**12.14**	**22.22**	**23.2**	**35.66**	**55.58**	**101.6**	**32.7**	**36.45**	**27.17**

Source: Annual Season Crop Report, directorate of Land Records Kusumpti, Shimla.

Outturn of Fresh Fruits has fluctuated from 4,44,609 tons in 1998-99 to 9,28,830 tons in 2015-16.The data depicts that during 1998-99 to 2015-16, the outturn of fresh fruits in Himachal Pradesh has grown by 39.05 percent while, in Lahaul & Spiti, it has grown by 25.28 percent and in Kinnaur, by 7.96 percent. Data indicates that outturn of fresh fruits in the State as well as in these districts did not remain stagnant particularly till 2001-02.

Outturn of Crops (Continued)

	Outturn of Dry Fruits			Outturn of Fresh Fruits			Outturn of Non Food Crops		
Year	**H.P**	**K**	**L&S**	**H.P**	**K**	**L&S**	**H.P**	**K**	**L&S**
1998-1999	2456 (100)	325 (13.23)	4 (0.20)	444609 (100)	24713 (5.58)	94 (0.02)	5687 (100)	5 (0.09)	23 (0.40)
1999-2000	3075 (100)	482 (15.67)	7 (0.20)	875200 (100)	18572 (2.12)	70 (0.007)	11451 (100)	72 (0.63)	746 (6.51)
2000-01	1895 (100)	364 (19.21)	4 (0.20)	425294 (100)	15528 (3.65)	67 (0.01)	12688 (100)	11 (0.09)	562 (4.43)
2001-02	2755 (100)	512 (18.58)	8 (0.30)	258878 (100)	21918 (8.46)	123 (0.05)	10595 (100)	102 (0.96)	698 (6.59)
2002-03	4568 (100)	773 (16.92)	16 (0.40)	454420 (100)	18861 (4.15)	117 (0.02)	10547 (100)	6 (0.06)	30 (0.28)
2003-04	5203 (100)	1195 (22.97)	7 (0.10)	552825 (100)	22211 (4.01)	44 (0.007)	10142 (100)	19 (0.19)	31 (0.31)
2004-05	7152 (100)	1342 (18.76)	8 (0.11)	685870 (100)	33168 (4.83)	158 (0.02)	9783 (100)	2 (0.02)	24 (0.25)
2005-06	6141 (100)	886 (14.43)	19 (0.31)	689353 (100)	38132 (5.53)	219 (0.03)	9922 (100)	0 (0.00)	16 (0.16)
2006-07	6164 (100)	459 (7.45)	22 (0.36)	263423 (100)	41173 (15.62)	205 (0.07)	9283 (100)	1 (0.01)	4 (0.04)
2007-08	5680 (100)	412 (7.25)	15 (0.26)	706612 (100)	40379 (5.71)	197 (0.02)	8138 (100)	0 (0.00)	0 (0.00)
2008-09	6227 (100)	403 (6.47	7 (0.11)	621306 (100)	41644 (6.70)	484 (0.07)	8696 (100)	1 (0.01)	14 (0.16)
2009-10	6770 (100)	396 (5.84)	5 (0.07)	377226 (100)	55271 (14.65)	585 (0.15)	10018 (100)	0 (0.00)	101 (1.01)
2010-11	5011 (100)	765 (15.26)	15 (0.29)	1020860 (100)	40529 (3.97)	196 (0.01)	6444 (100)	1 (0.02)	93 (1.44)
2011-12	6991 (100)	287 (4.10)	4 (0.05)	367897 (100)	63886 (17.36)	208 (0.05)	8658 (100)	0 (0.00)	109 (1.25)
2012-13	4926 (100)	210 (4.26)	10 (0.20)	549637 (100)	53371 (9.71)	140 (0.02)	7180 (100)	0 (0.00)	0 (0.00)
2013-14	6071 (100)	348 (5.73)	72 (1.18)	859701 (100)	52087 (6.05)	185 (0.02)	15442 (100)	2 (0.01)	75 (0.48)
2014-15	6643 (100)	259 (3.89)	26 (0.39)	866330 (100)	54134 (6.24)	209 (0.02)	9066 (100)	10 (0.11)	138 (1.52)
2015-16	7118 (100)	407 (5.71)	33 (0.46)	928830 (100)	59295 (6.38)	287 (0.03)	9001 (100)	0 (0)	122 (1.35)
Mean	**5269.22**	**545.83**	**15.656**	**608237.28**	**38604**	**199.33**	**9596.72**	**12.89**	**154.78**
S.D	**1699.41**	**318.17**	**16.02**	**235033.45**	**15534.16**	**138.39**	**2239.98**	**27.91**	**242.78**
C.V	**32.88**	**59.92**	**105.67**	**38.64**	**40.23**	**69.34**	**23.34**	**216.52**	**156.85**

Source: Annual Season Crop Report, directorate of Land Records Kusumpti, Shimla.

Moreover, standard deviation in respect of outturn of fresh fruits in Himachal Pradesh has been calculated 2,35,033.45 metric tons with C.V. 38.64 percent indicating a fluctuating trend of outturn of fresh fruits in the State.

The outturn of dry fruits in the tribal districts (Kinnaur and Lahaul & Spiti) has almost similar trend like fresh fruits. The average outturn of dry fruits is 5,269.22 metric tons in Himachal Pradesh with coefficient of variance of 32.88 percent and standard deviation 1,699.41 metric tons. Data indicates that out of average 5,269.22 metric tons, 545.83 metric tons (10.35%) was in Kinnaur and 15.65 metric tons (0.29%) was in Lahaul & Spiti. Therefore, Kinnaur is ahead in production of dry fruits as compared to Lahaul & Spiti.

The average outturn of non- food crops in the State included Sesamum, Mustard and Soyabeen, has been analyzed to be 9,596.72 metric tons with standard deviation of 2,239.98 metric tons, and coefficient of variance of 23.34 percent which indicates less variance in production of non-food crops in the State as compared to both the districts while the S.D. is 2,239.98 metric tons. Further, the growth of these crops in the State is calculated 8.66 percent.

In Kinnaur, an average of 12.89 metric tons of non- food crops is produced every year and in Lahaul & Spiti, it is 154.78 metric tons. The production of non-food crops is very less in Kinnaur as compared to Lahaul & Spiti. The coefficient of variance of outturn in non food crops is more than 150 percent in both the districts, showing least uniformity in the production of non food crops in these districts in comparison to other districts of the State. However, coefficient of variance is less in Lahaul & Spiti in comparison to Kinnaur, depicting slightly more uniformity in the production of non- food crops in this district.

3.26 Outturn of Cereals

Outturn of cereals is analysed as under:

As per table 3.26 shown in Average Outturn of cereals.

Table-3.26 : Outturn of Cereals

(in metric tons)

Year	Himachal Pradesh		Kinnaur		Lahaul & Spiti	
	Cereals	Growth	Cereals	Growth	Cereals	Growth
1998-99	1377603 (100)		4419 (0.32)		1595 (0.01)	
1999-2000	1317679 (100)	-4.35	5255 (0.40)	18.91	1123 (0.01)	-29.59
2000-01	1303459 (100)	-1.08	5148 (0.39)	-2.04	1172 (0.09)	4.36
2001-02	1434071 (100)	10.02	5394 (0.38)	4.78	1255 (0.01)	7.08
2002-03	1298460 (100)	-9.46	5850 (0.45)	8.45	1055 (0.01)	-15.94
2003-04	1427477 (100)	9.94	4428 (0.31)	-24.31	1112 (0.01)	5.40
2004-05	1362166 (100)	-4.58	5112 (0.38)	15.45	760 (0.01)	-31.65
2005-06	1585480 (100)	16.39	4563 (0.29)	-10.74	1145 (0.01)	50.66
2006-07	1100979 (100)	-30.56	4028 (0.37)	-11.72	1006 (0.01)	-12.14
2007-08	1385706 (100)	25.86	6708 (0.48)	66.53	859 (0.01)	-14.61
2008-09	1476702 (100)	6.57	4522 (0.31)	-32.59	1248 (0.01)	45.29
2009-10	1058785 (100)	-28.30	2975 (0.28)	-34.21	979 (0.01)	-21.55
2010-11	1450517 (100)	36.99	3823 (0.26)	28.50	1044 (0.07)	6.64
2011-12	1404658 (100)	-3.16	4656 (0.33)	21.78	804 (0.05)	-22.99
2012-13	1214531 (100)	-13.53	3495 (0.28)	-24.93	735 (0.06)	-8.58
2013-14	1038710 (100)	-14.47	2514 (0.24)	-28.08	587 (0.05)	-20.14
2014-15	1553630 (100)	49.57	3700 (0.23)	47.17	1087 (0.07)	85.17
2015-16	1574500 (100)	1.34	3625 (0.24)	-2.02	979 (0.06)	-11.03
C.G.		**2.77**		**-2.41**		-1.06
Mean	**1353617.39**		**4456.38**		**1030.28**	
SD	**164391.71**		**1035.66**		**231.68**	
CV	**12.14**		**22.27**		**23.2**	

Source: Annual Season Crop Report, Directorate of Land Records, Kusumpti, Shimla.

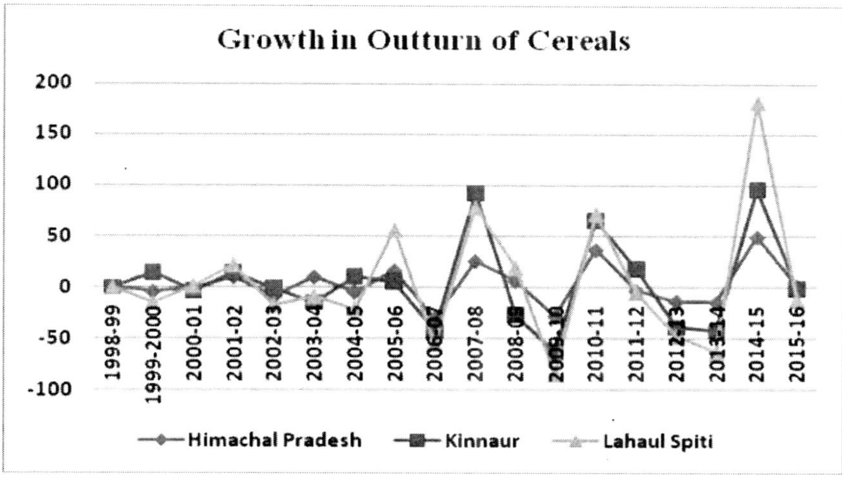

Figure-3.5 : Growth in Outturn of Cereals

The average outturn of cereals was 13,53,617.39 metric tons ranged between 15,85,480 metric tons in 2005-06 and 10,38,710 in the year 2013-14 with 2.77 percent compound growth. The coefficient of variance is 12.14 percent.

On the contrary, in Kinnaur, average turnover of cereals during the study period was 4,456.38 metric tons (only 0.32% of average production of State) and in Lahaul & Spiti 1,030.27 metric tons (only 0.07% of average production of State). Surprisingly, outturn of cereals has recorded a decline over the research period as the compound growth has shown a decline by 2.41 percent in Kinnaur and 1.06 percent in Lahaul & Spiti.

3.27 Outturn of Pulses

As per table 3.27, average outturn of pulses during the study period in Himachal Pradesh was 18,338.41 metric tons. Highest outturn was 33,663 metric tons in the year 2002-03 and minimum was 5,426 metric tons in the year 2014-15. The coefficient of variance was 35.66 percent with Standard Deviation of 6,541.67 metric tons. The growth trend of pulses is fluctuating during these years.

In Kinnaur, the average outturn of pulses was 1,020.33 metric tons (5.56% of the State) and the highest outturn was 2,024 metric tons in the year 2007-08.

Outturn of pulses was 1,556 metric tons in Lahaul & Spiti in the year 1998-99, which decreased to 15 metric tons in the year 2015-16. However, average outturn was 3,665.41 metric tons. It is analysed from the data that Lahaul & Spiti is much ahead as compared to Kinnaur in production of pulses.

Table-3.27 : Outturn of Pulses

(in metric tons)

Year	Himachal Pradesh		Kinnaur		Lahaul & Spiti	
	Pulses	Growth	Pulses	Growth	Pulses	Growth
1998-99	15335 **(100)**		961 **(6.27)**		1556 **(10.15)**	
1999-2000	18611 **(100)**	21.36	778 **(4.18)**	-19.04	6468 **(34.75)**	**315.68**
2000-01	22888 **(100)**	22.98	341 **(1.49)**	-56.17	6446 **(28.16)**	**-0.34**
2001-02	25717 **(100)**	12.36	1634 **(6.35)**	379.18	6835 **(26.58)**	**6.03**
2002-03	33663 **(100)**	30.90	1452 **(4.31)**	-11.14	6694 **(19.89)**	**-2.06**
2003-04	24316 **(100)**	-27.77	1322 **(5.44)**	-8.95	7829 **(32.20)**	**16.96**
2004-05	20322 **(100)**	-16.43	1665 **(8.19)**	25.95	8862 **(43.61)**	**13.19**
2005-06	22542 **(100)**	10.92	1716 **(7.61)**	3.06	8130 **(36.07)**	**-8.26**
2006-07	19206 **(100)**	-14.80	1361 **(7.09)**	-20.69	8149 **(42.43)**	**0.23**
2007-08	13884 **(100)**	-27.71	2024 **(14.58)**	48.71	20 **(0.14)**	**-99.75**
2008-09	13335 **(100)**	-3.95	1106 **(8.29)**	-45.36	13 **(0.10)**	**-35.00**
2009-10	14464 **(100)**	8.47	949 **(6.56)**	-14.20	17 **(0.12)**	**30.77**
2010-11	12164 **(100)**	-15.90	981 **(8.06)**	3.37	15 **(0.12)**	**-11.76**
2011-12	20147 **(100)**	65.62	0 **(0)**	-100	451 **(2.23)**	**2906.67**
2012-13	17642 **(100)**	-12.43	867 **(4.91)**	100	790 **(4.47)**	**75.17**
2013-14	12091 **(100)**	-31.46	570 **(4.71)**	-34.25	20 **(0.16)**	**-97.46**
2014-15	5426 **(100)**	**-55**	352 **(6.5)**	**-38.24**	17 **(0.31)**	**-15**
2015-16	5955 **(100)**	**9.74**	287 **(4.81)**	**-18.46**	15 **(.25)**	**-13.33**
C.G.		**-1.35**		**11.39**		**181.27**
Mean	**18338.41**		**1020.33**		**3665.41**	
SD	**6541.67**		**567.05**		**3725.71**	
CV	**35.66**		**55.58**		**101.6**	

Source: Annual Season Crop Report, Directorate of Land Records, Kusumpti, Shimla, 1998-99 to 2015-16.

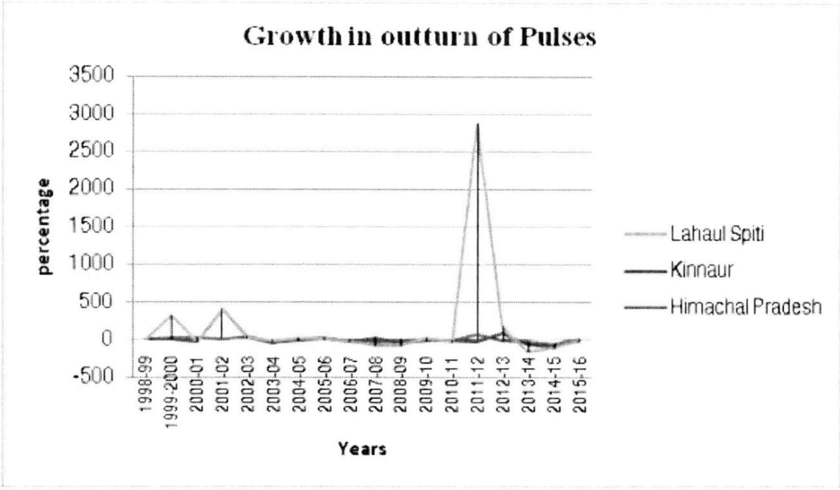

Figure-3.6 : Growth in Outturn of Pulses

3.28 Outturn of Vegetables

Outturn of vegetables is as shown in Table 3.28. The average outturn of vegetables in Himachal Pradesh is 1,92,289.65 metric tons with S.D. = 62,885.55 metric tons and C.V. = 32.7 percent. It was 1,30,795 metric tons in the year 1998-99, which increased to 1,60,855 metric tons in 2015-16.

Further, highest production of, 3,07,384 metric tons was in 2011-12 and minimum was 1,08,207 metric tons in 2005-06. A positive compound growth of 4.93 percent is calculated in these years.

In Kinnaur, average outturn is 1,657.53 metric tons which is 0.86 percent of the State. In Lahaul & Spiti, it is 20,010.29 metric tons which is 10.40 percent of the State. Both the districts have recorded a positive compound growth with Kinnaur at 12.21 percent and Lahaul & Spiti at 3.06 percent and it is concluded that the production of vegetables is more in Lahaul & Spiti as compared to Kinnaur.

Table-3.28 : Outturn of Vegetables

(in metric tons)

Year	Himachal Pradesh		Kinnaur		Lahaul & Spiti	
	Vegetables	Growth	Vegetables	Growth	Vegetables	Growth
1998-99	130795 **(100)**		1390 **(1.06)**		15675 **(11.98)**	
1999-2000	124718 **(100)**	-4.65	2892 **(2.32)**	108.06	18027 **(14.45)**	15.00
2000-01	149416 **(100)**	19.80	1708 **(1.14)**	-40.94	23988 **(16.05)**	33.07
2001-02	122653 **(100)**	-17.91	1450 **(1.18)**	-15.11	19403 **(15.82)**	-19.11
2002-03	153303 **(100)**	24.99	1100 **(0.72)**	-24.14	20123 **(13.13)**	3.71
2003-04	182543 **(100)**	19.07	1441 **(0.79)**	31.00	23068 **(12.64)**	14.63
2004-05	191453 **(100)**	4.88	2927 **(1.53)**	103.12	18496 **(9.66)**	-19.82
2005-06	108207 **(100)**	-43.48	1000 **(0.92)**	-65.84	11738 **(10.85)**	-36.54
2006-07	143054 **(100)**	32.20	1779 **(1.24)**	77.90	11136 **(7.78)**	-5.13
2007-08	229421 **(100)**	60.37	1328 **(0.58)**	-25.35	16848 **(7.34)**	51.59
2008-09	264750 **(100)**	16.58	2452 **(0.92)**	84.64	19475 **(7.28)**	15.09
2009-10	215550 **(100)**	-19.41	1849 **(0.86)**	-24.59	22413 **(10.40)**	3.90
2010-11	264804 **(100)**	22.85	1673 **(0.63)**	-9.51	33159 **(12.52)**	47.94
2011-12	307384 **(100)**	16.07	1815 **(0.59)**	8.48	22712 **(7.38)**	-31.50
2012-13	243704 **(100)**	-20.71	1002 **(0.41)**	-44.79	24192 **(9.92)**	6.51
2013-14	279524 **(100)**	14.69	1427 **(0.51)**	42.41	25408 **(9.08)**	5.02
2014-15	157645 **(100)**	-43.60	945 **(0.60)**	-33.77	14314 **(9.08)**	-43.66
2015-16	160855 **(100)**	2.03	1286 **(.8)**	36.08	15924 **(9.90)**	11.24
C.G.		**4.93**		**12.21**		**3.06**
Mean	**192289.65**		**1657.53**		**20010.29**	
SD	**62885.55**		**604.64**		**5437.57**	
CV	**32.7**		**36.45**		**27.17**	

Source: Annual Season Crop Report, Directorate of Land Records, Kusumpti, Shimla, 1998-99 to 2015-16.

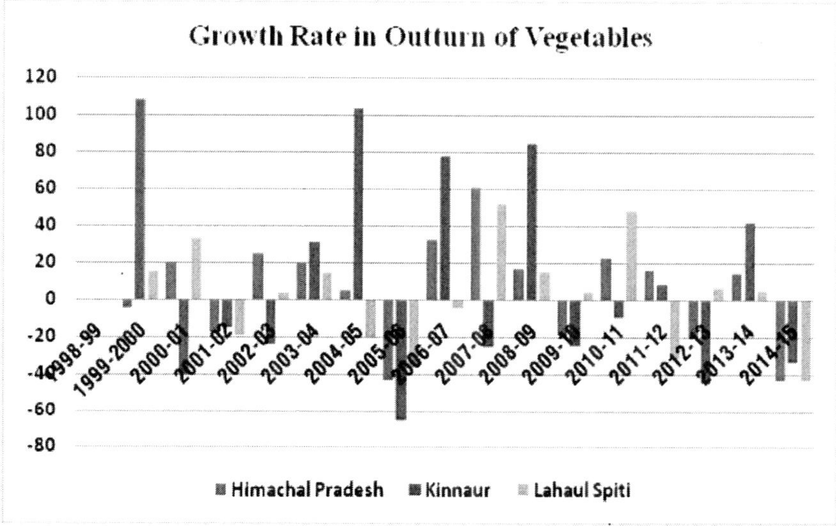

Figure-3.7 : Growth Rate in Outturn of Vegetables

3.29 Outturn of Fresh Fruits

Outturn of fresh fruits has recorded fluctuation from 4,44,609 tons in 1998-99 to 9,28,830 tons in 2015-16. The data depicts that during 1998-99 to 2015-16, the outturn of fresh fruits in Himachal Pradesh has grown by 39.05 percent while, in Lahaul & Spiti, it has grown by 25.28 percent and in Kinnaur, by 7.96 percent. Data indicates that outturn of fresh fruits in the State as well as in these districts did not remain stagnant particularly till 2001-02. It is pertinent to mention that out of average (6,08,237.28 tons) outturn of fresh fruits in Himachal Pradesh, 38,604.36 metric tons was in Kinnaur and 199.33 metric tons was in Lahaul & Spiti.

Further, there has been a variance of 40.23 percent in Kinnaur and 69.34 percent in Lahaul & Spiti. It is analysed that the least coefficient of variance in district Kinnaur shows consistency in the production of fresh fruits in Kinnaur as compared to Lahaul & Spiti.

Moreover, the outturn of fresh fruits in Himachal Pradesh has recorded standard deviation of 2,35,033.45 tons which shows a big gap between average production and actual production, with C.V. 38.64 percent indicating a fluctuating trend of outturn of fresh fruits in Himachal Pradesh.

Table-3.29 : Outturn of Fresh Fruits

(in metric tons)

Year	Himachal Pradesh		Kinnaur		Lahaul & Spiti	
	Fresh Fruits	Growth	Fresh Fruits	Growth	Fresh Fruits	Growth
1998-99	444609 (100)		24713 (5.58)		94 (0.02)	
1999-2000	875200 (100)	-80.32	18572 (2.12)	-24.84	70 (0.007)	-25.53
2000-2001	425294 (100)	385.94	15528 (3.65)	-16.39	67 (0.01)	-4.29
2001-02	258878 (100)	-39.13	21918 (8.46)	41.15	123 (0.05)	83.58
2002-03	454420 (100)	75.53	18861 (4.15)	-13.95	117 (0.02)	-4.88
2003-04	552825 (100)	21.66	22211 (4.01)	17.76	44 (0.007)	-62.39
2004-05	685870 (100)	24.07	33168 (4.83)	49.33	158 (0.02)	259.09
2005-06	689353 (100)	0.51	38132 (5.53)	14.97	219 (0.03)	38.61
2006-07	263423 (100)	-61.79	41173 (15.62)	7.97	205 (0.07)	-6.39
2007-08	706612 (100)	168.24	40379 (5.71)	-1.93	197 (0.02)	-3.90
2008-09	621306 (100)	-12.07	41644 (6.70)	3.13	484 (0.07)	145.69
2009-10	377226 (100)	-39.28	55271 (14.65)	32.72	585 (0.15)	20.86
2010-11	1020860 (100)	170.62	40529 (3.97)	-26.67	196 (0.01)	-66.49
2011-12	367897 (100)	-63.96	63886 (17.36)	57.63	208 (0.05)	6.12
2012-13	549637 (100)	49.39	53371 (9.71)	-16.45	140 (0.02)	-32.69
2013-14	859701 (100)	56.41	52087 (6.05)	-2.40	185 (0.02)	32.14
2014-15	866330 (100)	0.77	54134 (6.24)	3.92	209 (0.02)	12.97
2015-16	928830 (100)	7.21	59295 (6.38)	9.53	287 (0.03)	37.32
C.G.		**39.05**		**7.96**		**25.28**
Mean	**608237.28**		**38604**		**199.33**	
SD	**235033.45**		**15534.16**		**138.38**	
CV	**38.64**		**40.23**		**69.34**	

Source: Horticultural Development Facts & Figures, Horticulture Department Himachal Pradesh, Nigam Vihar, Shimla, 1998-99 to 2015-16.

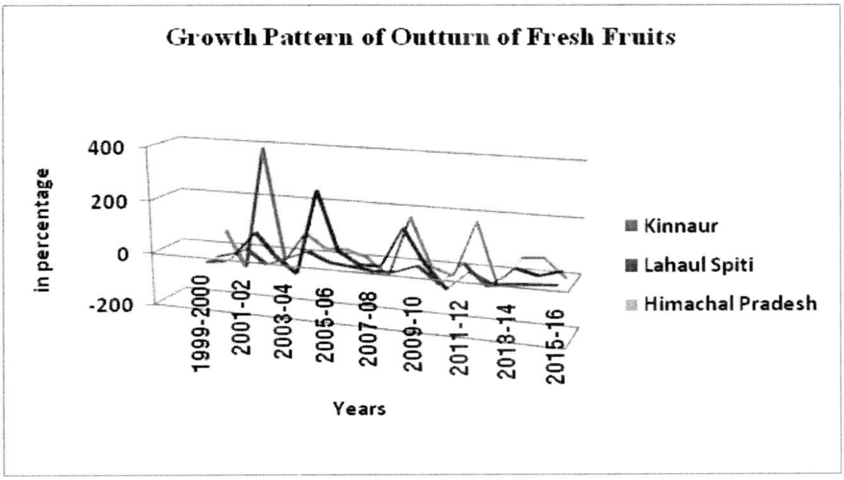

Figure-3.8 : Growth Pattern of Outturn of Fresh Fruits

3.30 Outturn of Dry Fruits

The outturn of dry fruits in the tribal districts (Kinnaur and Lahaul & Spiti) has recorded almost similar trend for fresh fruits. The table 3.30 shows total outturn of dry fruits.

As shown in the table 3.30, positive compound growth for dry fruits was 7.96 percent in Himachal Pradesh, whereas, 58.67 percent in Lahaul & Spiti and 11.70 percent in Kinnaur. The highest growth rate was recorded 93.18 percent in the year 2010-11, and lowest growth rate which was negative -62.48 percent, was in the year 2011-12 in Kinnaur.

In Lahaul & Spiti, the highest growth rate was 620 percent in the year 2013-14, whereas, the lowest was -73.33 percent was recorded in the year 2011-12. Data indicates that outturn of dry fruits in the State and two districts did not remain uniform. It is pertinent to state that out of average 5,269.22 tons, 545.83 tons (10.35%) was in Kinnaur and 15.65 tons (0.29%) was in Lahaul & Spiti. Therefore, Kinnaur is ahead in production of dry fruits as compared to Lahaul & Spiti.

Table-3.30 : Outturn of Dry Fruits

(in metric tons)

Year	Himachal Pradesh		Kinnaur		Lahaul & Spiti	
	Dry Fruits	Growth	Dry Fruits	Growth	Dry Fruits	Growth
1998-99	2456 (100)		325 (13.23)		4 (0.20)	
1999-2000	3075 (100)	25.20	482 (15.67)	48.31	7 (0.20)	75.0
2000-01	1895 (100)	-38.37	364 (19.21)	-24.48	4 (0.20)	-42.86
2001-02	2755 (100)	45.38	512 (18.58)	40.66	8 (0.30)	100.0
2002-03	4568 (100)	65.81	773 (16.92)	50.98	16 (0.40)	100.0
2003-04	5203 (100)	13.90	1195 (22.97)	54.59	7 (0.10)	-56.25
2004-05	7152 (100)	37.46	1342 (18.76)	12.30	8 (0.11)	14.29
2005-06	6141 (100)	-14.14	886 (14.43)	-33.98	19 (0.31)	137.50
2006-07	6164 (100)	0.37	459 (7.45)	-48.19	22 (0.36)	15.79
2007-08	5680 (100)	-7.85	412 (7.25)	-10.24	15 (0.26)	-31.82
2008-09	6227 (100)	9.63	403 (6.47	-2.18	7 (0.11)	-53.33
2009-10	6770 (100)	8.72	396 (5.84)	-1.73	5 (0.07)	-28.57
2010-11	5011 (100)	-25.98	765 (15.26)	93.18	15 (0.29)	200
2011-12	6991 (100)	39.51	287 (4.10)	-62.48	4 (0.05)	-73.33
2012-13	4926 (100)	-29.53	210 (4.26)	-26.82	10 (0.20)	150
2013-14	6071 (100)	23.24	348 (5.73)	65.71	72 (1.18)	620
2014-15	6643 (100)	9.42	259 (3.89)	-25.57	26 (0.39)	-63.88
2015-16	7118 (100)	7.15	407 (5.71)	57.14	33 (0.46)	26.92
C.G.		7.96		11.70		58.67
Mean	5269.22		545.83		15.656	
SD	1699.41		318.17		16.02	
CV	32.88		59.92		105.67	

Source: Horticultural Development Facts & Figures, Horticulture Department Himachal Pradesh, Nigam Vihar, Shimla, 1998-99 to 2015-16.

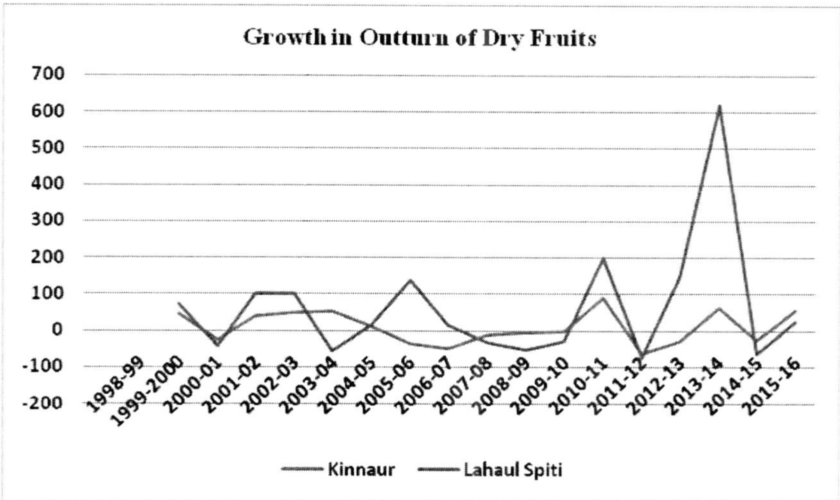

Figure-3.9 : Growth in Outturn of Dry Fruits

3.31 Outturn of Non Food Crops

Sesamum, Mustard and Soyabeen are included in non food crops. The detail of outturn of non food crops in the two tribal districts is shown in table 3.31. The average outturn of non food crops in the State has been analyzed to be 9,596.72 metric tons with standard deviation of 2,239.98 metric tons, and coefficient of variance of 23.34 percent which indicates less variance in production in the State as compared to both the districts while the S.D. is (2,239.98 metric tons). Further, the growth of these crops in the State is recorded 8.66 percent.

In Kinnaur, an average of 12.89 metric tons are produced every year and in Lahaul & Spiti it is 154.78 metric tons. The production of non food crops is very less in Kinnaur as compared to Lahaul & Spiti.

The coefficient of variance of outturn in non food crops is more than 150 percent in both the districts, showing least uniformity in the production of non food crops in these districts in comparison to other districts of the State.

However, coefficient of variance is less in Lahaul & Spiti in comparison to Kinnaur, depicting slightly more uniformity in the production of non food crops in this district.

Table-3.31 : Outturn of Non Food Crop

(in metric tons)

Year	Himachal Pradesh		Kinnaur		Lahaul & Spiti	
	Non Food Crops	Growth	Non Food Crops	Growth	Non Food Crops	Growth
1998-99	5687 (100)		5 (0.09)		23 (0.40)	
1999-2000	11451 (100)	101.35	72 (0.63)	1340.00	746 (6.51)	3143.48
2000-01	12688 (100)	10.80	11 (0.09)	-84.72	562 (4.43)	-24.66
2001-02	10595 (100)	-16.50	102 (0.96)	827.27	698 (6.59)	24.20
2002-03	10547 (100)	-0.45	6 (0.06)	-94.12	30 (0.28)	-95.70
2003-04	10142 (100)	-3.84	19 (0.19)	216.67	31 (0.31)	3.33
2004-05	9783 (100)	-3.54	2 (0.02)	-89.47	24 (0.25)	-22.58
2005-06	9922 (100)	1.42	0 (0.00)	-100	16 (0.16)	-33.33
2006-07	9283 (100)	-6.44	1 (0.01)	-	4 (0.04)	-75.00
2007-08	8138 (100)	-12.33	0 (0.00)	-100	0 (0.00)	-100
2008-09	8696 (100)	6.86	1 (0.01)	-	14 (0.16)	-
2009-10	10018 (100)	15.20	0 (0.00)	-100	101 (1.01)	621.43
2010-11	6444 (100)	-35.68	1 (0.02)	-	93 (1.44)	-7.92
2011-12	8658 (100)	34.35	0 (0.00)	0	109 (1.25)	17.20
2012-13	7180 (100)	-17.07	0 (0.00)	0	0 (0.00)	-100
2013-14	15442 (100)	115.06	2 (0.01)	100	75 (0.48)	-
2014-15	9066 (100)	-41.28	10 (0.11)	400	138 (1.52)	84
2015-16	9001 (100)	-0.71	0 (0)	-100	122 (1.35)	-11.59
C.G.		8.66		158.26		228.19
Mean	9596.72		12.89		154.78	
SD	2239.98		27.91		242.78	
CV	23.34		216.52		156.85	

Source: Annual Season Crop Report, Directorate of Land Records, Kasumpti, Shimla, 1998-99 to 2015-16.

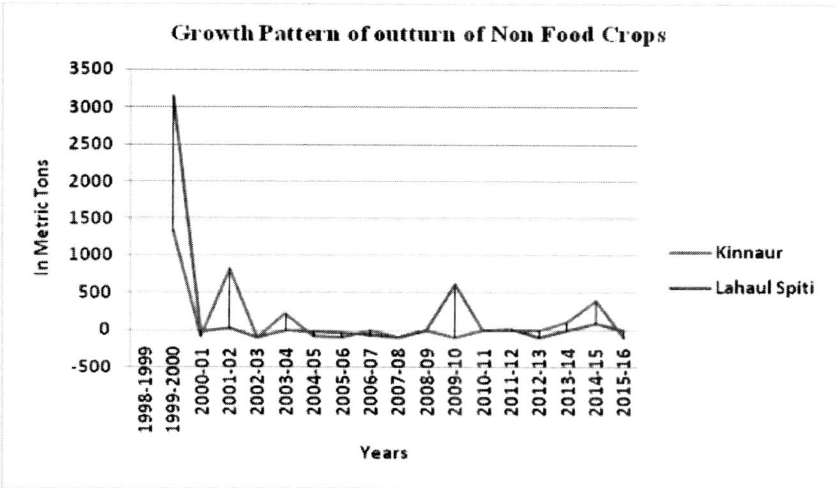

Figure-3.10 : Growth Pattern of Outturn of Non Food Crops

SUMMARY

The total geographical area of Himachal Pradesh is 55,673 sq. kms, out of which 45,756.38 sq.kms. (82.19%) is utilised area for different purposes of production. Out of utilised area i.e. only 20.88 percent is used for cropping activities. It is summarized that 0.97 percent area in Kinnaur and 0.34 percent area in Lahaul & Spiti is cultivated area of the State. The cropping intensity in Kinnaur is more consistent as compared to Lahaul & Spiti despite of the fact that both the districts have less irrigation intensity as compared to the State. In the areas of these districts which are considered as irrigated, kulh is the major source of irrigation, Lahaul & Spiti has expansion of land used for production of pulses as that of Kinnaur, whereas, Kinnaur leads in terms of area under production of cereal crops. In context of, area under production of fresh fruits, Kinnaur is much ahead from Lahaul & Spiti as about 97 percent area in Kinnaur is covered under production of apple crop. Kinnaur is known for production of dry fruits. However, the area covered under production of dry fruits has declined in the District. The analysis drawn in the study summarise that out of average area under vegetables in the State, 1.43 percent area is cultivated in Kinnaur and 4.35 percent is in Lahaul & Spiti. Though production of rice and wheat is negligible in both the districts, Kinnaur is much consistent in production of rice and wheat as compared to Lahaul &

Spiti. Further, standard yield of black gram in Kinnaur is higher in comparison to all other pulses, whereas the standard yield of peas summarizes that it is the most dominating crop of Lahaul & Spiti.In aggregate Lahaul & Spiti is much ahead in terms of per hectare production of vegetables as compared to Kinnaur.

The average turnover of cereals during the study period was 4,456.38 metric tons (only 0.32% of average production of the State) and 1,030.27 metric tons (only 0.07% of average production of the State) in Lahaul & Spiti. In Kinnaur, the average outturn of pulses was 1,020.33 metric tons (5.56% of the State) and 3,665.41 (19.98% of the State) metric tons in Lahaul & Spiti which is 19.98 percent of the State. Thus, Lahaul & Spiti is much ahead in production of pulses. In terms of production of vegetables in Kinnaur, average outturn was 1,657.53 metric tons which is 0.86 percent of total production of the State. In Lahaul & Spiti, it is 20,010.29 metric tons which is 10.40 percent of the State. Hence, in Lahaul & Spiti, production of vegetables is more as compared to Kinnaur. The average outturn of fresh fruits was 6,08,237.28 metric tons in Himachal Pradesh, out of which 38,604.36 metric tons (6.34% of the State's production) was in Kinnaur and 199.33 metric tons (0.32% of the State) in Lahaul & Spiti. Further, as per analysis Kinnaur district is contributing 10.35 percent of the total production of dry fruits while Lahaul-Spiti is producing 0.29 percent. However, production of non food crops is very less in Kinnaur as compared to Lahaul & Spiti i.e. 12.89 metric tons in Kinnaur (0.13% of the State) and 154.78 metric tons (1.61%) in Lahaul & Spiti. Overall, it is summarised that Kinnaur (12.34%) and Lahaul- Spiti consist of 17.34 percent utilized land area of Himachal Pradesh. Lahaul- Spiti is wider in comparison to Kinnaur in terms of land area but production and yield of different crops is much high in district Kinnaur in comparison to district Lahaul- Spiti.

4

Empirical Analysis of Cropping Pattern and Socio-Economic Development

On the basis of analysis drawn in the preceding chapter, it is evident that there has been a massive decline in the factors of influencing tribal population towards agriculture and horticulture. Till date, irrigation facilities have not found any expansion and there has been a shift of the tribal population from the regions of tribes. Moreover, crop production, intensity and yield has not depicted much attractive results. All such findings indicate that people of the tribal regions have apprehensions and expectations from the occupations in such circumstances where Government has special schemes and programmes of assistance in occupations for them so that the tribal communities are strengthened. A moderate attempt has been made in this chapter to know about the perceptions of tribal population with regard to analysis of cropping pattern and socio-economic development.

4.1 General Information about the Respondents

The general information taken from the heads of the families from the two districts Kinnaur and Lahaul & Spiti as shown in table 4.1, shows the gender wise, educational qualification wise, marital status wise, age wise and residential status -wise distribution of the respondents.

Table-4.1 : General Information about the Responents

Profile		Kinnaur	L & S	Total
Gender-wise	Male	201(69.79) (95.7)	87 (30.20) (96.66)	288(100) (96)
	Female	9(75) (4.3)	3(25) (3.33)	12(100) (4)
	Total	210(70) (100.0)	90(30) (100)	300(100) (100)
Marital Status-wise	Married	199(69.58) (94.74)	87(30.41) (96.66)	286(100) (95.33)
	Unmarried	2(100) (.95)	-	2(100) (.66)
	Widow	6(66.66) (2.85)	3(33.33) (3.33)	9(100) (3)
	Separated	3(100) (1.42)	-	3(100) (1)
	Total	210(70) (100)	90(30) (100)	300(100) (100)
Educational Qualification-wise	Illiterate	35(50) (16.7)	35(50) (38.9)	70(100) (23.33)
	Matriculate	123(78.84) (58.6)	33(21.15) (36.7)	156(100) (52)
	Graduate	43(72.88) (20.5)	16(27.11) (17.8)	59(100) (19.66)
	Post Graduate	9(69.23) (4.3)	4(30.76) (4.4)	13(100) (4.33)
	Others	-	2(100) (2.2)	2(100) (.66)
	Total	210(70) (100)	90(30) (100)	300(100) (100)
Age-wise	18-30	22 (64.70) (10.5)	12 (35.29) (13.3)	34 (100) (11.33)
	31-45	77(74.03) (36.7)	27 (25.96) (30)	104 (100) (34.66)
	46-60	70 (68.33) (33.3)	32 (31.37) (35.6)	102 (100) (34)
	Above 60	41(68.33) (19.5)	19 (31.66) (21.1)	60 (100) (20)
	Total	210 (70) (100)	90 (30) (100)	300 (100) (100)
Residential Status-wise	Residence of District by Birth	209(69.89) (99.5)	90(30.10) (100)	299(100) (99.66)
	Migrated to the District	1(100) (.5)	-	1(100) (.33)
	Total	210(70) (100)	90(100) (100)	300 (100)

Source: Data collected through interview schedule.

- Horizontal data in parentheses denotes percentage out of total in particular districts.
- Vertical data in parentheses denotes percentage of respondents, in each district.

Out of 300 respondents of both the districts, 210 are from Kinnaur and 90 are from Lahaul & Spiti district. In Kinnaur, 95.1 percent are males and 4.6 percent are females. Similarly, in Lahaul & Spiti, 97.66 percent are males and 3.33 percent are females. In overall, 96 percent respondents of both the districts are male respondents and only 4 percent respondents are females. Study reveals that in these regions families are patriarchal in nature.

Further, 94.87 percent are married and 0.95 percent respondents in Kinnaur are unmarried and out of 9 female respondents, 2.85 percent are widows and 3.33 percent are separated. In Lahaul & Spiti, 96.66 percent are married and 1.42 percent are widows.

Educational status wise, in Kinnaur out of 210 respondents, 16.7 percent are illiterate, 58.6 percent are matriculate, 20.5 percent are Graduates and 4.3 percent are Post Graduates.

In Lahual & Spiti, out of 90 respondents, 38.9 percent are illiterate, 36.7 percent are matriculate, 17.8 percent are Graduates, 4.4 percent are Post Graduates and only 2.2 percent have stated that they have other qualifications.

Out of 300 respondents in both the districts, 23.33 percent are illiterate, 52 percent are matriculate, 19.66 percent are graduates, 4.33 percent are post graduates and only 0.66 percent have professional qualifications. It is analysed from the data that, majority of the respondents are matriculate in both the districts.

In Kinnaur, 10.5 percent respondents belong to the age group between 18-30 years, 36.7 percent up to 45 years, 33.3 percent between 46-60 years and 19.5 percent above 60 years of age. In Lahual & Spiti, 13.3 percent respondents are aging between 18-30 years, 30 percent between 31-45 years, 35.6 percent between 46-60 years and 21.1 percent above 60 years.

The majority 34.66 percent respondents of both the districts, are in the age group of 31-45 years, 34 percent are in the age group 46-60, 20 percent respondents are age group above 60 years and very few 11.33 percent informants of both the districts are in the age group of 18-30 years.

From residential status wise, 99.5 percent respondents of district Kinnaur are residents of district by birth and only 0.5 percent (1) migrated to the district whereas, all the respondents of Lahual and Spiti are residents of the district by birth.

4.2 Occupation-wise Classification of the Respondents

Table-4.2 : Shows the Occupation wise Distribution of Informants

Occupation	Kinnaur	L & S	Total
Government/Private job / Agriculture / Horticulture	17(53.12) (8.09)	15(46.87) (16.7)	32(100) (10.66)
Government/Private job / Horticulture	71(95.94) (33.8)	3(4.05) (3.3)	74(100) (24.66)
Agriculture	8(11.42) (3.8)	62(88.57) (68.9)	70(100) (23.33)
Horticulture	67(100) (31.9)	-	67(100) (22.33)
Agriculture / Horticulture	31(93.93) (14.8)	2(6.06) (2.2)	33(100) (11)
Agri / Horti / Any Other(Business, Handloom, Contractor)	16(66.67) (7.6)	8(33.33) (8.9)	24(100) (8)
Total	210(70) (100)	90(30) (100)	300(100) (100)

Source: Data collected through interview schedule.

- Horizontal data in parentheses denotes percentage out of total in particular districts.
- Vertical data in parentheses denotes percentage of respondents, in each district.

From the table 4.2, out of 300 respondents, 10.66 percent in both the districts are employed in government or private sector, agriculture or horticulture, 24.66 percent stated that they are engaged in government, private job or horticulture, 23.33 percent in agriculture only, 22.33 percent in horticulture, 11 percent in horticulture and agriculture and 8 percent in agriculture, horticulture along with others including business, handloom and are contractors.

In Kinnaur, out of 210 informants, 8.09 percent are in government/ private jobs, agriculture or horticulture, 33.8 percent in horticulture with private/government job, 3.8 percent in only agriculture, 31.9 percent in horticulture, 14.8 percent are engaged in both agriculture/ horticulture, 7.6 percent in horticulture/agriculture, handloom, business, or contractors.

In Lahual & Spiti, out of 90 informants, 16.7 percent are having government/private job agriculture and horticulture, 3.3 percent in horticulture with private/government job, 68.9 percent in agriculture, 2.2 percent in both agriculture/horticulture, 8.9 percent in horticulture, agriculture, handloom, business, and contactor.

The respondents in great majority are involved in horticulture or agriculture as their main occupation. It is pertinent to mention that majority of respondents of Kinnaur district are involved in employment and horticulture as compared to Lahaul and Spiti. While respondents of Lahaul & Spiti are involved in business and other occupations in adition to agriculture.

4.3 Crops Grown in the Tribal Regions

Table 4.3 shows cropping pattern of the Tribal region. The Climatic conditions of both the regions determine the kinds of crops being produced.

There are two seasons of crops in Kinnaur region, spread as Kharif crops which are being sown in the month of April-May and the Rabi crops which are sown in the month of November and December in the region. During the kharif season, vegetables are also grown. In Lahaul and Spiti, the climate during spring and summer seasons (April-October) is rather mild during which both Rabi and Kharif crops are grown simultaneously. The raining is scanty and humidity remains low during this period.

However, during winters (November-March), the climate is extremely cold and mercury drops even up to minus 350C. During this period, heavy snowfall occurs and this area remains cut-off from rest of the World.

Table-4.3 : Crops Grown in The Tribal Regions

Crops		Kinnaur	L & S	Total
Kharif crops	Maize, Razmah	36(97.29) (17.1)	1(2.70) (4.54)	37(100) (15.94)
	Maize, Razmah, Fafra, Ogla	79(96.34) (37.6)	3(3.65) (13.66)	82(100) (35.34)
	Razmah	19(90.47) (9)	2(9.52) (9.09)	21(100) (9.05)
	Fafra, Ogla	76(82.60) (36.2)	16(17.39) (72.72)	92(100) (39.65)
	Total	210(90.51) (100)	22(9.48) (100)	232(100) (100)
Rabi Crops	Wheat	87(91.57) (47.54)	8(8.42) (11.42)	95(100) (37.55)
	Barley	48(94.11) (26.22)	3(5.88) (4.28)	51(100) (20.16)
	Wheat & Barley	48(44.85) (26.22)	59(55.14) (84.28)	107(100) (42.30)
	Total	183(72.33) (100)	70(27.67) (100)	253(100) (100)
Vegetables Grown	Tomato, Cabbage, Beans	51(100) (25.12)	-	51(100) (17.52)
	Potato, Peas	45(45.91) (22.16)	53(54.08) (60.22)	98(100) (33.67)
	Tomato, Cabbage, Potato	30(93.75) (14.77)	2(6.25) (2.27)	32(100) (10.99)
	Potato	27(93.10) (13.30)	2(77.14) (2.27)	29(100) (9.96)
	Peas	8(22.85) (3.94)	27(77.14) (30.68)	35(100) (12.02)
	All of the Above	42(91.30) (20.68)	4(8.69) (4.54)	46(100) (15.80)
	Total	203(69.75) (100)	88(30.24) (100)	291(100) (100)
Medicinal plants	Kuth		14(100) (26.92)	14(100) (26.92)
	Manu	-	8(100) (15.38)	8(100) (15.38)
	Hops	-	17(100) (32.69)	17(100) (32.69)
	Charma	-	13(100) (25)	13(100) (25)
	Total	-	52(100) (100)	52(100) (100)

Source: Data collected through interview schedule.

- Horizontal data in parentheses denotes percentage out of total in particular districts.
- Vertical data in parentheses denotes percentage of respondents, in each district.

In district Kinnaur, 17.1 percent respondents stated that they are producing Maize and Rajmah, 37.6 percent are growing Maize, Razmah, Ogla, and Fafra, 9 percent only Rajmah, and 36.2 percent have revealed that they are producing the combination of Fafra and Ogla. The table also shows that Rabi Crops are grown in the region stating that 183 are growing Rabi crops. Majority of the respondents, (47.54%) are producing Wheat only, followed by Barley (26.22%) and overall 48 are producing the combination of both Wheat and Barley in the region. It is also evident from the table that in Kinnaur, total 203 respondents are growing vegetables, out of which majority of the informants (25.12%) are growing Tomato, Cabbage, and Beans. Further, according to 22.16 percent respondents Potato and Peas are being grown while 20.68 percent are growing combination of all varieties of vegetables mentioned in the table. Only 13.30 percent are growing Potato and 3.94 percent are producing only peas.

In Lahaul & Spiti, 13.66 percent are producing Maize, Rajmah, Fafra, Ogla, 9.09 percent are producing Rajmah and 72.72 percent Fafra & Ogla. The table also reveals that, 84.28 percent respondents are producing both Wheat and Barley, 11.42 percent stated that they are producing Wheat, 4.28 percent barley and 70 amongst the respondents are producing Rabi crops. Majority (84.28%) are producing both Wheat and Barley. It is analysed from the data, that majority of the respondents of Kinnaur are grown Kharif crops as compared to Lahaul & Spiti. Maize, rajmah, fafra and ogla are major kharif crops of Kinnaur, and fafra & ogla are produced in Lahaul & Spiti in terms of Kharif crops, whereas, Lahaul & Spiti leads to production of Rabi crops (wheat & Barley) as compared to Kinnaur.

In Lahaul & Spiti out of 88 respondents, 60.22 percent are producing potato and peas, followed by 30.68 percent producing only peas, 4.54 percent are producing Tomato, Cabbage and Potato and 4 percent are those who are producing all of the above vegetables. The respondents from Lahaul & Spiti district revealed that they are engaged in production of some medicinal plants, 26.92 percent producing Kuth, 15.38 percent producing Manu, 36.29 percent are producing Hops, and 25 percent are producing Charma. There is no respondent found in Kinnaur growing medicinal plants. It is needless to state that only in Lahaul & Spiti, out of these two districts, Kuth, Manu, Hops and Charma are being produced.

It is analysed from the data that peas and potato are the major agricultural crops in both the tribal districts, where as hops, kuth, and manu are produced in Lahaul & Spiti. Data further shows that although people of Lahaul & Spiti are more engaged in agriculture in comparison to Kinnaur and more agricultural crops are produced in Lahaul & Spiti, yet crops are almost same in both the districts.

4.4 Fruits Produced in Kinnaur and Lahaul-Spiti

Agricultural diversification towards fruit and vegetable crops in Himachal Pradesh, especially in some areas in the districts of Shimla, Kullu, Solan, Kinnaur and Lahaul & Spiti, started in the late sixties and continued in the seventies and the eighties. The process of crop diversification gained momentum in the nineties and has now encompassed many new areas in the low and mid hill districts. The two tribal regions are famous for cultivation of Apple, Almond, Chilgoza, Walnut, pears, Peach and Plum. In the Kinnaur region, apple is the only fruit crop which is produced in the whole district but in Lahaul & Spiti, production of fruits has been stated to be meager as shown in the table 4.4.

Table-4.4 : Fruits Produced in Kinnaur and Lahaul & Spiti

Fruits produced	Kinnaur	L & S	Total
Apple	74(90.24) (35.74)	8(9.75) (100)	82(100) (38.13)
Apple, Almond, Chilgoza	24(100) (11.59)	-	24(100) (11.16)
Apple, Apricot, Almond, Chilgoza, Walnut	57(100) (27.54)	-	57(100) (26.51)
Apple, Pears, Peach, Plum	27(100) (13.04)	-	27(100) (12.55)
Any other fruits	25(100) (12.07)	-	25(100) (11.62)
Total	207(96.27) (100)	8(3.72) (100)	215(100) (100)

Source: Data collected through interview schedule.

- Horizontal data in parentheses denotes percentage out of total in particular districts.
- Vertical data in parentheses denotes percentage of respondents, in each district.

In Kinnaur, out of 207 respondents, 35.2 percent are producing apple only, followed by, 11.4 percent growing the combination of apple, almond, chilgoza, 27.1 percent growing apple, apricot, almond, chilgoza, and walnut, 12.9 percent producing the combination of apple, pears, peach, and plum and 11.9 percent producing other types of local fruits i.e. Luchi, Grapes, Bemi, chulli etc. In Lahaul & Spiti only 3.72 percent respondents are producing apple fruit. It indicates that apple is the only fruit which is being highly produced. However, in Lahaul and Spiti, the number of horticulturists is found to be meager.

4.5 Classification According to Crops Grown, Marketing and Annual Income

In tribal areas, cropping pattern has changed and to know about cropping pattern, marketing of crops and annual income from crops of the households, as shown in the table 4.5.Classification according to crops grown, marketing and annual income has been made and analyzed.

Table-4.5 : Classification According to Crops Grown, Marketing and Annual Income

Cash Crops grown Responses	 Yes	 No	 Total	Marketing of Crops Local/within the State	 Outside State	 Other	 Total	Annual income from crops Up to Rs. 1lakh	 Rs.1,00,001- 2 lakhs	 Rs. 2,00,001- 5 lakhs	 Rs. 5,00,001- 10 lakhs	 Above Rs.10 lakhs	 Total
Kinnaur	200	10	210	63	136	1	200	66	51	68	20	5	210
	-95.2	-4.8	-100	-31.5	-68	-0.5	-100	-31.4	-24.3	-32.4	-9.5	-2.4	-100
	- 69.93	- **71.42**	-70	**-43.75**	**-96.45**	**-100**	**-69.9**	- **57.89**	**-68.91**	**-86.07**	-74.07	**-83.33**	**-70**
Lahaul & Spiti	86	4	90	81	5	-	86	48	23	11	7	1	90
	-95.6	-4.4	-100	-94.18	-5.81		-100	-53.3	-25.6	-12.2	-7.8	-1.1	-100
	- 30.06	- **28.57**	**-30**	**-56.25**	**-3.54**		- 30.06	**-42.1**	**-31.08**	**-13.92**	**-25.92**	**-16.67**	**-30**
Total	286	14	300	144	141	1	286	114	74	79	27	6	300
	- 95.33	-4.66	-100	-50.34	-49.3	-0.34	-100	-38	-24.66	-26.33	-9	-2	-100
	-100	**-100**	**-100**	**-100**	**-100**	**-100**	**-100**	**-100**	**-100**	**-100**	**-100**	**-100**	**-100**

Source: Data collected through interview schedule.

- Horizontal data in parentheses denotes percentage out of total in particular districts.
- Vertical data in parentheses denotes percentage of respondents, in each district.

From the table 4.5, it is analyzed that out of total 300 respondents, 286 (95.33%) were growing cash crops. In Kinnaur, 95.2 percent and in Lahaul & Spiti 95.6 percent informants revealed that they are growing cash crops. It indicates that in both the tribal districts almost all of the respondents have cash crops. Further, the table shows the nature of market access for food products specifically the cash crops. In Kinnaur, out of 200 respondents, 31.5 percent are selling their crops in the Local market or in market within the State. Whereas, 68 percent sell the crops outside the State.

In Lahaul & Spiti, majority of the respondents (94.18%) sell their crops locally or within the State. The responses reveal that in Kinnaur 31.4 percent respondents have income from cropping up to Rs. 1 lakh, 24.3 percent having Rs. 1 to 2 lakhs, 32.4 percent between Rs. 2 to 5 lakhs, and only 11.9 percent have above Rs. 5 lakhs. In both the districts, the annual income of 114 respondents is up to Rs. 1 lakh, followed by 74 who have annual crop income between Rs. 1 to 2 lakhs, 79 have Rs. 2 to 5 lakhs, and 33 have above Rs. 5 lakhs annual cropping income.

The data shows that out of 114 respondents of both the districts having up to Rs. 1 lakh annual cropping income, 57.89 percent are from Kinnaur and 42.10 percent are from Lahaul & Spiti indicating more percentage of Kinnaur having the annual cropping income, up to Rs. 1 lakh. Study also reveals that majority of the respondents of Lahaul & Spiti have annual cropping income up to Rs. 2 lakhs whereas, majority of the respondents of district Kinnaur falls between annual cropping income of Rs. 2 to 5 lakhs.

4.6 Annual Income wise Classification of Respondents

As per the table 4.6, the population in the tribal regions of Himachal Pradesh in a great majority (47%) have their Annual Income below Rs. 1 lakh.

Table-4.6 : Annual Income - wise Classification of Respondents

Annual Income	Kinnaur	L & S	Total
Up to Rs.1,00,000	123(82.23) **(58.57)**	18(12.76) **(20)**	141(100) **(47)**
Rs. 1,00,001-Rs. 2,00,000	27(30.33) **(12.9)**	62(69.66) **(68.88)**	89(100) **(29.66)**
Rs. 2,00,001-Rs. 5,00,000	43(95.55) **(20.5)**	2(4.44) **(2.2)**	45(100) **(15)**
Above Rs. 5,00,000	17(68) **(8.1)**	8(32) **(8.9)**	25(100) **(8.33)**
Total	210(100) **(100)**	90(100) **(100)**	300(100) **(100)**

Source: Data collected through interview schedule.

- Horizontal data in parentheses denotes percentage out of total in particular districts.
- Vertical data in parentheses denotes percentage of respondents, in each district.

In Kinnaur, 58.6 percent respondents revealed to have their annual income below Rs. 1 lakh whereas, 12.9 percent between Rs. 1,00,001 to Rs. 2,00,000, 20.5 percent between Rs. 2,00,001 to Rs. 5,00,000, and 8.1 percent are earning above Rs. 5,00,000 per year. This analyzes that in Kinnaur district, majority of the population which is actually residing in the region, has annual income below Rs. 1 lac which is not a good signal of development. Similarly, in Lahaul & Spiti, 68.9 percent are earning between Rs. 1,00,001 to Rs. 2,00,000, 8.9 percent are earning above Rs. 5,00,000 and 2.2 percent between Rs. 2 lakhs to Rs. 5 lakhs.

Out of total 141 respondents of both the districts, 82% having income upto Rs. 1 lakh are from Kinnaur and the remaining are from Lahaul & Spiti. Similarly, 69.66 percent respondents falling in the income group of Rs.1, 00,001 to Rs. 2 lakhs are from Kinnaur and the remaining are from Lahaul & Spiti. About 95 percent respondents of Kinnaur are in the income group of Rs. 2,00,001 to Rs. 5,00,000 and only 5 percent are from Lahaul & Spiti. In the income group above Rs. 5 lakhs, 68 percent are from Kinnaur and the rest are from Lahaul & Spiti. It is evident from the responses that majority of the respondents of Lahaul & Spiti have income between Rs. 1,00,001 to Rs. 2,00,000 whereas, Kinnaur is much ahead in all other income groups.

4.7 Income of the Family Members: Occupation-wise

Despite of emerging cash crops as the source of income, tribal communities are engaged in different occupations and investment sources including job, business, pension and farm labour. These investment avenues and occupations are adding to the income of the families.

Out of total 300 respondents of the present study, 127 have revealed that in their families, other members are involved in different occupations adding to the income of the family as shown in the table 4.7.

Table-4.7 : Income of the Family Members: Occupation wise

Income	Kinnaur				Lahaul and Spiti				
	Job	Business	Pension	Farm labour	Job	Business	Pension	Farm labour	Total
Up to Rs. 50,000	7(17.5) **(15.90)**	1(2.5) **(16.67)**	6(15) **(31.58)**	13(32.5) **(54.2)**	4(10) **(23.52)**	1(2.5) **(25)**	1(2.5) **(50)**	7(17.5) **(63.63)**	40(100) **(31.50)**
50,001-1,00,000	9(20.93) **(20.45)**	3(6.97) **(50)**	10(23.25) **(52.63)**	9(20.93) **(37.5)**	6(13.95) **(35.29)**	3(6.97) **(75)**	1(2.32) **(50)**	2(4.65) **(18.18)**	43(100) **(33.85)**
1,00,001-2,00,000	23(63.88) **(52.27)**	1(2.77) **(16.66)**	3(8.33) **(15.79)**	2(5.55) **(8.34)**	5(13.88) **(29.41)**		-	2(5.55) **(18.18)**	36(100) **(28.35)**
Above 2,00,000	5(62.5) **(11.36)**	1(12.5) **(16.66)**	-	--	2(25) **(11.76)**		-	-	8(100) **(6.30)**
Total	44(34.64) **(100)**	6(4.72) **(100)**	19(14.96) **(100)**	24(18.89) **(100)**	17(13.38) **(100)**	4(3.14) **(100)**	2(1.57) **(100)**	11(8.66) **(100)**	127(100) **(100)**

Source: Data collected through interview schedule.

- Horizontal data in parentheses denotes percentage out of total in particular districts.
- Vertical data in parentheses denotes percentage of respondents, in each district.

In Kinnaur, 166 (79%) families are not having income from job whereas, 52.27 percent families are earning between Rs. 1,00,001 to Rs. 2,00,000, 20.45 percent from Rs. 50,001 to Rs. 1,00,000 and 15.90 percent earning up to Rs. 50,000. Only11.36 percent families are earning above Rs. 2,00,000.

From business, only one respondent is earning up to Rs. 50,000, between Rs. 50,001-Rs. 1,00,000, and one each between Rs. 1,00,001-Rs. 2,00,000 and above Rs. 2,00,000. Further, 19 families are getting pension from government, out of whom, 52.63 percent are getting pension between Rs. 50,001 to 1,00,000, 1.4 percent between Rs. 1,00,001 to Rs. 2,00,000 and 15.79 percent up to Rs. 50,000. It is noted that 24 families are earning their livelihood by working as farm labour and minimum income of 13 families is Rs. 50,000 per year whereas, 37.55 percent families are earning between Rs. 50,001 to Rs. 1,00,000. Only 8.24 percent families are earning between Rs. 1,00,001 to Rs. 2,00,000 from farm labour. A huge number of (186) respondent (86%) are not earning from farm labour.

In Lahaul & Spiti, only 34 families have income from other sources, it has been found that 17 families are earning from job, 11 from farm labour, 4 from business, and 2 from pension. It is analysed that majority of the respondents of both the districts are earning up to Rs. 1,00,000. This reveals that the family income is low in both the districts and the socio -economic development of the families is due to the involvement of the members in different occupations in addition to their involvement in agriculture. According to the responses, 56.66 percent families are not having additional earning members.

4.8 Total Family Income of the Respondents

Total family income of the respondents is including income of the head of the family, income earned by other family members, and income of the concerned respondent. Table 4.8 shows the aggregate of income of all the three components.

Table-4.8 : Total Family Income of the Respondents

Family income	Kinnaur	L & S	Total
Up to 2,00,000	67(57.26) **(31.9)**	50(42.73) **(55.6)**	117(100) **(39)**
2,00,001-5,00,000	77(72.64) **(36.7)**	29(27.35) **(32.2)**	106(100) **(35.33)**
5,00,001-8,00,000	48(87.27) **(22.9)**	7(12.72) **(7.8)**	55(100) **(18.33)**
Above 8,00,000	18(8.18) **(8.6)**	4(18.81) **(4.4)**	22(100) **(7.33)**
Total	210(70) **(100)**	90(30) **(100)**	300(100) **(100)**

Source: Data collected through interview schedule.

- Horizontal data in parentheses denotes percentage out of total in particular districts.
- Vertical data in parentheses denotes percentage of respondents, in each district.

Table 4.8 shows that family income in a great majority falls below Rs. 5,00,000 in both the districts. In Kinnaur, 31.9 percent respondents have income up to Rs. 2,00,000, followed by 36.7 percent having Rs. 2 to Rs. 5 lakhs, 22.9 percent have Rs. 5-8 lakhs and only 8.6 percent have above Rs. 8 lakhs income per annum. The family income stated by the respondents of Lahaul & Spiti has been in a great majority (55.6%) falling upto Rs. 2 lakhs.

However, 32.2 percent have family income between Rs. 2 to 5 lakhs, 7.8 percent between Rs. 5-8 lakhs and only 4.4 percent have above Rs. 8 lakhs. Thus in Lahaul & Spiti, majority of the families are earning up to Rs. 2 lakhs while in Kinnaur, the family income is between Rs. 2 to Rs. 5 lakhs. In both the districts, the annual income of 117 respondents is stated by them up to Rs. 2 lakhs, while 106 have between Rs. 2 to Rs. 5 lakhs, 48 have stated their family income between Rs. 5 to Rs. 8 lakhs and 22 have above Rs. 8 lakhs.

4.9 Responses Regarding Family Structure

Based on the responses from the study regions, the following table 4.9 explains the type of family structure and number of family members of the respondents.

Table-4.9 : Responses Regarding Family Structure

Family Structure				Number of Family Members				
Responses	**Joint**	**Nuclear**	**Total**	**2members**	**3-5members**	**6-8members**	**Above 8members**	**Total**
Kinnaur	97(46.2) **(57.05)**	113(53.8) **(86.92)**	210(100) **(70)**	7(3.3) **(63.63)**	106(50.47) **(72.10)**	65(31) **(69.89)**	32(15.23) **(65.30)**	210(100) **(70)**
Lahaul & Spiti	73(81.1) **(42.94)**	17(18.9) **(13.07)**	90(100) **(30)**	4(4.4) **(36.36)**	41(45.6) **(27.89)**	28(31.1) **(30.10)**	17(18.9) **(34.69)**	90(100) **(30)**
Total	170(56.66) **(100)**	130(43.33) **(100)**	300(100) **(100)**	11(3.66) **(100)**	147(49) **(100)**	93(31) **(100)**	49(16.33) **(100)**	300(100) **(100)**

Source: Data collected through interview schedule.

- Horizontal data in parentheses denotes percentage out of total in particular districts.
- Vertical data in parentheses denotes percentage of respondents, in each district.

As per the table 4.9, there is enormous gap in the family structure of both the districts as 81.1 percent informants of Lahaul & Spiti district stated that they live in joint families against 46.2 percent living in joint families in Kinnaur. Thus in Lahaul & Spiti, the concept of joint family is still surviving in comparison to that in Kinnaur district.

As many as, 106 respondents of Kinnaur have revealed that they have 3-5 family members, 31 percent have 6 to 8 members, 16.7 percent have above 8 members and only 3.3 percent informants have 2 members.

In Lahaul & Spiti, 4 percent informants have revealed that their families have only 2 family members, followed by 45.6 percent having 3-5 members, 31.1 percent have 6-8 and 18.9 percent have above 8 members. In both the districts, 49 percent respondents have 3-5 family members, followed by 31 percent who have 6-8 members, and 16.33 percent have above 8 family members. It is noted that in Kinnaur, the great majority (exceeding 50%) belongs to such families where the number of family members is between 3-5 against Lahaul & Spiti, where the number of family members exceeding above 8 members, is more that of Kinnaur.

4.10 Classification of Land Area: Land Use Wise

In terms of land area, Lahaul & Spiti is wide spread although, in terms of land use, Kinnaur district is much ahead. According to 59 percent informants, table (4.10) in Kinnaur, they have up to 5 bighas of agricultural land, 36 percent having 6-10 bighas, 4 percent having 11-20 bighas and 1 informant has 20 bighas of agricultural land. Thus, in Kinnaur, majority have below 10 bighas of land which they use for agriculture. In Lahaul & Spiti, 28.91 percent respondents stated to have up to 5 bighas agricultural land and 36.14 percent have 6-10 bighas, 12.05 percent have 11-20 bhigas and 22.89 percent have more than 20 bighas of agricultural land. In Lahaul & Spiti, households have much more area for agriculture in comparison to those in Kinnaur district.

Further, it is revealed that in Kinnaur district 50.78 percent respondents have used 6-10 bighas of land for horticulture, followed by 41.45percent having up to 5 bighas. Only 7.78 percent have 11-20 bighas of horticultural land. On the contrary, in Lahaul & Spiti only, 9.09 percent respondents have horticultural land up to 5 bighas. It clearly indicates that in comparison to Lahaul & Spiti, respondents of Kinnaur have stated more horticultural land and in Lahaul & Spiti, it is negligible. Moreover, in both the districts, the respondents have revealed that they have uncultivated land.

Table-4.10 : Classification of Land Area: Land Use Wise

Use of Land	Total Land	5orbelow5	6-10Bhigas	11- 20Bhigas	Above20Bhigas	Total
Agricultural Land	K	59(59) **(71.08)**	36(36) **(54.54)**	4(4) **(28.57)**	1(1) **(5)**	100(100) **(54.65)**
	L	24(28.91) **(28.91)**	30(36.14) **(45.45)**	10(12.05) **(71.42)**	19((22.89) **(95)**	83(100) **(45.35)**
	T	83(45.35) **(100)**	66(36.06) **(100)**	14(7.65) **(100)**	20(10.93) **(100)**	183(100) **(100)**
Horticultural Land	K	80(41.45) **(90.90)**	98(50.78) **(100)**	15(7.78) **(100)**	-	193(100) **(96.01)**
	L	8(9.09) **(100)**	-	-	-	8(100) **(3.98)**
	T	88(43.78) **(100)**	98(48.75) **(100)**	15(7.46) **(100)**	-	201(100) **(100)**

Contd. ...

Uncultivated Land	K	98(89.90) **(68.53)**	11(10.09) **(78.57)**	-	-	109(100) **(69.42)**
	L	45(93.75) **(31.46)**	3(6.25) **(21.42)**	-	-	48(100) **(30.57)**
	T	143(91.08) **(100)**	14(8.91) **(100)**	-	-	157(100) **(100)**
Total Land	K	54(25.71) **(75)**	125(59.52) **(75.75)**	30(14.28) **(62.5)**	1(.47) **(8.33)**	210(100) **(70.70)**
	L	18(20.68) **(25)**	40(45.97) **(24.24)**	18(20.68) **(37.5)**	11(12.64) **(91.67)**	87(100) **(29.29)**
	T	72(24.24) **(100)**	165(55.55) **(100)**	48(16.16) **(100)**	12(4.04) **(100)**	297(100) **(100)**

Source: Data collected through interview schedule.

- Horizontal data in parentheses denotes percentage out of total in particular districts.
- Vertical data in parentheses denotes percentage of respondents, in each district.

Out of 157 respondents of both the districts, 143 have land up to 5 bighas, followed by 14 respondents having 6-10 bhigas of uncultivated land. In Kinnaur, 69.42 percent respondents have uncultivated land up to 10 bhigas. On the contrary, 30.57 percent from Lahaul & Spiti have uncultivated land. There is no respondent in both the districts who has above 20 bhigas of uncultivated land. Kinnaur district has more uncultivated land as compared to Lahaul and Spiti. Since majority of the respondents have revealed the total land below 10 bhigas in both the districts, it indicates that in both the tribal districts, farmers have very small land holdings.

4.11 Irrigation Facilities

It is already discussed earlier that the source of irrigation in the tribal regions of Himachal Pradesh (Kinnaur and Lahaul & Spiti) is 'Kulh' i.e. the system through which water is channeled by making small drain like landscape from the available water source to the fields. It is a traditional method developed by farmers from the available water source in slight slopes on the land connecting fields and it contains very limited amount of water flow. The responses regarding irrigation facilities are depicted in table 4.11.

Table-4.11 : Irrigation Facilities

	Irrigation Facility			Sources of Irrigation		
Responses	Yes	No	Total	Kulh	Any other (Tanks, IPH Lifts)	Total
Kinnaur	151(71.9) **(63.17)**	59(28.1) **(96.72)**	210(100) **(70)**	141(93.37) **(62.94)**	10(6.62) **(66.67)**	151(100) **(63.17)**
Lahaul & Spiti	88(97.8) **(36.82)**	2(2.2) **(3.27)**	90(100) **(30)**	83(94.31) **(37.05)**	5(5.6) **(33.33)**	88(100) **(36.82)**
Total	239(79.66) **(100)**	61(20.33) **(100)**	300(100) **(100)**	224(93.72) **(100)**	15(6.27) **(100)**	239(100) **(100)**

Source: Data collected through interview schedule.

- Horizontal data in parentheses denotes percentage out of total in particular districts.
- Vertical data in parentheses denotes percentage of respondents, in each district.

Dependency on rain water in the tribal areas is reflected through the responses as in Kinnaur district 28.1 percent respondents have revealed that they have no irrigation facility, against Lahaul & Spiti where only 2.2 percent respondents have revealed that there is no irrigation facility.

Out of 151 respondents of Kinnaur district who admitted that they are availing irrigation facility, 93.37 percent of them admitted that irrigation is through Kulh and rest of 6.62 percent are using other sources for irrigation. In Lahaul & Spiti, 92.2 percent out of 88 are using kulh system and the rest of 5.68 percent are using other sources of irrigation.

4.12 Responses Regarding Area under Irrigation

Table 4.12 depicts the profile of respondents in terms of irrigated land available. It shows the number of respondents owning irrigated land, in both the districts along with the percentage of total irrigated land in the districts individually and total irrigated land in both districts. This table includes the respondents having irrigated land only. Out of 151 respondents of district Kinnaur, 13.25 percent have irrigated land up to 2 bhigas, 38.41 percent have 3 to 5 bhigas, 27.81 percent have 6 to 10 bhigas, 6.62 percent have 11 to 20 bhigas and 13.90 percent respondents have irrigated land above 20 bhigas.

Table-4.12 : Classification of Respondents in Terms of Total Irrigated Land

Total irrigated Land	Kinnaur	L & S	Total
Up to 2 Bighas	20(86.95) **(13.25)**	3(13.04) **(3.44)**	23(100) **(9.66)**
3-5 Bighas	58(67.44) **(38.41)**	28(32.55) **(32.18)**	86(36.13) **(36.13)**
6-10 Bighas	42(67.74) **(27.81)**	20(32.25) **(22.98)**	62(100) **(26.05)**
11-20 Bighas	10(41.66) **(6.62)**	14(58.33) **(16.09)**	24(100) **(10.08)**
Above 20 Bighas	21(48.83) **(13.90)**	22(51.16) **(25.28)**	43(100) **(18.06)**
Total	151(63.44) **(100)**	87(36.55) **(100)**	238(100) **(100)**

Source: Data collected through interview schedule.

- Horizontal data in parentheses denotes percentage out of total in particular districts.
- Vertical data in parentheses denotes percentage of respondents, in each district.

It is apparent from the table that majority 38.41 percent respondents have only 3 to 5 bhigas irrigated land which is very small area and only 13.90 percent have irrigated land above 20 bhigas. It may be noted that 20 bhigas of irrigated land is not a big deal.

In Lahaul & Spiti majority of the respondents i.e 32.18 percent have 3-5 bhigas land area followed by, 25.28 percent having 20 bhigas, and 16.09 percent have 11-20 bhigas land area. Only 3.44 percent have below 2 bhigas of irrigated land. In both the districts, most of the respondents (36.13%) have irrigated land between 3-5 bhigas, followed by 26.05 percent between 6-10 bhigas, 18.06 percent have above 20 bhigas followed by, 10.08 percent respondents between 11-20 bhigas of irrigated land and only 9.66 percent have up to 2 bhigas of irrigated land.

It is analysed from the table that 41.37 percent respondents of Lahaul & Spiti have above 10 bhigas of irrigated land. Whereas, in Kinnaur it is 20.52 percent which is half that of Lahaul and Spiti. It indicates that there is huge disparity in the irrigated land area covered in both the study regions.

4.13 Responses Regarding Labour Engaged for Cultivated Land

Land cultivation has not remained confined occupation for self but has emerged as a source of employment generation for others as per the responses of informants. This is perhaps due to engagement of the land owners in different employment avenues also. However, the responses regarding labour engaged for cultivated land are explained as per the following table 4.13.

Table-4.13 : Response Regarding Labour Engaged for Cultivated Land

(Per Annum)

Labour Engaged				Amount Spent on Labour				
Responses	Yes	No	Total	Up to Rs. 10,000	Rs. 10,001 to 20,000	Rs. 20,001 to 40,000	Above 40,000	Total
Kinnaur	152(72.38) **(71.02)**	58(27.6) **(67.44)**	210(100) **(70)**	21(13.81) **(63.63)**	34(22.36) **(50.74)**	46(30.26) **(74.19)**	51(33.55) **(87.93)**	152(100) **(69.09)**
Lahaul & Spiti	62(68.89) **(28.97)**	28(31.1) **(32.55)**	90(100) **(30)**	12(19.35) **(36.36)**	33(53.22) **(49.25)**	10(14.70) **(17.85)**	7(11.29) **(12.06)**	62(100) **(30.90)**
Total	214(71.33) (100)	86(28.67) (100)	300(100) (100)	33(15.42) (100)	67(31.30) (100)	56(26.16) (100)	58(27.10) (100)	214(100) (100)

Source: Data collected through interview schedule.

- ➢ Horizontal data in parentheses denotes percentage out of total in particular districts.
- ➢ Vertical data in parentheses denotes percentage of respondents, in each district.

Great majority of the respondents (71% spread as 72.38% of Kinnaur and 68.89%) revealed that they have engaged labour for their cultivated land. Further, cultivated land is proved to be instrumental in terms of generating employment of more than Rs. 10,000 per annum for 85 percent labour. The respondents from Kinnaur district revealed that more than 86 percent labour engaged for land cultivation is earning more than Rs. 10,000 per annum. Needless to state that more than one fourth of the respondents who admitted to have labour engaged for cultivation have stated that the labour is earning above Rs. 40, 000 per annum due to cultivation of their land which is a handsome amount of employability. Moreover, there is similarity in responses of both the districts with regard to labour engaged for cultivation of land.

4.14 Major Changes in Cropping Pattern

Cropping pattern of a region is closely influenced by the geo-climatic, socio-economic, historical and political factors. In the instance of the present research, since both the study regions are considered as geographically tribal areas, the geo-climatic factors and socio-economic conditions are causes of changes in cropping pattern of these areas. Table 4.14 shows the major changes in cropping pattern of the selective tribal districts during the last 18 years.

Table-4.14 : Response Regarding Major Changes in Cropping Pattern

Changes in Cropping Pattern				New Crops Grown						
Responses	Yes	No	Total	Apple	Rajmah	Potato	Green peas	Apple /Rajmah	Potato Green peas	Total
Kinnaur	109 (51.9) **(56.77)**	101 (48.1) **(93.51)**	210 (100) **(70)**	42 (38.53) **(97.67)**	35 (32.11) **(79.54)**	13 (11.92) **(76.47)**	-	19(18.81) **(82.60)**	-	109(100) **(56.77)**
L & S	83 (92.2) **(43.22)**	7(7.8) **(6.48)**	90(100) **(30)**	1 (1.16) **(2.32)**	9 (10.84) **(20.45)**	4 (4.65) **(23.52)**	5(6.02) **(100)**	4 (4.65) **(17.39)**	60(72.28) **(100)**	83 (100) **(43.22)**
Total	192 (64) **(100)**	108 (36) **(100)**	300 (100) **(100)**	43 (39.44) **(100)**	44 (22.91) **(100)**	17 (8.85) **(100)**	5(2.60) **(100)**	23(11.97) **(100)**	60(31.25) **(100)**	192 (100) **(100)**

Source: Data collected through interview schedule.

- Horizontal data in parentheses denotes percentage out of total in particular districts.
- Vertical data in parentheses denotes percentage of respondents, in each district.

The respondents in a great majority, (64%) have admitted that they have switched over from production of one crop to another crop. Such a great shift has been recorded in Lahaul & Spiti where more than 92 percent respondents have advocated that they have shifted to produce new crops than the crops being already produced on their land. Such a change is stated by almost one half of the respondents of

Kinnaur. It is needless to mention that Rajmah (pulse) is the most preferred crop of production in both the regions as 32.11 percent of the respondents of Kinnaur and 10.84 percent of the respondents of Lahaul & Spiti who agreed that there is change in their cropping pattern, have revealed that they have changed from production of their existing crops to the production of Rajmah. However, in Lahaul & Spiti, the most dominating crops being produced are potato and peas which are admitted to be produced by 72.28 percent of the respondents. On the contrary, apart from Rajmah, Apple has been admitted as the most preferred crop being produced in Kinnaur according to 38.53 percent respondents.

4.15 Health Facilities in Tribal Areas

With a view to identify socio-economic development of the tribal population in terms of the health facilities available in the study area, attempt has been made to examine the availability of health facilities in these regions as shown in the following table 4.15.

Table-4.15 : Response Regarding Health Facility

	Health Facility			Type of Health Facility				
Responses	Yes	No	Total	Sub Centre	P.H.C	Rural Dispensary	Ayurvedic Dispensary	Total
Kinnaur	200 (95.2) **(86.95)**	10 (4.8) **(14.28)**	210 (100) **(70)**	53 (26.5) **(79.10)**	75 (37.5) **(92.59)**	43 (21.5) **(87.75)**	29 (14.5) **(87.87)**	200 (100) **(86.95)**
L &S	30 (33.3) **(13.04)**	60 (66.7) **(85.71)**	90 (100) **(30)**	14 (46.66) **(20.89)**	6 (20) **(7.40)**	6 (20) **(12.24)**	4 (13.33) **(12.12)**	30 (100) **(13.04)**
Total	230 (76.66) **(100)**	70 (23.33) **(100)**	300 (100) **(100)**	67 (29.13) **(100)**	81 (35.21) **(100)**	49 (21.30) **(100)**	33 (14.34) **(100)**	230 (100) **(100)**

Source: Data collected through interview schedule.

- Horizontal data in parentheses denotes percentage out of total in particular districts.
- Vertical data in parentheses denotes percentage of respondents, in each district.

It is apparent from the table that 95.2 percent of the respondents in Kinnaur district have basic health facilities in their villages. On the contrary, in Lahaul and Spiti, 66.7 percent respondents have no basic health facilities in their villages. This clearly indicates the difference of social development in both the regions in point of view of the availability of health facilities in these two regions.

Further, for tribal regions, Government of India has provided different types of health facilities. In both the districts out of 230 respondents who have health centres in their villages, (Sub Centre, PHC, Rural Dispensary, and Ayurvedic dispensary) 26.5 percent have sub centres; followed by 37.5 percent having PHCs' and 21.5 percent having Rural Dispensaries. Only 13.8 percent respondents have Ayurvedic Dispensaries in their villages. This shows that there are more allopathic health facilities available in District Kinnaur as compared to Ayurvedic health facilities. In Lahaul and Spiti district out of 30 respondents who have availability of health facilities, 46.66 percent have sub centres, followed by 20 percent having PHCs' 20 percent having rural dispensaries, and only 13.33 percent have Ayurvedic dispensaries.

Moreover, in both the districts 81 have PHCs' followed by, 67 who have sub centre, 49 have rural dispensaries, and 33 have Ayervedic dispensaries. It is analysed that in the study regions Primary Health Centres are provided by the government in almost all the villages of district Kinnaur, but ignored in case of Lahaul and Spiti region.

4.16 Contribution of Crops in Socio-Economic Development

It is obvious that abundant sources of income particularly highly productive traditional occupations due to high land fertility, have led to improve the income of people. The table 4.16 examines the percentage contribution of cropping income in total income of these tribal regions to analyze comparative change in the social and economic status of farmers residing at the adjoining regions of these areas.

Table-4.16 : Responses Regarding Contribution of Crops on Socio-Economic Development

Crops and Socio-Economic Development				Contribution of Crops in Income				
Responses	Yes	No	Total	Up to 30%	31-50%	51-70%	71-100%	Total
Kinnaur	197 (93.8) **(69.12)**	13 (6.2) **(86.66)**	210 (100) **(70)**	29 (14.72) **(93.54)**	52 (26.39) **(78.78)**	44 (22.33) **(78.57)**	72 (36.54) **(54.54)**	197 (100) **(69.12)**
L & S	88 (97.8) **(30.87)**	2 (2.2) **(13.33)**	90 (100) **(30)**	2(2.2) **(6.45)**	14 (15.90) **(21.21)**	12 (13.63) **(21.42)**	60 (68.18) **(45.45)**	88 (100) **(30.87)**
Total	285 (95) **(100)**	15(5) **(100)**	300 (100) **(100)**	31 (10.88) **(100)**	66 (23.15) **(100)**	56 (19.65) **(100)**	132 (46.31) **(100)**	285 (100) **(100)**

Source: Data collected through interview schedule.

- Horizontal data in parentheses denotes percentage out of total in particular districts.
- Vertical data in parentheses denotes percentage of respondents, in each district.

The responses of table 4.16 depict that crops have contributed to develop people economically due to which, they could improve their quantity of lives their by improved their status in the society as 95 percent of the respondents from both the districts have admitted it.

In Kinnaur, out of 93.8 percent of the respondents who admitted that due to production of crops, their socio- economic lives have changed, 36.54 percent are those who believe that the qualitative change in their socio-economic lives due to production of crops is to the extent of more than 70 percent. Whereas, more than two- third (68.18%) of such respondents (97.8%) from Lahaul & Spiti have stated more than 70 percent contribution of crops income in changing their socio-economic lives. It can be stated that in these two districts of the research, production of crops has contributed to add income and a socio-economic change as except 5 percent of the respondents who are not of this view and except 10.88 percent of those who are admitting socio-economic change due to crops, rest of the respondents from both the districts accept more than 30 percent change in their socio-economic lives due to production of crops.

4.17 Road Structure in Tribal Areas

It is true that good roads connectivity leads to boost- up social set up by strengthening economic network and infrastructure and encouraging markets. The relevance of efficiency of cropping outturn is obviously dependent upon road structure. Keeping in view, the correlation between cropping in the tribal regions of Kinnaur and Lahaul & Spiti and cropping has been tried to be understood with the help of the feedback of the informants. The following table 4.17 shows how road structure is ranked by the respondents.

Table-4.17 : Response Regarding Road Structure in Tribal Areas

Responses	Total Respondents	Percent
Poor	159	53.0
Below Average	24	8.0
Average	87	29.0
Moderate	23	7.7
Excellent	7	2.3
Total	300	100.0

Source: Data collected through interview schedule.

Road structure of the tribal regions has been stated to be poor by 53% respondent, followed by 29 who have stated that it is average. As per 90% responses, the fact is that road structure is average or below average which analyses that poor road structure is a hurdle in the researched tribal regions.

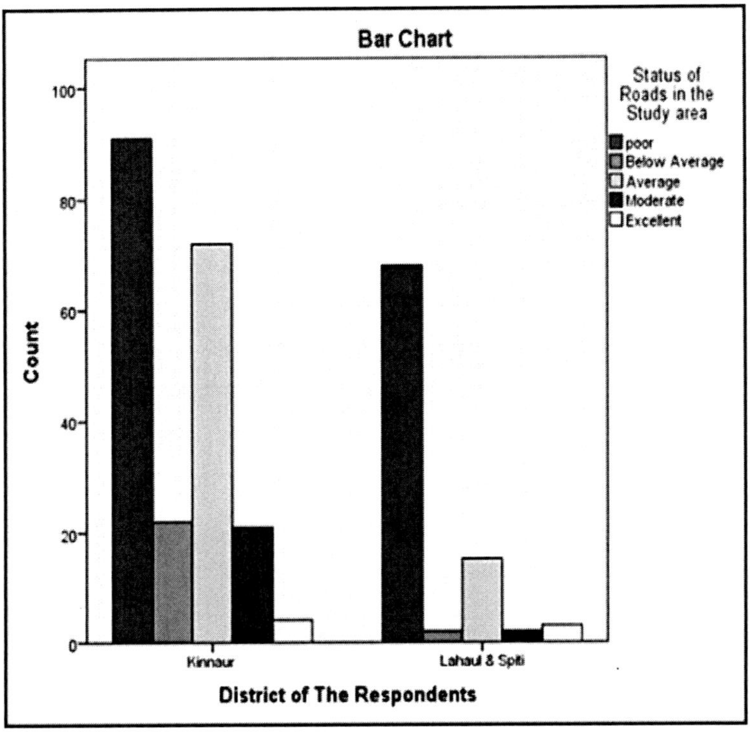

Figure 4.1 : Road Structure in the Study Areas

4.18 Annual Income-wise Types of Houses

The responses reflect that cropping pattern is contributing to socio-economic development. But the conformity of such responses necessitates to know about annual income, facilities being availed and status of properties particularly the types of houses of the respondents. Attempt has been made to study annual income and types of houses of the informants as per table 4.18.

Table-4.18 : Annual Income-wise Types of Houses

(per annum)

Annual income of family	Kachcha	Kachcha-Packcka	Packcka-Small	Packcka-Large	Packcka-Wooden	Total
Up to 2,00,000	44(37.3) (83)	27(22.9) (50)	10(8.5) (25.64)	21(17.8) (18.4)	16(13.6) (40)	118(100) (39.3)
2,00,001-5,00,000	9(8.6) (17)	19(18.09) (35.18)	24(22.85) (61.15)	41(39) (36)	11(10.5) (27.5)	105(100) (35)
5,00,001-10,00,000	0(0) (0)	5(9.09) (9.25)	4(7.3) (10.25)	36(65.5) (31.6)	10(18.2) (25)	55(100) (18.3)
Above 10,00,000	0(0) (0)	2(9.1) (3.7)	1(4.5) (2.6)	16(72.7) (14)	3(13.6) (7.5)	22(100) (7.3)
Total	53(17.7) (100)	54(18) (100)	39(13) (100)	114(38) (100)	40(13.3) (100)	300
C=.484 Chi -value 91.623 p.Value.000						

Source: Data collected through interview schedule.

- Horizontal data in parentheses denotes percentage out of total in particular districts.
- Vertical data in parentheses denotes percentage of respondents, in each district.

Amongst 118 respondents falling under the category of annual family income upto Rs. 2 lakhs, 74 percent have revealed that their houses are characterized to have kachcha as well as packcka houses. Further, respondents having annual income between Rs. 2 to 5 lakhs have in a great majority (35%), stated to have packcka large houses, whereas, all others having income above Rs. 5 lakhs, have packcka large houses. Overall, majority have (38%) packcka large houses. It is pertinent to state that those having kachcha houses, kachcha & packcka houses and packcka small houses, in majority, are having income between Rs. 2 to 5 lakhs and those having packcka large and packcka wooden houses, have annual income in majority between Rs. 5 to 10 lakhs.

Chi-square value is 91.623 and indicates asymptotic significance (i.e., p-value) 0.000 which is highly significant at 0.01 level of confidence. Hence it may be concluded that there is a significant impact of income on the family and type of house constructed in the tribal regions. It analyses that higher income leads to contain large sized packcka houses.

4.19 Occupation wise Annual Income

The table 4.19 depicts the occupation wise annual income from agriculture or horticulture. Income from agriculture has not remained the only source but people are engaged in government jobs and other occupations also. The 32 respondents have revealed that they are earning from govt. Job along with cropping income out of whom, 31.2 percent have earned between Rs. 1 lakh to Rs. 2 lakhs, followed by 25 percent each up to Rs. 1,00,000, and between Rs. 2 to 5 lakhs and only 3.1 percent respondent is revealed earning above Rs. 10 lakhs. Further, 74 respondents are those who have earning from government job along with horticultural income, out of which, 32.43 percent are earning between Rs. 1 to 2 lakhs, followed by 29.72 percent having income up to Rs. 1,00,000, 28.37 percent between Rs. 2 to 5 lakhs, 8.10 percent are those who have earning between Rs. 5 to 10 lakhs and only 1 (1.4%) informant is earning above Rs. 10,00,000.

Table-4.19 : Occupation Wise Annual Income

Occupation	Up to Rs.1,00,000	Rs.1,00,001 to Rs.2,00,000	Rs.2,00,001 to Rs.5,00,000	Rs.5,00,000 to Rs.10,00,000	Above 10,00,000	Total
Government job/Agriculture/ Horticulture	8(25) **(7)**	10(31.2) **(13.5)**	8(25) **(10.1)**	5(15.6) **(18.5)**	1(3.1) **(16.7)**	32(100) **(10.7)**
Government job/Horticulture	22(29.7) **(19.3)**	24(32.4) **(32.4)**	21(28.4) **(26.6)**	6(8.1) **(22.2)**	1(1.4) **(16.7)**	74(100) **(24.7)**
Agriculture	41(58.6) **(36)**	16(22.85) **(21.6)**	8(11.4) **(10.1)**	4(5.7) **(14.8)**	1(1.4) **(16.7)**	70(100) **(23.3)**
Horticulture	26(38.8) **(22.8)**	12(17.9) **(16.2)**	21(31.3) **(26.6)**	6(9) **(22.2)**	2(3) **(33.3)**	67(100) **(22.3)**
Agrculture/ Horticulture	7(21.2) **(6.1)**	8(24.2) **(10.8)**	13(39.4) **(16.5)**	5(15.2) **(18.5)**	0(0.0) **(0.0)**	33(100) **(11)**
Agri / Horti / Any Other (Business, Handloom, Contractor)	10(41.7) **(8.8)**	4(16.7) **(5.4)**	8(33.3) **(10.1)**	1(4.2) **(3.7)**	1(4.2) **(16.7)**	24(100) **(8)**
Total	114(38) **(100)**	74(24.7) **(100)**	79(26.3) **(100)**	27(9) **(100)**	6(2) **(100)**	300(100) **(100)**
C= .316 chi-value 33.188 p. value .032						

Source: Data collected through interview schedule.

- Horizontal data in parentheses denotes percentage out of total in particular districts.
- Vertical data in parentheses denotes percentage of respondents, in each district.

As many as 70 respondents have revealed that they have only agricultural income, out of which majority of the respondents (58.6%) have earning up to Rs. 1,00,000, followed by 22.85 percent having income between Rs. 1 to Rs. 2 lakhs, 11.4 percent have income between Rs. 2 to Rs. 5 lakhs, 5.71 percent between Rs. 5 to Rs. 10 lakhs and only 1.42 percent (1) is earning above Rs. 10,00,000. Horticulture is also the main traditional occupation of both the districts. Out of 67 respondents, 38.80 percent have stated that their earning is up to Rs. 1,00,000, followed by 31.34 percent between Rs. 2 to Rs. 5 lakhs, 17.9 percent between Rs. 1 to Rs. 2 lakhs, 9 percent between Rs. 5 to Rs. 10 lakhs and only 2.98 percent have earning above Rs. 10,00,000. Only 33, respondents are those who have both agriculture as well as horticultural income. Out of which, 39.4 percent have earning between Rs. 2 to Rs. 5 Lakhs, followed by 24.24 percent who are earning between Rs. 1 to Rs. 2 lakhs, 21.21 percent have earning up to Rs. 1 lakh and 15.2 percent are earning between Rs. 5 to Rs. 10 lakhs.

It is worth to state that both the tribal districts of Himachal Pradesh are known for traditional cottage industry and handloom. Consequently, a major chunk of population was traditionally involved in these activities and as such, they had an additional source of earning. The respondents have admitted that still these activities are instrumental in their annual income as 24 respondents are those who have earning from agriculture/horticulture as well as business, handloom and contracts. Amongst those whose income is from these activities, 10 have stated that they are earning up to Rs. 1,00,000, 8 between Rs. 2 to Rs. 5 lakhs, 4 between Rs. 1 to Rs. 2 lakhs, 1 between Rs. 5 to Rs. 10 lakhs and 1 is earning above Rs. 10 lakhs. It is analysed from the table that the people of tribal districts are not only dependent on the cropping income but with the employment as well as business. Influence of occupation on cropping income has been analyzed by applying chi-square test. The Chi-square value is 91.623 and p. value is 0.032 which is significant at 0.05 level of confidence. Hence it may be concluded that there is a significant influence of occupation on cropping income. Therefore, the null hypothesis is rejected. It leads to the conclusion that respondents have different opinion regarding occupation and agriculture income.

4.20 Marketing of Crops: Education Qualification Wise Distribution

The respondents have stated that their crops are being marketed in different market places of the State as well as outside. However, selection of the market place has been found to be influenced by the educational status. Table 4.20 shows that out of 69 illiterate respondents, 60.86 percent are selling their crops within the State, against 39.13 percent outside. A huge number of respondents (156) are educated up to senior secondary level, out of which majority of the respondents 54.5 percent have sold their crops outside the State, followed by 45.5 percent selling within the State. It has been revealed by 60 graduate households that, 50 percent have sold their crops outside the State, followed by 48.33 percent selling locally and only 1.7 percent is selling crops through other source i.e. standing crops to the thekedar.

Table-4.20 : Marketing of Crops: Education Qualification wise Distribution

Qualification	Local within the State	Outside State	Other	Total
Illiterate	42(**60.9**) (28.19)	27(**39.1**) (18)	0 (0.0)	69(**100**) (23)
Up to +2	71(**45.5**) (47.65)	85(**54.5**) (56.67)	0 (0.0)	156(**100**) (52)
Graduate	29(**48.3**) (19.46)	30(**50**) (20)	1(**1.7**) (100)	60(**100**) (20)
Post Graduate	7(**53.8**) (4.69)	6(**46.2**) (4)	0 (0.0)	13(**100**) (4.33)
Other	0 (0.0)	2(**100**) (1.33)	0 (0.0)	2(**100**) (0.66)
Total	149(**49.7**) (100)	150(**50**) (100)	1(**0.3**) (100)	300(**100**) (100)
Chi –value 10.643 df=8 p. Value .223				

Source: Data collected through interview schedule.

- Horizontal data in parentheses denotes percentage out of total in particular districts.
- Vertical data in parentheses denotes percentage of respondents, in each district.

Further, out of 13 post graduate respondents, 53.8 percent have stated that they sell their crops within the State and 46.2 percent outside the State. Only 2 stating to have other qualification (i.e. professional courses), have stated that they sell their crops outside the State. While applying cross tab, chi square-value is calculated 10.643 with p value i.e. 0.223 is not significant on the 0.05 level of confidence. Thus, it is analysed that educational qualification influences pattern of marketing of crops.

4.21 Factors Affecting Crops

Table 4.21 depicts the factors which affect production of crops in both the tribal regions. From the table 4.21, it is clear that in Kinnaur, production and marketing of crops is mainly affected by lack of irrigation facility, non availability of labour and inefficient road networking as per the responses of 82.78 percent respondents. Whereas, in Lahaul & Spiti, apart from the above mentioned factors, majority (53.3%) have stated that soil and weather as well as transportation are responsible for less efficiency of production and marketing status of crops. Moreover, the value of correlation signifies that there is influence of different factors on production and marketing of crops in both the districts.

Table-4.21 : Factors Affecting Production and Marketing of Crops

Respondents of the districts	Lack of guidance/proper seeds/ fertilizer /credit facilities	Irrigation Facility/soil and weather/Labour/ Transportation/ Road Networking	Irrigation Facility/Labour/ Road Networking	Proper seeds/ Fertilizer/ Irrigation Facility/Soil and Weather	Total
Kinnaur	6 (2.9) 37.5	71 (33.8) 59.66	101 (48.1) 82.78	32 (15.2) 74.41	210 (100) 70
Lahaul & Spiti	10 (11.1) 62.5	48 (53.3) 40.33	21 (23.3) 17.21	11 (12.2) 25.58	90 (100)
Total	16 (5.3) 100	119 (39.7) 100	122 (40.7) 100	43 (14.3) 100	300 (100) 100
C =.272 Chi –Value 24 df=3 P. Value .000					

Source: Data collected through interview schedule.

- Horizontal data in parentheses denotes percentage out of total in particular districts.
- Vertical data in parentheses denotes percentage of respondents, in each district.

4.22 Correlation between Annual Income and Types of Houses

Table-4.22 : Correlation between Annual Income and Types of Houses

		1	2	3	4	5	6	7	8	9
S.No.	Statements	Annual income from cropping	Type of house	Bathroom	Laterine	Electricity	Water	Radio/ Television/ Telephone	Gas/ Stove/ Culah	Store
1	Annual cropping Income	1								
2	Type of House	.351**	1.00							
3	Bathroom	0.218**	0.162**	1.00						
4	Laterine	0.259**	0.128**	0.494**	1.00					
5	Electricity	0.085	.159**	.310**	.179**	1.00				
6	Water	0.206**	.280**	.246**	.315**	0.090	1.00			
7	Radio/T.V.	.121*	.110*	.090	.103	.282**	.139*	1.00		
8	Gas/Stove/Culah	.171**	.100	.150**	.169**	.201**	.150**	.219**	1.00	
9	Store	.327**	.238**	.296**	.310**	.163**	.099	.100	.266**	1.00

Source: Data collected through interview schedule.

Table 4.22 presents the correlation matrix of nine statements. It is revealed from the table that statements 1 to 9 are positively correlated with each other at 1 percent and 5 percent level of significance. These statements are related to annual agricultural income of the households and type of house of the respondents. Further, annual income of the households is showing positive relationship with type of house, latrine, bathroom, electricity, water, gas/stove/chulah and store. Majority of the statements relating to facilities available in houses have shown significant positive relation at 1 percent level of significance, only statement 7 i.e. Radio/Television has been significant at 5 percent level of significance. It leads to the conclusion that in tribal areas people are more concerned with television facility.

4.23 Correlation between Annual Income and Crops Grown

Table-4.23 : Correlation between Annual income and Crops Grown

	Statements	1	2	3	4	5	6
Kendall's tau-b		Annual income from agri/horti crops	Kharif Crops Grown	Rabi Crops Grown	Vegetables Grown	Fruits	Any other vegetables and medicinal plants
1	Annual income from agri/horti crops	1.000					
2	Kharif crops grown	.251**	1.000				
3	Rabi Crops Grown	-.189**	-.303**	1.000			
4	Vegetables grown	-.046	-.067*	-0.70	1.000		
5	Fruits	.221**	.343**	.175	.103**	1.000	
6	Any other Vegetables and Medicinal plants	-.72	-.289**	.123	.080	-.418**	1.000

Source: Data collected through interview schedule.

It is revealed from the table that statements 1, 2 and 5 are positively correlated with each other at 1 percent level of significance. These statements have shown contribution of Kharif crops and fruits produce. Further, annual income of the households has been negative correlation with Rabi crops, vegetables and other vegetables and

Medicinal plants. It leads to the conclusion that only Kharif crops and fruits are commercialised in both the districts leading to income generation whereas, Rabi crops and vegetables are not contributing to income generation.

4.24 Correlation between Annual Income and Average Annual Expenditure

Table 4.24 shows the Kendall's correlation coefficient for Agricultural income with Average Annual Expenditure. It may be analysed from the table that the agricultural income and Average Annual Expenditure have high and positive significant correlation (r=.517) at 0.01 level of confidence. It shows that as the income increases, expenditure also increases to the extent of 51 percent.

Table-4.24 : Correlation between Annual Income and Average Annual Expenditure

	Annual income from Agriculture/Horticulture Crops	Average Annual Expenditure
Annual income from Agriculture/Horticulture Crops	1.000	.517**
Average Annual Expenditure	.517**	1.000

Source: Data collected through interview schedule.

Table-4.25 : Major Factors Affecting Cropping Pattern

Statements	Large Extent	Some Extent	Not at all	Total	Mean	Sd	Sk	Kt	Chi	P.value
More Floods	163	110	27	300	2.45	.655	-7.96	-.444	93.980	**.000**
More Soil -erosion	127	135	38	300	2.30	.681	-.450	-.814	57.980	**.000**
More Land slide	228	40	32	300	2.65	.664	-1.680	1.345	246.080	**.000**
Less rain	152	88	60	300	2.31	.784	-.599	-1.126	44.480	**.000**
Less snow fall	117	92	91	300	2.09	.830	-.163	-1.529	4.340	**.114**
Erratic rain	154	108	38	300	2.39	.702	-703	-.710	68.240	**.000**
Drought	147	81	72	300	2.25	.818	-.491	-1.337	33.540	**.000**
Global warming	154	93	53	300	2.34	.761	-.652	-.990	51.740	**.000**
Hydro electric project	188	58	54	300	2.45	.781	-.969	-.672	116.240	**.000**
Deforestation	121	123	56	300	2.22	.738	-.368	-1.093	29.060	**.000**
Over grazing	114	136	50	300	2.21	.709	-.332	-.975	39.920	**.000**

Contd. ...

Hyd seeds	90	154	56	300	2.11	.689	-.152	-.891	49.520	**.000**
Fertilizer	124	96	80	300	2.15	.813	-.275	-1.435	9.920	**.007**
Pesticides	96	128	76	300	2.07	.756	-.111	-1.237	13.760	**.001**
Availing Agricultural Loan	153	105	42	300	2.37	.718	-.684	-790	61.980	**.000**
Availing Subsidies	146	112	42	300	2.35	.713	-.618	-832	56.240	**.000**
Availing Crop insurance	60	96	114	300	1.72	.777	**.533**	-1.154	35.520	**.000**
Irrigation facilities	127	88	85	300	2.14	.830	-.267	-1.500	10.980	**.004**
Lack of awareness about the above said facilities	133	122	45	300	2.29	.713	-.496	-.923	45.980	**.000**
Traditional mindset	138	121	41	300	2.32	.703	-.547	-.847	53.660	**.000**
Land division	202	50	48	300	2.51	.756	-1.167	-.248	156.080	**.000**
Nuclear family	115	149	36	300	2.26	.660	-.344	-.758	67.220	**.000**
Small land holdings	130	139	31	300	2.33	.655	-.465	-718	71.820	**.000**
Total				300		.				

Source: Data collected through interview schedule.

It is the well known fact that the horticulture and agriculture is a biggest growing industry in rural economy of the state. The livelihood of majority of the respondents of study area is depending on the crops grown by them, either it is for commercial purpose or for self consumption. As far as the cropping pattern is concerned it depends on the many factors like climatic factors, manmade factors, government provided facilities and social factors. The factors affecting cropping pattern includes floods, soil erosion, land slide, less rain, less snow fall, erratic rain, drought, global warming, hydro electric projects, excess running of vehicle, deforestation, overgrazing, HYD Seeds, fertiliser, pesticides, availing agricultural loan, subsidies, crop Insurance, lack of irrigation facilities, lack of awareness, traditional mindset, land division, nuclear family and small land holdings. These aforesaid factors made researcher to analyze various factors fostering problems towards changes in cropping pattern and its impact of the socio-economic life of the people of the study areas.

In the study regions, there is a uncertainty in occurrence of the factors like floods, soil erosion, land slide, less rain, less snow fall which effects the crop pattern and crop production. It is the fact that due to the adverse effects of these climatic factors farmers are compelled to shifting there cropping pattern. And as per the responses, the man made factors like Hydro electric projects, deforestation and overgrazing is also affects the crop production and cropping pattern in these regions. Along with this there is also lack of awareness among farmers about technological and scientific knowledge, farmers are still practising traditional methods of farming and facing the problem of unavailability of HYD seeds, fertiliser and pesticides in the study regions. Furthermore, the opinion regarding lacking awareness of the credit facilities provided by government like agricultural loan (kcc), subsidies to buy new agricultural equipments, and crop insurance schemes also affects the cropping pattern of these regions, the majority of the farmers of these regions admitted that, they are availing the agricultural loans, about subsidies majority admitted that they are aware about subsidies provided by the government, but they also revealed that the process of availing these facilities is taking long time . In context of crop insurance, majority of the respondents are admitted that they are not aware about the crop insurance schemes. There are some social factors which are also affects the cropping pattern, majority of the respondents are admitted that the factors like traditional mindset, regarding cultivation of crops, traditional farming techniques, trend of nuclear family and small land holdings are also responsible for shifting of cropping pattern and less production of crops. As exhibited in table 4.25 when examined floods, soil erosion, land slide, less rain, less snow fall, erratic rain, drought, global warming, hydro electric projects, excess running of vehicle, deforestation, overgrazing, hyd seeds, fertiliser, pesticides, the climatic and manmade factors affecting cropping pattern and crop production. The mean score of above factor arrived at three point likert scale is (2.45, 2.30, 2.65, 2.31, 2.09, 2.39, 2.25, 2.34, 2.45, 2.22, 2.21, 2.11, 2.15 and 2.07) respectively which is greater than the standard mean score, which explains that the opinions of respondents are bent towards higher side. Furthermore, the negative value of skewness and kurtosis is platykurtic which confirms the above results. Also when test of goodness of fit is applied the chi square value arrived is significant at 0.01 percent level of significance. The other factors in the same context above mention is availing agricultural loan, subsidies, crop insurance, lack of irrigation facilities, lack of awareness, traditional mindset, land division, nuclear family and small land holdings. The result reflects that the calculated mean score of above factors is (2.07, 2.37, 2.35, 2.14, 2.29, 2.32, 2.51, 2.26 and 2.33) respectively which is greater than the standard mean score, which show that the opinion of respondent towards higher side. Moreover, kurtosis is leptokurtic while the chi square value is significant at 0.05 percent level of significance. In nutshell, it is evidently inferred that all these factors are affecting the cropping pattern of the study regions and crop production of these regions.

SUMMARY

On the basis of the analysis drawn in the chapter, Kinnaur district is much ahead in education and employment as compared to Lahaul and Spiti. Majority of Kinnaur is engaged in horticulture along with employment in government and private sectors, whereas in Lahaul & Spiti, majority is engaged in agricultural occupation. The traditional occupations like handloom and cultivation of traditional crops, are decreasing in both the districts and the people are shifting towards the modern occupations and cultivation of commercial crops. The major agricultural crops in both the districts are peas, potato, rajmah, and hops etc. and the major horticultural crops include apple, pear, walnut and grapes etc. Further, some other crops in uncultivated land in both the districts are, chilgoza (neyoza), kala zira, rattanjot, kuth, manu, and wild mushroom etc. Majority of the crops in Lahaul & Spiti region are sold within the State whereas, majority in Kinnaur are sold outside the State.

In respect of agricultural income, majority of Kinnauras' are earning income between Rs. 2,00,001 to Rs. 5,00,000 whereas, majority of Lahaulis' are earning between Rs. 1,00,001 to Rs. 2,00,000 annually. It indicates that the earning from agriculture is low and joint families are still in prevalence.

Agriculture and horticulture are major occupations in both the districts. Further, the cropping pattern and crop production of both the districts are affected by climatic conditions, manmade factors, social factors and scientific factors. which require improving road networking, transportation, guidance and help from government agencies to establish local markets and crop insurance facility etc.

5

Conclusion, Findings and Suggestions

Agriculture provides and sustains the food supply and fulfils other basic needs of human beings. It is associated with the production of various crops. However, 'Agricultural Operations' include animal husbandry, dairy farming and poultry farming also. Similarly, 'Agriculture Produce' includes all produce of the agriculture or horticulture and all articles of food or drink wholly or partly manufactured from any such produce and fleeces and the skins of animals. Agriculture is the art, science and occupation of cultivating the field, producing crops and raising livestock and in varying degrees, the preparation and marketing of the resulting products. Hence, the term agriculture also includes the process of financing, processing, marketing and distribution of agricultural products; services of other sectors, health, nutrition and food consumption, proper use of land and water resources their conservation, development and maintenance of recreational resources.

The agricultural sector in India, has occupied almost 43 percent of the total geographical area of the Country. It contributes to nearly one-fourth to the National Gross Product (NGP) and provides employment opportunities to about two- third of the population.

Majority of the Indian population resides in villages. Rural development is a priority which implies equitable economic growth. Rural development includes increased participation of people in the rural development process, decentralization of planning, better enforcement of land reforms and greater access to credit and inputs as well as improvements in health, education, drinking water, energy supply, sanitation and housing coupled with attitudinal changes. The country has a great diversity in terms of Caste, Creed, Region, Culture and other considerations which are influencing development of society.

Scheduled Tribes are classified on the basis of geographical areas of land, economic conditions of people, region and culture etc. The total population of Scheduled Tribes in India is 8.61 percent of the total population. Their population has increased more rapidly than the total population growth of the Country except for the state of Nagaland. The dominating regions of Scheduled Tribes in terms of geographical considerations are in the Himalayan ranges including the State of Himachal Pradesh, Uttarakhand, Bihar, Jammu and Kashmir, Uttar Pradesh, Assam, Meghalya, Arunachal Pradesh and Sikkim.

The tribes of Himachal Pradesh are natives of the borders of other countries. They are in the Districts of Kinnaur and Lahaul-Spiti and some parts of Chamba and Kangra Districts. The tribal communities of the region are Lahaulis, Kinnauras, Pangwals, Spitians, Bodh, Khampa, Jad, Lamba and Swangwals. The topographical conditions of the tribal regions of the State are quite tough. However, the sloppy landscape is fertile and the dependence of people is mainly upon agricultural and horticultural production.

The continuous population pressure on land, lack of rural non-farm employment opportunities, liberal laws of inheritance and resultant sub-division of holdings, etc. are some constraints in boosting-up agricultural production and productivity and raising the level of living of Indian farmers. With a view to encourage agriculture, land reforms were made to revamp the institutional framework by redistributing land in favour of the poor, providing security of tenure, regularity of rent on land and consolidating small and fragmented holdings. The crops are categorized on the physical and economic basis consisting of Kharif, Rabi, food crops, oilseeds, fibre crops, plantation crops and horticultural crops. During the period of green revolution in the late sixties and early seventies, there was a continuous surge in diversified agriculture on techno- economic considerations.

This study endeavors to understand the cropping pattern of tribal districts (Kinnaur and Lahaul-Spiti) of Himachal Pradesh, in context of socio-economic development of inhabitants of these regions. Cropping pattern refers to the distribution of cultivated land among different crops. It also reveals the nature of agricultural operations, including the importance of food- crops and cash- crops. Cropping pattern varies from region to region and country to country. It also refers to the change in cultivation and distribution of crops and change in the area under crop cultivation over a period of time.

The difficulty in mountainous states like Himachal Pradesh is that there is less availability of cultivable land and prevalence of small land holdings. Only 22.12 percent of the total utilised area in Himachal Pradesh is cultivable. Besides this, Himachal Pradesh is famous for production and selling of apple, peach, almond, pears, mango, lichi, potato, peas etc. and the study regions have unique feature of production of both, cash as well as traditional crops like kuth, manu, chilgoza, walnut, hops, charma, fafra, ogla, wheat, buckwheat, takk, kodha, and dhankhar etc.

Researchers have studied cropping patterns of different regions with respect to different climatic conditions, topographical variations and other variables. The scholars have stated that relatively less time is required to increase productivity of crops by bringing in new technology and services. Further, studies reveal that there is influence of natural forces like storm, drought, wind, rain etc. on productivity of crops, which are beyond the control of farmers and that there is a need to shift from food crops to commercial crops. However, the researchers have not paid attention upon discussing crop intensity, dependency on cropping and its impact on employment and as such, these reasons prompted to conduct this research with reference to the tribal areas of Himachal Pradesh.

The process of shifting of cropping pattern has gained momentum in the tribal areas in nineties and has now encompassed many new areas in the low and mid hill districts. The total geographical area of Himachal Pradesh is 55,673 sq. kms, out of which 45,756.38 Sq. kms (82.19%) is utilised area for different purposes of production. Out of the average Used Area, 22.12 percent is Cropped Area, and only 9.83 percent is Irrigated Area. Further, out of the average Used Area, in Kinnaur only 1.74 percent area is Cropped Area 49.67 percent of which is Irrigated Area. On the contrary, out of the average Used Area in Lahaul & Spiti, an average of 0.45 percent i.e. 3397.31 hectares area is Cropped Area. It is concluded that 0.97 percent area of Kinnaur and 0.34 percent area of Lahaul & Spiti is cultivated area of the State.

The average Cropping Intensity of Himachal Pradesh was 173.84 percent and the average Irrigation Intensity was 174.13 percent. In Kinnaur, average Cropping Intensity was 122.50 percent which ranged between maximum cropping intensity of 131.20 percent in the year 2000-01 and minimum 116.10 percent in the year 2004-05 and the Average Irrigation Intensity was 124.10 percent, with considerable fluctuation (maximum 135.39% and minimum 118.40%). In Lahaul & Spiti, the average Cropping Intensity was 104.19 percent and Average Irrigation Intensity of the district was 106.25 percent.

It is concluded that both the districts have less Irrigation Intensity as compared to the State. However, Kinnaur has recorded an increase in Irrigation Intensity. Whereas, Lahaul & Spiti has recorded slight decline. The study finds that the cropping intensity in Kinnaur is more consistent as compared to Lahaul & Spiti and irrigation is based upon traditional systems of kulh as the major source of irrigation.

One of the objectives of the study was to know about the outturn of crops grown in district Kinnaur and district Lahaul & Spiti. The study finds that the average outturn of cereals was 4456.38 metric tons i.e. 0.32 percent of average production of the State in Kinnaur and 1030.27 metric tons i.e. 0.07 percent of average production of the State in Lahaul & Spiti. In Kinnaur, the average outturn of pulses was 1020.33 metric tons (5.56% of the State) and 3665.41 metric tons in Lahaul & Spiti which is 19.98 percent of the State. In terms of production of vegetables in Kinnaur, average outturn was 1657.53 metric tons which is 0.86 percent of total production of vegetables in the State. In Lahaul & Spiti, it was 20,010.29 metric tons which is 10.40 percent of the State. The average outturn of fresh fruits was 608237.28 metric tons in Himachal Pradesh, out of which 38604.36 metric tons (6.34% of the State's production) was in Kinnaur and 199.33 metric tons (0.32% of the State) in Lahaul & Spiti. Further, Kinnaur district is contributing 10.35 percent to the total production of dry fruits while Lahaul -Spiti is producing 0.29 percent. However, production of non food crops is very less in Kinnaur as compared to Lahaul & Spiti i.e. 12.89 metric tons in Kinnaur (0.13% of the State) and 154.78 metric tons (1.61%) in Lahaul & Spiti. Thus it is found that in production of cereals, fresh fruits and dry fruits district Kinnaur is ahead of Lahaul & Spiti whereas, in production of pulses, vegetables and non-food crops, district Lahaul-Spiti is ahead of district Kinnaur. Overall, it is concluded that Kinnaur consists of 12.34 percent and Lahaul-Spiti consists of 17.34 percent utilized land area of Himachal Pradesh, respectively. Lahaul-Spiti is bigger in comparison to Kinnaur in terms of total land area but production and yield of different crops is higher in district Kinnaur.

Findings

It was found from the primary data collected from 300 respondents that 77 percent harvested Kharif crops (maize, rajmah, fafra, ogla), 84 percent harvested Rabi crops (wheat, barley), 97 percent harvested vegetables (potato, peas, tomato, cabbage, beans) and 8 percent harvested medicinal plants (kuth, manu, hops, charma). The analysis of the empirical data of the research reveals that the socio-economic condition of the tribal people is directly influenced by their agricultural income. A positive co-relation is found between the agricultural income and the quantity and quality of amenities and facilities available in the houses of tribal people.

However, majority of population has total cultivated land ownership below 10 bhigas in both the districts. It concludes that in both the tribal districts, farmers have small land holdings despite the difference in the total land area of the districts.

The study finds that there is an impact of education and employment on cropping pattern of the region. It is found that Kinnaur district is much ahead in education and employment as compared to Lahaul and Spiti. Majority of people of Kinnaur district is engaged in horticulture along with employment in government and private sector jobs, whereas in Lahaul & Spiti, majority is engaged in agricultural occupations. The traditional occupations like handloom and cultivation of traditional crops, are decreasing in both the districts and the people are shifting towards the modern occupations and cultivation of commercial crops. The major agricultural crops in both the districts are peas, potato, rajmah, and hops etc. and the major horticultural crops include apple, pear, walnut and grapes etc. Further, some other crops in uncultivated land in both the districts are, chilgoza (neyoza), kalazira, rattanjot, kuth, manu, and wild mushroom etc. In terms of marketing of crops it is found that, majority of Lahaulis sell their crops within the State whereas, majority of Kinnauras sold their crops outside the State.

In context of agricultural income, majority of Kinnauras are earning annual income between Rs. 2,00,001 to Rs. 5,00,000, whereas, majority of Lahaulis are earning between Rs. 1,00,001 to Rs. 2,00,000 annually. It concludes that the earning from agriculture is low in Lahaul & Spiti district in comparison to Kinnaur district though it is low in both the districts.

The study finds that joint families are still in prevalence in both the districts and agriculture and horticulture are the major occupations in both the districts.

Further, cropping pattern and crop production of both the districts are affected by factors like climatic factors, manmade factors, facilities provided by government and social factors including floods, soil erosion, land slide, less rain, less snow fall, erratic rain, drought, global warming, construction of hydro electric projects, excess running of vehicles, deforestation, overgrazing, use of pesticides, agricultural loans, imbalances causing diversion of occupation preferring daily wages, lack of irrigation facilities, lack of awareness, traditional mindset, land division, and small land holdings. The study concludes that due to the uncertainty in occurrence of these factors the cropping pattern and crop production is adversely affected.

Farmers are still practicing traditional methods of farming and facing the problem of unavailability of HYD seeds, fertilizers and pesticides. Cumbersome procedure of getting loan for agriculture along with long time delay for availing loan, low level of outturn, influences of environmental and social factors on crop yields, low level of infrastructure, low level of earnings from agriculture and use of land for production of similar crop repeatedly causing low level of productivity, are found to be the causes of change in cropping pattern. Further, introduction and implementation of new technologies, horticultural crops of high yield and stigma related to social status of the employed personnel and other occupations for which, government facilitated regulatory and financial support, is found to be responsible for a change of occupation and preference of agriculturists to engage in other occupations also. The above mentioned factors have been found to be responsible for change in cropping pattern by those who are dependent upon use of land holdings for better returns. The change in cropping pattern in the tribal areas of Himachal Pradesh has influenced socio-economic life of these regions.

Primary Health Centres are available in almost all the villages studied in Kinnaur disrict, but in Lahaul and Spiti region, still health services have not reached. Cropping pattern has been found instrumental in income generation for nearly one third population in Kinnaur and two third in Lahaul- Spiti. Thus dependency on cropping has though declined yet it is the occupation leading to employment generation in tribal areas. It can be stated that in Kinnaur and Lahaul-Spiti, production of crops has contributed to add income thereby socio-economic change.

- The study finds that Agriculture and Horticulture are the major sources of earning and employment in the tribal districts of Himachal Pradesh.
- In Kinnaur only 1.74 percent of Utilised Area is Cropped Area out of which 49.67 percent is Irrigated Area. In Lahaul & Spiti an average of 0.45 percent i.e. 3397.31 hectares area is Cropped Area and above 95 percent (3278.78 hectares) of the Cropped Area is Irrigated Area. It is found that 0.97 percent area of Kinnaur and 0.34 percent area of Lahaul & Spiti is cultivated area of the State.
- The average Cropping Intensity of Himachal Pradesh has been found 173.84 percent. In Kinnaur, it was 122.50 percent and was 104.19 percent in Lahaul & Spiti. The cropping intensity is found to vary from 116.10 percent to 131.20 percent in Kinnaur district and 102.40 percent to 106 percent in Lahaul & Spiti.
- The average Irrigation Intensity has been found 174.13 percent in Himachal Pradesh. It has been found 124.10 percent in Kinnaur and 106.25 percent in Lahaul & Spiti.
- It has been found that households have very small land holdings below 10 bhigas in both the districts.
- It is found that Apple crop is contributing maximum in household income, followed by potato and peas, almond crop, chilgoza and kuth, manu and hops in the tribal areas of Himachal Pradesh.
- The study finds that people are growing horticultural crops also and there is a shift in the cropping pattern due to which, the household income has increased and thereby, families could improve quality of their lives and could seek better education and respectable occupations. Thus following of new cropping pattern has influenced the socio-economic life of tribal population in the State.
- Both the tribal regions are known for production of chilgoza, ratanjot, kuth, manu, and hops, which cannot be marketed without obtaining license. This is causing decline in interest of people to produce and collect such crops.

- It has been found that there is abundance of water sources in the lower reaches of the tribal regions. But the villagers do not use such sources for irrigation. The Government should introduce funding schemes for construction of irrigation system from such water sources under subsidized loan scheme. This would motivate people to avail such loan and constructing such system, they would be benefited by irrigation.

Based upon the conclusion and findings of the research, following measures have been suggested:

Suggestions

- The tribal regions are still following the traditional methods of irrigation which are quite meager. On the other hand, cropping patterns have been changed to boost- up household income. In order to get a multiplier effect of production of crops, a need arises to install irrigation facilities by pumping river water or by any other modern technique for providing irrigation facility.
- There is a decline in the production and yield of traditional crops in the tribal regions whereas; some of the traditional crops have a special identity in the Country.
- There is a need to convince producers about the peculiarity of traditional medicinal crops for which twin initiatives are required (a) the procedure of issuing licences for sale of such crops by the residents of the tribal regions need to be liberalized for them and (b) Linkages with banks need to be developed for providing subsidies and loans for production and growth of these crops.
- The reservation in education and employment scheduled tribes is availed by the tribal regions of Kinnaur and Lahaul & Spiti. However, the benefit of reservation is being availed by those who could avail the opportunity to get education of the school level. The households having sources of income to send their children outside for higher education, are able to avail the reservation in education and then in employment. Cropping has emerged as the source of income for such households. Surprisingly, this process which starts from use of crops for income followed by availing reservation in education and then

employment is not much spread particularly in Lahaul- Spiti. After decades of the reservation policy and the beneficiaries are benefited generation to generation and are settled in areas outside these regions. Where there is no justification of the reservation for successor generations. There is a need to amend reservation policy to be employable for those who are residing in these regions so that they help others in socio-economic development by sustaining inherited occupations, culture and crops.

- Soil erosion due to construction of hydro-electric project and cutting of trees is causing environmental threats. The climate is gradually changing and to increase productivity of crops, the use of pesticides, fertilizers and chemicals is increasing. Thus, the existing horticulture and agriculture is not sustaining productivity and quality of production. Further, due to cutting of trees, there is increase in the volume of barren land area. In order to utilize barren land, there is a need to grow fruit crops by planting fruits like apple and peas which would compensate the loss due to cutting of trees to the environment and would be useful to add economy to the region and to the State.
- The scientific agricultural practices like inter cropping system and crop rotation should be followed to enhance soil fertility as well as crop production and crop productivity.
- Uncultivated areas are mostly under different Government bodies of Himachal Pradesh. If such areas are converted into cultivated land. Which leads to increase farming area, many commercial crops can be grown in such farms and can also ensure employment generation.
- Use of land for agriculture can be sustained by maintaining joint family system. As joint family system is a great boon with regard to agriculture, family members are indulging in agriculture activities there is no need to hire outside labour. Due to which family members get employment on their own land and crops are grown constantly. People who are living in nuclear families and involved in other employment are not actively indulged in agriculture. Their land remain uncultivated. In this regard, it is the moral duty of the religious and spiritual heads of the regions to encourage families to

sustain the inherited cultural values and to pay importance to the bondages of joint family system.

- There is a need to seek help of agriculture and horticulture departments to know about the characteristics of the soil and to select crops to be produced. The experts of the related departments should visit the regions and interact with farmers. It would also help the farmers to get guidance about the fertilizers to be used.
- Emphasis should be drawn by the growers of horticultural crops to grow such crops which are suitable in terms of the climatic conditions. This would be useful for getting high level of production and thereby more earnings.
- Commercial crops have changed the socio-economic set-up of the tribal regions due to which, people could avail better avenues of education and employment. However, it has been the cause of massive transformation. To sustain use of land and also to avail the better employment avenues. There is a need to encourage people of the tribal regions to serve in their native regions. This would be justifiable as per the motive of the reservation policy to encourage society as also to avail better employment avenues and sustained of land use which would have a prolonged effect of maintaining the dependency on land use.

There is a need to correlate cropping with their processing, marketing and Government support in the native regions of the tribal areas so that all kinds of traditional and changed crops grown by the farmers are ensured to be sold and processed there and in case of losses, the farmers are supported by the Government. It would lead to divert attention of the farmers to look for other employment avenues and would feel safe in terms of earnings from crops.

Bibliography

A. BOOKS

Attri, Rajender, Himachal Pradesh: A Himalayan Dreamland, Shimla: Sarla Publications, 2015.

Bakshi, S.R. and Kiran, Bala, Social and Economic Development of Scheduled Tribes, New Delhi: Deep and Deep Publication Pvt. Ltd., 2000.

Balokhra, Jag Mohan, The Wonderland – Himachal Pradesh, New Delhi: H.G. Publications, 2016.

Baradwaj, A.N., Problems of Scheduled Caste and Scheduled Tribes in India, New Delhi: Light and Life Publishers, 1985.

Bggichi, T., Profile of some Indian Tribes, Calcutta: Punti Pustak, 1994.

Bhange, N.P., Tribal Commissions and Committees in India, Bombay: Himalaya Publishing House, 1993.

Bose, Nirmal Kumar, Some Indian Tribes, New Delhi: National Book Trust, 1997.

Chatopadhyaya, Kamala Devi, Tribalism in India, New Delhi: Vikas Publishing House,1979.

Choudhary Mamata, Tribes of Ancient India, Calcutta: Indian Museum, 1977.

Desai, A.R., Rural India in Transition, Bombay: Popular Book Depot, 1961.

Devendra, Thakur, Socio-economic Development of Tribes in India, New Delhi: Deep and Deep Publications, 1986.

Dhondyal, S.P., Problem of Indian Agriculture, Meerut: Friends Publication, 1995.

Furer, Haimendorf, Tribes of India, Bombay: Oxford University Press, 1982.

Ghurye, G.S., The Tribals So Called, Bombay: Popular Book Depot, 1959.

Govind, N., Regional Perspectives in Agricultural Development, New Delhi: Concept Publishing Company, 1986.

Grigg, D., An Introduction to Agriculture Geography, New York: Routledge Printing in London, 1975.

Grigg, D., The Dynamics of Agricultural Change, The Historical experience, London: Hutchinson, 1982.

Gupta, K.R., Water Crisis in India, New Delhi: Atlantic Publishers & Distributors Ltd., 2008.

Hasnain, Nadeem, Tribal India, Delhi: Palaka Prakashan, 2009.

Husain, M., Systematic Agricultural Geography, Jaipur: Rawat Publications, 1996.

Jain, C.K., Pattern of Agricultural Development, New Delhi: Northern Book Centre, 1988.

Jain, S.C., Agricultural Development in India, Allahabad: Kitab Mahal, 1967.

Jhodha, N.S., and Vyas, V.S., Condition of Stability and Growth in Arid Agriculture, Gujrat: Agro Economic Research Centre, 1969.

Jodha, N.S. et al., (ed.), Sustainable Mountain Agriculture, New Delhi: IBH Publishing Co., 1992.

Jules, N. Pretty, Regenerating Agriculture, New Delhi: Vikas Publishing House, 1996.

Kalla, Aloke and Joshi, P.C., (ed.), Tribal Health and Medicines, Delhi: Concept Publishing Company, 2004.

Kalpana Rajaran, Geography of India, New Delhi: Spectrum Books Pub. Ltd., 2005.

Khusro, A.M., Factors Affecting Cropping Pattern, Agriculture Engineering, Madras: Research Centre, 1962.

Kunhaman, M., Development of Tribal Economy, New Delhi: Classical Publishing Company, 1989.

M.H., Qureshi, India Agriculture & Rural Development, Delhi: B.R. Publishing Corporation, 1985.

M.L., Dewan, Agriculture & Rural Development in India, New Delhi: Concept Publishing Company, 1982.

Majumdar, D.N., The Affairs of a Tribe: A Study in Tribal Dynamics, Lucknow: University Publishers, 2002.

Mamgain, M.D., District Gazetteers: Kinnaur, Chandigarh: Punjab Press, 1975.

Mohammad, A., (ed.), Dynamics of Agricultural Development in India, New Delhi: Concept Publishing Company, 1978.

Moseman, Albert H., (ed.), Agricultural Science for the Developing Nations, Delhi: Radhika Krishan Prakashan, 1964.

Pandey, A.K., Tribal Society in India, New Delhi: Manak Publishers, 1997.

Prasad, Chandra Shekhra, Agriculture and Rural Development in India Since 1947, Delhi: New Century Publications, 2009.

Raj, K.N., Organisational Issues in Indian Agriculture, New Delhi: S.K. Mookerjee, 1990.

Rastyannikov, V.G., Agrarian Evolution in A Multi Form Structure Society, London: RKP Publishers, 1981.

Ray, P.K., Agricultural Insurance, London: Peegamin Press Ltd., 1967.

Redeppa, L., Food Security in India, New Delhi: Kanishka Publishers, 2011.

Sadhu, A.N. & Mehajam, R.K., Technology changes and Agriculture Development in India, Bombay: Himalaya Publishing House, 1985.

Sanker Kumar Bhaumik (ed.), Reforming Indian Agriculture, New Delhi: Sage Publications, 2008.

Shah, K.T., Crops-Planning and Production, Bombay: Vora & Co. Publishers Pvt. Ltd., 1948.

Sharda, N.K., Sharma, V.P. and Gupta, S.K., Tribal Development; Appraisal and Alternatives, New Delhi: Indus Publishing Co., 1998.

Sharma, L.R., The Economy of Himachal Pradesh, New Delhi: Mittal Publications, 1987.

Sharma, M.L. and Singh, Ranveer, et al., "Impact of Irrigation on Socio Economic Farm Families of Himachal Pradesh," Shimla: Agro-Economic Research Centre, H.P.U, 1992.

Sharma, Manorma, Tribal Melodies of Himachal Pradesh: Lahaul Valley, New Delhi: A.P.H. Publishing Corporation, 1998.

Singh, Jasbir and Dhillon, S.S., Agricultural Geography, New Delhi: McGraw-Hill Publishing Company Limited, 1998.

Singh, Katar, Rural Development Principals, Policies and Management, New Delhi: Sage publications, 2013.

Singh, Y.P., Key Communicators of Agricultural Innovation, Agra: Satish Book Enterprise, 1973.

Tarique, M.D., Economic Reforms and Indian Agriculture, New Delhi: Regal Publications, 2009.

Tewari, S.C. and Awasthi, O.P., Analysis of Integrated Resource Inventory and Inventory of Resource, Kangra District, Himachal Pradesh, Palampur: Himachal Pradesh Krishi Vidyalaya, 1978.

Vyas, V.S., India's Agrarian Structure Economic Policies and Sustainable Development, Delhi: Academic Foundation, 2003.

B. JOURNALS / ARTICLES

Aggarwal, P.K. and Moudgil, A., "Structural Change and Growth of Agriculture in Haryana", International Journal of Applied Research, Vol. 1, No. 13, 2015.

Ahlawat, Vanita and Renu, "Regional Disparity in Cropping Intensity and Relative Impact of Irrigation in Haryana" IOSR Journal of Business and Management, Volume 18, Issue 9, September, 2016.

Akhter, Rubeenah and Acharya, Rekha, "Changes in Cropping Pattern in Jammu and Kashmir" International Journal of Advanced Research in Education & Technology, Vol. 2, Issue 4, Oct. - Dec. 2015.

Arif, H. Shah and Hakim F. Ahmad, et al., "Changing Land Use and Cropping Pattern in Budgam District of Jammu and Kashmir- A Spatio-Temporal Analysis", International Journal of Scientific & Engineering Research, Vol. 4, No. 2, February, 2013.

Asha, V. Latha K., et al., "Impact of Climate Change on Rainfed Agriculture in India: A Case Study of Dharwad", International Journal of Environmental Science and Development, Vol. 3, Issue No. 4, August, 2012.

Baba, S.H:, "Substantial Hill Agricultural Practices through Watershed Development", Agricultural Economics, 2010.

Barla Marcus, "The Impact of New Agricultural Technology on Tribal Farming: A Study of Ranchi District of Jharkhand State", Journal of Economic & Social Development, Vol. IX, No.1, 2013.

Bhati, J.R., et al., "Diversity of Mountain Farming System in Himachal Pradesh", in N.S. Jodha, et al., (ed.), Sustainable Mountain Agriculture, New Delhi: IBH Publishing Co., 1992.

Desai, A.R. and Mutalik, V.R., "Our food Problem", in V.R. Mutalik (ed.), The Strategy of food and Agriculture in India, Bombay: Western Printers and Publishers, 1969.

Deshpande, B.R., Low Returns to Cultivators, in V.R. Mutalik (ed.),The Strategy of food and Agriculture in India, Bombay: Western Printers and Publishers, 1969.

Ellot, C.M., "Role of Agriculture", in K. Warley (ed.), Agricultural Producers and their Markets, U.K.: Basil Blackwell Oxford, 1967.

Gupta, Amiya K., "Some Aspects of Input- Output Relationship in Indian Agriculture", in S.C. Jain (ed.), Changing Indian Agriculture, Bombay: Vora & Co. Pvt. Ltd., 1966.

Hill, F.F., "Developing Agricultural Institutions in Underdeveloped Countries", in Albert H. Moseman (ed.), Agricultural Science for the Developing Nations, Delhi: Radhika Krishan Prakashan, 1964.

Homer, Evans C., "The Apple Processing Industry" in R.D. Fraizer (ed.), Market Structure of the Agricultural Industries, USA.: The Iowa State University press Ames, 1966.

J.T., Coppock, "The Geography of Agriculture", Journal of Agriculture Economics, Volume 19, Issue 2, May 1968.

Jakhade, V.M., "Food Grain Marketing Zone in India", in R.T. Mirchandani, and G.J. Hiranandani (ed.), Marketing of Agricultural Commodities, Bombay: The Indian Societies of Agricultural Economics, 1965.

James Zivanomoya and Julius Mukarati, "Determinants of Choice of Crop Variety as Climate Change Adaptation in Arid Regions of Zimbabwe", Russian journal of Agricultural and socio-economic Sciences, Vol. 3, No. 15, 2013.

Jodhka, S. Surinder, "The Decline of Agriculture", in Sanker Kumar Bhaumik (ed.), Reforming Indian Agriculture, New Delhi: Sage Publications, 2008.

Joshi, P.C., "Poverty, Land Hunger and Emerging Class Conflicts in Rural India", in Steve Jones, P.C. Joshi, Miguel Murmis (ed.), Rural Poverty and Agrarian Reform, New Delhi: Allied Publishers Pvt. Ltd., 1982.

Kalaiselvi, V., "Pattern of Crop Diversification in Indian Scenario," Scholars Library Annals of Biological Research, 2012.

Kannan, Elumalai, and Sundaram, Sujata, "Analysis of Trends in India's Agricultural Growth", The Institute for Social and Economic Change, Bangalore, 2011.

Karamouzi, M., et al., "Development of Management Schemes in Irrigation Planning: Economic and Crop Pattern Consideration" Scientia Iranica, Vol. 16, No. 6, December 2009.

Kekane, Arjun, Maruti, "Indian Agriculture-Status, Importance and Role in Indian Economy" International Journal of Agriculture and Food Science Technology, Vol. 4, No. 4, 2013.

Kellog, Charles E., "Interactions and Agricultural Research", in Albert H. Moseman (ed.), Agricultural Science for the Developing Nations, Delhi: Radhika Krishan Prakashan, 1964.

Khan, Muhammad Tariq, Islam, Muhammad and Hussain, Thair, "Impact of Mini Dams on Socio-Economic Development of Farmers of Rainfed Region", Journal of Agriculture of Social Sciences. 2011.

Kuldeep Sharma & Sudhir Pradhan, "Organic farming Problems & Prospects", Yojana, Jan., 2011.

Kumar, Naveen, et al., "Kala Matar: an Indigenous Legume Crop of Spiti Valley in The Trans Himalyan Cold Desert of India Facing Threat of Extinction" International Journal of Current Research in Life Sciences, Vol. 4, No. 08, August 2015.

Kumari, Anita, Kaushal, P., Dubhey, J.K. and Sharma, D.K., "Climate Change-An impact study in Himachal Pradesh,"International Journal of Farm Sciences, Vol. 2, No. 2, 2012.

Long, J. Erven, "Institutional factors Limiting Progress in the Less Developed Countries", in Albert H. Moseman (ed.), Agricultural Science for the Developing Nations, Delhi: Radhika Krishan Prakashan, 1964.

M.S., Swaminathan, "Sustainable Food Society", Yojana, Vol. 54, Oct., 2010.

Madhu, G.R. and Uma, H.R., "A study on the Changing Cropping Pattern and Internal Migration Issues and Challenges," International journal of Applied Research, Vol. 4, No. 6, June 2014.

Mahato, Anupama, "Climate Change and its Impact on Agriculture," International Journal of Scientific and Research Publications, Vol. 4, No. 4, April, 2014.

Majumdar, N.A., "Agricultural growth in A Labour Surplus Economy", in S.C. Jain, (ed.), Changing Indian Agriculture, Bombay: Vora & Co. Pvt. Ltd., 1966.

Mathur, S. Archana and Das, Surajit, "SubhalakshmiSircar, Status of Agriculture in India Trends and Prospects", Economic and Political Weekly, Vol. XLI, No. 52, December 30, 2006.

Nadda, A.L. and Sharma, L.R., et al., "Optimising Crop Production Patterns in Different Agro-Climatic Zones of Himachal Pradesh", Indian Journal of Agricultural Economics, Vol. No. XXXIII (4), 1978.

Nagaraji, "Effect of Crop Mixtures on Income and Employment - Case Study of Anantapur District", Agricultural Situation in India, Vol. XVII, No. 11, 1989.

Patil, Jayanti, "Long Term Challenges in Indian Agriculture," in V.S. Vyas, and Pradeep Bhargava (ed.), Policies for Agricultural Development, Jaipur: Rawat Publications, 1997.

Patil, R.B., et al., "Impact of Water Percolation Tank on Changing Cropping Pattern: A Case Study of Rampur Village, Tal.-Jath, Dist: Sangli, Maharashtra", Online International Interdisciplinary Research Journal, Vol. II, No. VI, Dec., 2012.

Patil, R.B., "Displacement and Rehabilitation A Study of Change in Agricultural Practices of Dudhgangha Dam Affected People in Kolapur District (MH)". Research Directions, Vol. 1, No. 10, April, 2014.

Patil, Sachin Kumar, Patil, S.S. and Sathe, T.V., "Comparative Analysis of Cropping Pattern and Socio-Economic Status of Fisherman and Farmers", International Journal of Science, Environment and Technology, Vol. 3, No. 5, 2014.

Periasamy, G., "Erratic Monsoon and Indian Economy", Southern Economist, Volume 48, No. 18, January 15, 2010.

Prabha, Lakshmi U., "Impact of Farm Ponds on Cropping Pattern- A Case Study on Vembedu Village in Tamilnadu", International Journal of Innovative Research in Advanced Engineering, Vol. 1, No. 4, May, 2014.

Pratap, Tej, "Hill Agriculture: Challenges and Opportunities", Agricultural Economics, 2011.

R.D. Fraizer and J.B. Peterson, "Plant Agriculture in the Emerging Nations", in Albert H. Moseman (ed.), Agricultural Science for the Developing Nations, Delhi: Radhika Krishan Prakashan, 1964.

Ralph, W. Philips, "Animal Agriculture in the Emerging Nations", Albert H. Moseman (ed.), Agricultural Science for the Developing Nations, Delhi: Radhika Krishan Prakashan, 1964.

Randev, A.K., "Economic of Horticultural Crops in Tribal areas of Himachal Pradesh: A Case Study of Kinnaur District", Palampur: Unpublished Ph.D. Thesis, Department of Agriculture Economics, Himachal Pradesh Krishi Vishva Vidyalaya, 1986.

Ray, Shovan, "Economic Policy and Agriculture", in Shovan Ray (ed.), Hand Book of Agriculture, New Delhi: Oxford University Publishers, 2010.

Richard Bradfield, "The Role of Educated People in Agricultural Development", in Albert H. Moseman (ed.), Agricultural Science for the Developing Nations, Delhi: Radhika Krishan Prakashan, 1964.

Sangral, Chinky, "Changes in Cropping Pattern and Crop Diversification in Jammu and Kashmir" IOSR Journal of Humanities and Social Science, Vol. 20, No. 4, April, 2015.

Sangwan, P.S., "Changing Indian Agriculture-Epitomised Versionof Left-Over Problems", in S.C. Jain, (ed.), Changing Indian Agriculture, Bombay: Vora & Co. Pvt. Ltd., 1966.

Sharma, L.R. and Bhati, J.P., et al., "Emerging Farming Systems in Himachal Pradesh: Key Issues in Sustainability" Indian Journal of Agriculture Economics, Vol. No. XXVII (3), 1991.

Shastri, C.P., Factor influencing Cropping Pattern, in V.R. Mutalik (ed.), The Strategy of food and Agriculture in India, Bombay: Western Printers and Publishers, 1969.

Shivamaggi, H.B., "Impact of food Aid on Agricultural Development", in S.C. Jain, (ed.), Changing Indian Agriculture, Bombay: Vora & Co. Pvt. Ltd., 1966.

Singh, D.V. and Saraswat, S.P., "Impact of Irrigation on Cropping Pattern and Farm Income under Optimal Solution", Indian Journal of Agricultural Economics, Vol. 39, No. 3, 1984.

Singh, Harbans, "Development of Horticulture in Hill Regions of India", Paper presented in a Seminar on Development of Hilly Areas Problems and Potential, New Delhi: Vigyan Bhavan, 1975.

Singh, R., "Analysis of Spatial-Temporal Changes in Cropping Pattern and Cropping Intensity in Agriculture of Haryana." Online International Interdisciplinary Research Journal, Vol. 5, No. 6, 2015.

Srinivasan, P.V., "Agriculture and Food Security", in Shovan Ray (ed.), Hand Book of Agriculture, New Delhi: Oxford University Press, 2010.

Surridge, B.J., "Farmers Marketing Organizations", in K. Warley (ed.), Agricultural Producers and their Markets, U.K.: Basil Blackwell Oxford, 1967.

Swamy, Raju Narayan, "Tribal Land Question and Land Reforms in Kerala", Yojna, 2011.

Thakur, D.R., "Impact of Investment on Agricultural Growth and Rural Development in Himachal Pradesh: Dynamics of Public and Private Investment", Agricultural Economics, 2010.

Thomas, K.V., "Climate Change and Indian Agriculture", Vol. 55, Yojana, Jan. 2011.

Tiwari, K.N. and Tiwari, Rakesh, "Balanced Fertilization Real Benefits for Agriculture Sustainability", Kurukshetra, July, 2011.

Tripathy, K.K. & Mishra, K.C., "Food Security in India Policy issues & Challenges", Kurukshetra, A Journal of Rural Development Vol. 59, No. 5, March, 2011.

Uma, H.R., "Land Reform a Panacea for Agricultural Development", Yojana, 2011.

Uma, Madhu, H.R. and Pushpa, G.R., Nanaiah. K., "Changing Cropping Pattern: A Boon or a Bane to Food Security", International Journal of Humanities and Social Science Invention, Volume 2, No. 8, August, 2013.

Vishwanath A. Khot and Talwar Sabanna, "Scenario of Cropping Pattern and Crop Diversification: A Study of Gokak Taluk in Belgaum District, Karnataka, India". International Journal of Research in Management, Economics and Commerce, Volume 07, Issue 04, April, 2017.

Wani, M.H., "Hill Agriculture in India: Problems and Prospects of Mountain Agriculture", Agricultural Economics, 2011.

C. REPORTS

Annual Season and Crop Report 2010-11.

Annual Season and Crop Report, Directorate of Land Record, Kasumpti Shimla Himachal Pradesh –09.

Brief Facts – Himachal Pradesh (2011), Economics and Statistics Department, Himachal Pradesh, Shimla-9.

Census of India, 2011.

Jodha, N.S., Inter-Cropping in Traditional Farming Systems, Economic Progress Report-3. ICRISAT, Patancheru, AP, India, 1979.

Ministry of Tribal Affairs Statistical Division Government of India, 2013.

Singh, Padam, Agriculture in the Hill Regions of North India, New Delhi: Directorate of Extension, Ministry of Food and Agriculture, 1962.

State Statistical Abstract of Himachal Pradesh, Department of Economics and Statistics Kasumpti Shimla-09.

D. NEWS PAPERS

Amar Ujala

Danik Jagran

Hindustan Times

Times of India

The Hindu

E. WEBSITES

http://mrunal.org/2012/07/culture-tribes.,p.1,dated,1/08/2015.

http//www.ecoindia.com/tribes/dated,2/07/2015.

Glossary

Sr. No.	Words	Meaning
1	**Fafra**	Buckwheat
2	**Ogla**	Variety of Buckwheat
3	**Bhemi**	Wild peaches
4	**Takk**	Barley
5	**Jodh**	Wheat
6	**Dankhar**	Amaranthus
7	**Kodro**	Amaranth
8	**Chuli**	Wild Apricots
9	**Luchi**	Variety of Plum
9	**Dhakhang**	Grapes
10	**Nyoza**	Chilgoza
11	**Kim**	House
12	**Chaliya**	Maize
13	**Charma**	A Variety of Plant from which Tea Leaves are obtained.
15	**Rad**	Proso millet
16	**Kinnauras**	A community resides in Kinnaur
17	**Lahaulas**	A community resides in Lahaul

Index

***